IN ASSOCIATION WITH

SQA

Hodder Gibson Model Practice Papers WITH ANSWERS

PLUS: Official SQA Specimen Paper & 2014 Past Paper With Answers

National 5
English

2013 Specimen Question Paper, Model Papers & 2014 Exam

HODDER GIBSON
AN HACHETTE UK COMPANY

This book contains the official 2013 SQA Specimen Question Paper and 2014 Exam for National 5 English, with associated SQA approved answers modified from the official marking instructions that accompany the paper.

In addition the book contains model practice papers, together with answers, plus study skills advice. These papers, some of which may include a limited number of previously published SQA questions, have been specially commissioned by Hodder Gibson, and have been written by experienced senior teachers and examiners in line with the new National 5 syllabus and assessment outlines, Spring 2013. This is not SQA material but has been devised to provide further practice for National 5 examinations in 2014 and beyond.

Hodder Gibson is grateful to the copyright holders, as credited on the final page of the Answer Section, for permission to use their material. Every effort has been made to trace the copyright holders and to obtain their permission for the use of copyright material. Hodder Gibson will be happy to receive information allowing us to rectify any error or omission in future editions.

Hachette UK's policy is to use papers that are natural, renewable and recyclable products and made from wood grown in sustainable forests. The logging and manufacturing processes are expected to conform to the environmental regulations of the country of origin.

Orders: please contact Bookpoint Ltd, 130 Park Drive, Abingdon, Oxon OX14 4SE. Telephone: (44) 01235 827720. Fax: (44) 01235 400454. Lines are open 9.00–5.00, Monday to Saturday, with a 24-hour message answering service. Visit our website at www.hoddereducation.co.uk. Hodder Gibson can be contacted direct on: Tel: 0141 848 1609; Fax: 0141 889 6315; email: hoddergibson@hodder.co.uk

This collection first published in 2014 by
Hodder Gibson, an imprint of Hodder Education,
An Hachette UK Company
2a Christie Street
Paisley PA1 1NB

¡BrightRED Hodder Gibson is grateful to Bright Red Publishing Ltd for collaborative work in preparation of this book and all SQA Past Paper, National 5 and Higher for CfE Model Paper titles 2014.

Typeset by PDQ Digital Media Solutions Ltd, Bungay, Suffolk NR35 1BY

Printed in the UK

A catalogue record for this title is available from the British Library

ISBN: 978-1-4718-3701-2

3 2 1

2015 2014

Introduction

Study Skills – what you need to know to pass exams!

Pause for thought

Many students might skip quickly through a page like this. After all, we all know how to revise. Do you really though?

Think about this:

"IF YOU ALWAYS DO WHAT YOU ALWAYS DO, YOU WILL ALWAYS GET WHAT YOU HAVE ALWAYS GOT."

Do you like the grades you get? Do you want to do better? If you get full marks in your assessment, then that's great! Change nothing! This section is just to help you get that little bit better than you already are.

There are two main parts to the advice on offer here. The first part highlights fairly obvious things but which are also very important. The second part makes suggestions about revision that you might not have thought about but which WILL help you.

Part 1

DOH! It's so obvious but …

Start revising in good time

Don't leave it until the last minute – this will make you panic.

Make a revision timetable that sets out work time AND play time.

Sleep and eat!

Obvious really, and very helpful. Avoid arguments or stressful things too – even games that wind you up. You need to be fit, awake and focused!

Know your place!

Make sure you know exactly **WHEN and WHERE** your exams are.

Know your enemy!

Make sure you know what to expect in the exam.

How is the paper structured?

How much time is there for each question?

What types of question are involved?

Which topics seem to come up time and time again?

Which topics are your strongest and which are your weakest?

Are all topics compulsory or are there choices?

Learn by DOING!

There is no substitute for past papers and practice papers – they are simply essential! Tackling this collection of papers and answers is exactly the right thing to be doing as your exams approach.

Part 2

People learn in different ways. Some like low light, some bright. Some like early morning, some like evening / night. Some prefer warm, some prefer cold. But everyone uses their BRAIN and the brain works when it is active. Passive learning – sitting gazing at notes – is the most INEFFICIENT way to learn anything. Below you will find tips and ideas for making your revision more effective and maybe even more enjoyable. What follows gets your brain active, and active learning works!

Activity 1 – Stop and review

Step 1

When you have done no more than 5 minutes of revision reading STOP!

Step 2

Write a heading in your own words which sums up the topic you have been revising.

Step 3

Write a summary of what you have revised in no more than two sentences. Don't fool yourself by saying, "I know it, but I cannot put it into words". That just means you don't know it well enough. If you cannot write your summary, revise that section again, knowing that you must write a summary at the end of it. Many of you will have notebooks full of blue/black ink writing. Many of the pages will not be especially attractive or memorable so try to liven them up a bit with colour as you are reviewing and rewriting. **This is a great memory aid, and memory is the most important thing.**

Activity 2 — Use technology!

Why should everything be written down? Have you thought about "mental" maps, diagrams, cartoons and colour to help you learn? And rather than write down notes, why not record your revision material?

What about having a text message revision session with friends? Keep in touch with them to find out how and what they are revising and share ideas and questions.

Why not make a video diary where you tell the camera what you are doing, what you think you have learned and what you still have to do? No one has to see or hear it, but the process of having to organise your thoughts in a formal way to explain something is a very important learning practice.

Be sure to make use of electronic files. You could begin to summarise your class notes. Your typing might be slow, but it will get faster and the typed notes will be easier to read than the scribbles in your class notes. Try to add different fonts and colours to make your work stand out. You can easily Google relevant pictures, cartoons and diagrams which you can copy and paste to make your work more attractive and **MEMORABLE**.

Activity 3 – This is it. Do this and you will know lots!

Step 1

In this task you must be very honest with yourself! Find the SQA syllabus for your subject (www.sqa.org.uk). Look at how it is broken down into main topics called MANDATORY knowledge. That means stuff you MUST know.

Step 2

BEFORE you do ANY revision on this topic, write a list of everything that you already know about the subject. It might be quite a long list but you only need to write it once. It shows you all the information that is already in your long-term memory so you know what parts you do not need to revise!

Step 3

Pick a chapter or section from your book or revision notes. Choose a fairly large section or a whole chapter to get the most out of this activity.

With a buddy, use Skype, Facetime, Twitter or any other communication you have, to play the game "If this is the answer, what is the question?". For example, if you are revising Geography and the answer you provide is "meander", your buddy would have to make up a question like "What is the word that describes a feature of a river where it flows slowly and bends often from side to side?".

Make up 10 "answers" based on the content of the chapter or section you are using. Give this to your buddy to solve while you solve theirs.

Step 4

Construct a wordsearch of at least 10 X 10 squares. You can make it as big as you like but keep it realistic. Work together with a group of friends. Many apps allow you to make wordsearch puzzles online. The words and phrases can go in any direction and phrases can be split. Your puzzle must only contain facts linked to the topic you are revising. Your task is to find 10 bits of information to hide in your puzzle, but you must not repeat information that you used in Step 3. DO NOT show where the words are. Fill up empty squares with random letters. Remember to keep a note of where your answers are hidden but do not show your friends. When you have a complete puzzle, exchange it with a friend to solve each other's puzzle.

Step 5

Now make up 10 questions (not "answers" this time) based on the same chapter used in the previous two tasks. Again, you must find NEW information that you have not yet used. Now it's getting hard to find that new information! Again, give your questions to a friend to answer.

Step 6

As you have been doing the puzzles, your brain has been actively searching for new information. Now write a NEW LIST that contains only the new information you have discovered when doing the puzzles. Your new list is the one to look at repeatedly for short bursts over the next few days. Try to remember more and more of it without looking at it. After a few days, you should be able to add words from your second list to your first list as you increase the information in your long-term memory.

FINALLY! Be inspired...

Make a list of different revision ideas and beside each one write **THINGS I HAVE** tried, **THINGS I WILL** try and **THINGS I MIGHT** try. Don't be scared of trying something new.

And remember – "FAIL TO PREPARE AND PREPARE TO FAIL!"

National 5 English

The course

The National 5 English course aims to enable you to develop the ability to:

- Listen, talk, read and write, as appropriate to purpose, audience and context
- Understand, analyse and evaluate texts, including Scottish texts, as appropriate to purpose and audience in the contexts of literature, language and media
- Create and produce texts, as appropriate to purpose, audience and context
- Apply knowledge and understanding of language.

How the course is graded

The grade you finally get for National 5 English depends on three things:

- The two internal Unit Assessments you do in school or college: "Analysis and Evaluation" and "Creation and Production"; these don't count towards the final grade, but you must have passed them before you can get a final grade
- Your Portfolio of Writing – this is submitted in April for marking by SQA and counts for 30% of your final grade
- The two exams you sit in May – that's what this book is all about.

The exams

Reading for Understanding, Analysis and Evaluation

- Exam time: 1 hour
- Total marks: 30
- Weighting in final grade: 30%
- What you have to do: read a passage and answer questions about it.

Critical Reading

- Exam time: 1 hour 30 minutes
- Total marks: 40 (20 for each section)
- Weighting in final grade: 40%
- What you have to do: Section 1: read an extract from one of the Scottish Texts which are set for National 5 and answer questions about it; Section 2: write an essay about a work of literature you have studied during your course.

Reading for Understanding, Analysis and Evaluation

Three important tips to start with

- Since there will usually be a question asking you to summarise some or all of the passage, it is really important to read the whole passage before you even look at the questions. Doing this will give you a chance to get a rough idea of the main ideas in the passage, and you can add to this as you work your way through the questions.
- Pay close attention to the number of marks available for each question and make sure your answer is appropriate to the number of marks. In most questions, you will get 1 mark for each correct point.
- Some questions tell you to "use your own words". This means you mustn't just copy chunks from the passage – you have to show that you understand what it means by rephrasing it in your own words.

Questions which ask for understanding

- Keep your answers fairly short and pay attention to the number of marks available.

Questions about language features

- This type of question will ask you to comment on features such as Word Choice, Imagery, Sentence Structure and Tone.
- You should pick out a relevant language feature and make a valid comment about its impact. Try to make your comments as specific as possible and avoid vague comments (like "It is a good word to use because it gives me a clear picture of what the writer is saying"). Some hints:

  - **Word Choice:** always try to pick a single word and then give its connotations, i.e. what it **suggests**

  - **Sentence Structure:** don't just name the feature – try to explain what effect it achieves **in that particular sentence**

  - **Imagery:** try to explain what the image means **literally** and then go on to explain what the writer is **suggesting** by using that image

- **Tone**   this is always difficult – a good tip is to imagine the sentence or paragraph being read out loud and try to spot how the words or the structure give it a particular tone.

Summary questions

- Make sure you follow the instruction about what it is you are to summarise (the question will be as helpful as possible).
- Stick to the main ideas; avoid unimportant points and never include examples.
- Make sure you earn all the marks available for the question.

Critical Reading

Section 1 – Scottish Text

The most important thing to remember here is that there are two very different types of question to be answered:

- Three or four questions (for a total of 12 marks) which focus entirely on the extract
- One question (for 8 marks) which requires knowledge of the whole text (or of another poem or short story by the same writer).

The first type of question will often ask you to use the same type of close textual analysis skills you used in the Reading part of your Analysis and Evaluation Unit. There can also be a question asking for the type of summary skills you're used to in the Reading part of the exam. The golden rule is to read each question very carefully and do exactly as instructed.

The last question for 8 marks can be answered **either** in bullet points **or** as a "mini-essay". Choose whichever approach you are more comfortable with. Make as many relevant points as you can. If you look at the Marking Guide which is used for this type of question (see page 163), you'll get an idea of how this question is marked and this should help you in your approach.

Final bit of advice for the Scottish Text question: when you see the extract in the exam paper, don't get too confident just because you recognise it (you certainly should recognise it if you've studied properly!) And even if you've answered questions on it before, remember that the questions in the exam are likely to be different, so stay alert.

Section 2 – Critical Essay

A common mistake is to rely too heavily on ideas and whole paragraphs you have used in practice essays and try to use them for the question you have chosen in the exam. The trick is to come to the exam with lots of ideas and thoughts about at least one of the texts you have studied and use these to tackle the question you choose from the exam paper. You mustn't use the exam question as an excuse to trot out an answer you've prepared in advance.

Structure

Every good essay has a structure, but there is no "correct" structure, no magic formula that the examiners are looking for. It's **your** essay, so structure it the way **you** want. As long as you're answering the question all the way through, then you'll be fine.

Relevance

Be relevant to the question **all the time** – not just in the first and last paragraphs.

Central Concerns

Try to make sure your essay shows that you have thought about and understood the central concerns of the text, i.e. what it's "about" – the ideas and themes the writer is exploring in the text.

Quotations

In poetry and drama essays, you're expected to quote from the text, but never fall into the trap of learning a handful of quotations and forcing them all into the essay regardless of the question you're answering. In prose essays, quotation is much less important, and you can show your knowledge much more effectively by referring in detail to what happens in key sections of the novel or the short story.

Techniques

You are expected to show some understanding of how various literary techniques work within a text, but simply naming them will not get you marks, and structuring your essay around techniques rather than around relevant ideas in the text is not a good idea.

Good luck!

Remember that the rewards for passing National 5 English are well worth it! Your pass will help you get the future you want for yourself. In the exam, be confident in your own ability. If you're not sure how to answer a question, trust your instincts and just give it a go anyway – keep calm and don't panic! GOOD LUCK!

NATIONAL 5

2013 Specimen Question Paper

National
Qualifications
SPECIMEN ONLY

SQ13/N5/01

English
Reading for Understanding,
Analysis and Evaluation

Date — Not applicable

Duration — 1 hour

Total marks — 30

When you are told to do so, open the booklet, read the passage and attempt all the questions, using your own words as far as possible.

Before attempting the questions you must check that your answer booklet is for the same subject and level as this question paper.

On the answer booklet, you must clearly identify the question number you are attempting.

Use **blue** or **black** ink.

Before leaving the examination room you must give your answer booklet to the Invigilator. If you do not, you may lose all the marks for this paper.

The following article is about JK Rowling (the creator of Harry Potter) and the nature of fame.

Fame conveys the illusion of intimacy. We assume we know everything there is to know about the person concerned, from David Beckham's wardrobe to Prince William's childhood nicknames. The story of JK Rowling writing in a café with a prolonged cup of coffee to avoid a cold flat is almost as familiar as she is.

5   So it comes as a shock when an individual tone of voice penetrates those layers of gossip and assumption. The voices may not be quite what we imagined. Beckham, mythologised for his looks and skill, sounds insufficiently heroic when he speaks. A rare television interview with JK Rowling, broadcast this week, to mark the publication of *Harry Potter and the Order of the Phoenix*, revealed a thoroughly modern woman who speaks, not in
10   the modulated tones that might be expected of a children's classic author, but just like the rest of us.

Even the sound of Prince William chatting with his father and brother in a 21st birthday video is a surprise, after years when, like his mother, his image was familiar but his voice was rarely heard.

15   Rowling is loved for her stories, but also for her story. A contemporary Cinderella, she endured the cold flat and life on single-parent benefit. Then Harry happened and she went to the ball. Neil Murray, her husband, might be abashed to find himself cast as Prince Charming, but her life has changed as much as any scullery-maid turned princess.

The missing part of the Cinderella story is what happens when she puts on the glass
20   slipper and disappears into the palace. Rowling filled in the blanks, describing to Jeremy Paxman how she has to cope with begging letters, journalists rifling through her bins, photographers lurking on the beach, and strangers accosting her in the supermarket.

The writer was honest enough to admit that the massive success of Harry Potter had given her a sense of validation. "I don't feel like quite such a waste of space anymore." Like
25   David Beckham, taking care to thank Manchester United fans as his transfer to Real Madrid was announced, she is keenly aware of the true source of her popularity, guarding plots and characters in the interests of children who would be sad to have the story spoilt.

But Rowling was also frank about unexpected aspects of her fame. She feels guilty about
30   her wealth – denying she is worth the rumoured 280 million – and fears life after Harry, citing AA Milne, who could never get a book reviewed without Pooh and Tigger being mentioned.

Fame, as she implied, freezes you in one frame. Prince William will be lucky ever to take refuge in a proper job. David Beckham will always mean football, and Rowling, who
35   disclosed that she has tried her hand at a novel for adults, will have to write very brilliantly to discard the label of a children's writer.

Beckham exploits to his advantage the way in which the famous are transformed into products often with scant relation to their actual lives or personalities. He treats himself as a logo. In the week that his transfer was announced, he was touring Japan with his
40   wife, endorsing products.

This is a facet of celebrity that Rowling detests, describing the task of agreeing Potter merchandise as "horrible". But writers, unlike footballers, need not fear an early sell-by date for their skills.

45 William, of course, has nothing to sell – or has he? His face, youth and ease are guarantees that the monarchy can adapt and move into the 21st century. The palace both protects and carefully markets him, controlling access and exposure. Is he willing to surrender the chance of a relatively normal life to be the modern face of monarchy? For him, as for Rowling, the debate about a possible privacy law, kick-started this week by a committee of MPs, has intense personal relevance.

50 William at least has the consolation that his fame derives from his parentage, not from himself. Unless Britain turns republic, he will always be royal. But for those whose fame is built on personality, one crack brings the edifice crashing down.

JK Rowling is fortunate in that the reason for her fame exists at one remove from her. Harry is nothing to do with who her parents were, or how good she looks on television.
55 He is the product of her imagination, interacting with the imagination of millions of others. Just as the books, with their literary allusions and cultural quirks, borrow from other traditions, so the wizard world is held in common. Internet sites discuss the plot, translators try to render "Hogwarts" in other languages. Harry is public property in a way that his creator, despite the dustbins and long lenses, is not.

60 In an age of appearances, her story should reassure us. JK Rowling found success and made millions through trusting her own invention. We will never know her, but we know Harry, and his magic is likely to last.

Adapted from an article in the The Scotsman newspaper, June 2003.

MARKS

1. "Fame conveys the illusion of intimacy." **In your own words**, explain how examples the writer gives in the first paragraph illustrate this idea.   3

2. Look at lines 15–18. **In your own words**, explain what comparisons the writer draws between JK Rowling and Cinderella.   4

3. Explain how the writer's word choice in lines 19–22 helps to show the negative effects of fame.   4

4. For JK Rowling, what are the advantages and disadvantages of fame? Refer to lines 23–36 in your answer, **using your own words**.   4

5. Choose **one** of the two rhetorical questions in paragraph 11 (lines 44–49) and discuss its effect.   2

6. **In your own words**, explain fully in what ways JK Rowling feels she is "fortunate" (line 53). Give evidence from lines 53–62 to support your answer.   4

7. Read the last paragraph. Identify the writer's attitude to JK Rowling in this paragraph and give evidence to support your answer.   2

8. Choose **one** of the following images:

   "Fame, as she implied, freezes you in one frame." (line 33)

   "He treats himself as a logo." (lines 38–39)

   "But for those whose fame is built on personality, one crack brings the edifice crashing down." (lines 51–52)

   Explain what your chosen image means and analyse its effect.   3

9. Referring to the whole article, **in your own words** list the key points the writer makes about the nature of fame.   4

[END OF SPECIMEN QUESTION PAPER]

Acknowledgement of Copyright
Extract is adapted from an article titled "Reassuring message of Rowling's wizard world" taken from The Scotsman. Permission sought from Johnston Press plc.

National Qualifications
SPECIMEN ONLY

SQ13/N5/02

English
Critical Reading

Date — Not applicable

Duration — 1 hour and 30 minutes

Total marks — 40

SECTION 1 — Scottish Text — 20 marks

Read an extract from a Scottish text you have previously studied and attempt the questions.

Choose ONE text from either

Part A — Drama   Pages 2–7
or
Part B — Prose   Pages 8–17
or
Part C — Poetry   Pages 18–25

Attempt ALL the questions for your chosen text.

SECTION 2 — Critical Essay — 20 marks

Write ONE critical essay on previously studied text from Drama, Prose, Poetry, Film and Television Drama, or Language.

Your answer must be on a different genre from that chosen in Section 1.

You should spend approximately 45 minutes on each Section.

Before attempting the questions you must check that your answer booklet is for the same subject and level as this question paper.

On the answer booklet, you must clearly identify the question number you are attempting.

Use **blue** or **black** ink.

Before leaving the examination room you must give your answer booklet to the Invigilator. If you do not you may lose all the marks for this paper.

SECTION 1 — SCOTTISH TEXT — 20 marks

Choose ONE text from Drama, Prose or Poetry.

Read the text extract carefully and then attempt ALL the questions below the extract, using your own words as far as possible.

You should spend about 45 minutes on this question.

PART A — SCOTTISH TEXT — DRAMA

Text 1 — Drama

If you choose this text you may not write a critical essay on Drama in Section 2.

Read the extract below and then attempt the following questions.

***Tally's Blood* by Ann Marie di Mambro**

Rosinella seated, head in hands:
Looks up wearily when Massimo approaches:
Massimo looking at her very coldly; no sympathy at all.

	MASSIMO:	It's time we talked about Hughie—
5	ROSINELLA:	(*Interrupting*) Take me to Italy, Massimo.
	MASSIMO:	What?
	ROSINELLA:	I want to go to Italy.
	MASSIMO:	Why—all of a sudden?
	ROSINELLA:	Just to get away from here.
10	MASSIMO:	But why now?
	ROSINELLA:	Because I can't face it here. There's too much heartache.
	MASSIMO:	How long for?
	ROSINELLA:	I don't care.
	MASSIMO:	What about the shop?
15	ROSINELLA:	Do what you like with it. Shut it. Sell it. I don't care if we never come back.

Massimo looks at her with disbelief.

	MASSIMO:	You mean that, don't you?
	ROSINELLA:	I just want away.
20	MASSIMO:	When I think of the times I've asked you to come to Italy with me. Oh, but you always had an excuse ready. Now—because YOU'RE unhappy, because YOU miss Lucia—we've just to go. Just like that. To hell with the shop, to hell with everything I've worked for. To hell with everything except what YOU want.

MARKS

25 ROSINELLA: If you knew what I've been through.

    MASSIMO: Oh Rosie, Rosie, do you think I don't know. 'What you've been through'. It's all I've ever heard. But what about the rest of us? Do we not go through anything? What about Lucia—what about Hughie—what about me?

    ROSINELLA: Massimo . . . please. Don't do this to me.

30 MASSIMO: But you really don't care for anyone else's pain except your own, do you? I never realised that before and I wish to God I didn't now. All these years I've known what it meant to you, no being able to have a family. God knows, you never tried to hide it. Never. But did you ever once think what it's been like for me? Did you ever think maybe I would have liked a child.

35   A son to work alongside me, to plan things with. A son to leave my shop to . . . You know something else, Rosinella? It's only now I know what I must've put my father through. (*Voice breaks*) But you! You never think of anyone but yourself.

    ROSINELLA: Lucia. I want Lucia.

40 MASSIMO: (*With contempt*) Oh aye, 'Lucia, Lucia'. You love her that much you don't want her to love anyone else. You love her that much, nobody else has to get loving her. Oh aye, you love Lucia alright.

Questions

1. How do the stage directions in lines 1—3 prepare the audience for the conflict which follows in this scene?   **2**

2. Explain how sentence structure is used in lines 4—15 to reveal what the characters are thinking and/or feeling.   **4**

3. Re-read lines 20—38. Using your own words as far as possible, summarise the reasons why Massimo is angry and/or upset.   **4**

4. Explain what Massimo is saying to Rosinella in lines 40—42 of the extract.   **2**

5. This extract shows one moment in Rosinella and Massimo's relationship. With close reference to this extract and elsewhere in the play, explain how their relationship is portrayed.   **8**

OR

Text 2 — Drama

If you choose this text you may not write a critical essay on Drama in Section 2.

Read the extract below and then attempt the following questions.

***Bold Girls* by Rona Munro**

This extract is taken from scene two of the play. In the social club. Marie has just reluctantly joined Cassie on the dance floor.

	MARIE:	Cassie, what's wrong?
	CASSIE:	Oh, I'm just bad Marie, didn't you know?
5	MARIE:	No. I never knew that.
	CASSIE:	You remember that wee girl in Turf Lodge, the one Martin couldn't get enough of? She was a decent wee girl. She's bad now. Ask my mummy.
	MARIE:	Have you had words?
	CASSIE:	He's out in less than a year, Marie.
10	MARIE:	Martin!?
	CASSIE:	Joe.
	MARIE:	I know. It will be all right Cassie.

They stop dancing, they look at each other

It'll be all right, Cassie.

15	CASSIE:	I tell you Marie I can't stand the smell of him. The greasy, grinning beer bellied smell of him. And he's winking away about all he's been dreaming of, wriggling his fat fingers over me like I'm a poke of chips—I don't want him in the house in my *bed*, Marie.
	MARIE:	You'll cope.
20	CASSIE:	Oh I'm just bad. I am.
	MARIE:	Don't. Don't say that about yourself.
	CASSIE:	I'll go crazy.
	MARIE:	I won't let you. You won't get a chance Cassie, I'll just be across the road, I won't let you go crazy. You just see what you'll get if you try it.

25 *Slowly Cassie smiles at her*

(*Putting a hand on Cassie's arm*) Now will you come and sit down?

The doors at the back bang open

Hard white light floods everything

Oh Jesus it's a raid!

30 *All the women freeze, legs apart, arms raised as if they're being searched*

The same hard light stays on them

	DEIRDRE:	Brick in your hand, hard in your hand, hit skin and it will burst open and bleed, hit bones and they'll break, you can hear them break, hear them snap.

Page four

MARKS

MARIE: Why are you asking my name, you know my name.

35 DEIRDRE: Smell the petrol, lungs full of the smell of it. Blow it out again and you'll be
            breathing fire. Throw fire in a bottle and it runs everywhere like it's water.

MARIE: Everyone knows where I live.

DEIRDRE: Get a car, fast car, drive it till its wheels burn, leave it smoking, burning,
            exploding.

40 MARIE: Everyone knows all about me, don't they? So what do you want to know?
            What do you want?

DEIRDRE: The whole town's a prison, smash chunks off the walls 'cause we're all in a
            prison.

Cut the hard white light

Questions

6. Summarise what happens in this extract. Make at least three key points.   **3**

7. By close reference to **one** example of word choice, show how Cassie's attitude to
    Joe is made clear in this scene.   **2**

8. Look closely at the dialogue and stage directions and then explain what they tell us
    about:

    (a) the difference in personality between Cassie and Marie   **4**

    (b) Deirdre's personality.   **3**

9. By referring to both this extract and to the play as a whole, comment on the
    playwright's use of at least **two** different dramatic techniques used in the play.

    (*You may want to comment on: characterisation, setting, stage directions, lighting
    changes, monologues, cross conversations, use of colloquialisms, symbolism or any
    other dramatic technique.*)   **8**

OR

Text 3 — Drama

If you choose this text you may not write a critical essay on Drama in Section 2.

Read the extract below and then attempt the following questions.

Sailmaker **by Alan Spence**

Extract from Act Two

ALEC: But ah can feel the big black woman lookin at me. Tell me, she says—big deep voice like a man's—When did the Lord Jesus come into your heart? Pardon? I says. Terrified! She looks right at me. Ah said, when did the Lord Jesus come into your heart, child?

5   That was what I thought she'd said.

And she wanted an answer. From me!

I looked down at the floor.

I could feel myself blush,

What kind of question was that to ask?

10   How was I supposed to answer it?

Why didn't she ask me something straightforward?

Who carried Christ's cross on the way to Calvary?

Simon of Cyrene.

Into what estate did the fall bring mankind?

15   The fall brought mankind into an estate of sin and misery.

(*Tugs at collar*)

It's hot in here. Feelin a wee bit sick.

Ah'll just go outside for a minute, get some fresh air . . .

Ah'm trippin over ma own feet.

20   Knock over a pile of hymnbooks. Jesus Christ!

Out into the street, walkin faster, runnin, away fae the Mission, through a close, into the back court . . .

The night air was cool. I stopped and leaned against a midden wall. When did the Lord Jesus come into my heart? I could have said it was when my mother

25   died. That would have sounded pious.

But I didn't think it was true. I didn't know. That was it, I didn't know.

If the Lord Jesus had come into my heart, I should know.

The back court was quiet. Just the sound of the TV from this house or that.

Dark tenement blocks.

30   I kicked over a midden bin, and ran.

Page six

MARKS

Questions

10. In your own words, summarise the problem Alec faces in this extract and how he deals with it.   **4**

11. Alec is clearly uncomfortable in this extract. Show how the playwright's word-choice **and** sentence structure make this clear.   **4**

12. Alec speaks mainly in English in this extract.

    (a) Explain fully what this tells us about his character.   **2**

    (b) Explain why the playwright uses the occasional Scots word in Alec's speech in this extract.   **2**

13. The theme of social class is explored in this extract.

    Show how the theme of social class is developed here and elsewhere in the play.   **8**

PART B — SCOTTISH TEXT — PROSE

Text 1 — Prose

If you choose this text you may not write a critical essay on Prose in Section 2.

Read the extract below and then attempt the following questions.

The Telegram by Iain Crichton Smith

It was wartime and though the village appeared quiet, much had gone on in it. Reverberations from a war fought far away had reached it: many of its young men had been killed, or rather drowned, since nearly all of them had joined the navy, and their ships had sunk in seas which they had never seen except on maps which hung on the walls
5 of the local school which they all had at one time or another unwillingly attended. One had been drowned on a destroyer after a leave during which he had told his family that he would never come back again. (Or at least that was the rumour in the village which was still, as it had always been, a superstitious place.) Another had been drowned during the pursuit of the Bismarck.

10 What the war had to do with them the people of the village did not know. It came on them as a strange plague, taking their sons away and then killing them, meaninglessly, randomly. They watched the road often for the telegrams.

The telegrams were brought to the houses by the local elder who, clad in black, would walk along the road and then stop at the house to which the telegram was directed.
15 People began to think of the telegram as a strange missile pointed at them from abroad. They did not know what to associate it with, certainly not with God, but it was a weapon of some kind, it picked a door and entered it, and left desolation just like any other weapon.

The two women who watched the street were different, not only physically but socially.
20 For the thin woman's son was a sub-lieutenant in the Navy while the fat woman's son was only an ordinary seaman. The fat woman's son had to salute the thin woman's son. One got more pay than the other, and wore better uniform. One had been at university and had therefore become an officer, the other had left school at the age of fourteen.

When they looked out the window they could see cows wandering lazily about, but little
25 other movement. The fat woman's cow used to eat the thin woman's washing and she was looking out for it but she couldn't see it. The thin woman was not popular in the village. She was an incomer from another village and had only been in this one for thirty years or so. The fat woman had lived in the village all her days; she was a native. Also the thin woman was ambitious: she had sent her son to university though she only had a
30 widow's pension of ten shillings a week.

As they watched they could see at the far end of the street the tall man in black clothes carrying in his hand a piece of yellow paper. This was a bare village with little colour and therefore the yellow was both strange and unnatural.

The fat woman said: "It's Macleod again."

35 "I wonder where he's going today."

They were both frightened because he could be coming to their house. And so they watched him and as they watched him they spoke feverishly as if by speaking continually and watching his every move they would be able to keep from themselves whatever plague he was bringing.

MARKS

Questions

14. Look closely at lines 1—12.

    Give **two** examples of the writer's use of language to emphasise the effect of the war on the people of the village.

    4

15. "They watched the road often for telegrams." (line 12)

    Look closely at lines 13—18.

    By referring to **one** example, show how the writer uses word choice effectively to emphasise the significance of the telegrams to the people in the village.

    2

16. "The two women who watched the street were different." (line 19)

    From lines 19—30, summarise the differences between the two women. Use your own words as far as possible.

    4

17. "They were both frightened because he could be coming to their house." (line 36)

    Looking closely at lines 36—39, show how the writer's word choice helps to emphasise their fear.

    2

18. By referring to this story and **at least one** other story by Iain Crichton Smith, show how the writer is successful in building tension.

    8

OR

Text 2 — Prose

If you choose this text you may not write a critical essay on Prose in Section 2.

Read the extract below and then attempt the following questions.

A Chitterin' Bite **by Anne Donovan**

We go tae the pictures every week efter the swimmin, scramblin tae get the chummy seats up the back, sharing wer sweeties, grabbin each other's airms at the scary bits and gigglin at the love scenes. Then wan week, when we're walkin alang the road efter the baths, Agnes says:

5   *Ah said we'd meet Jimmy McKeown and his pal at the pictures.*

What?

He wants tae go wi me. He says he'll bring his pal for you.

Do you want tae go wi him?

Ah don't know, ah'll gie it a try.

10   Ah unlinked ma airm fae Agnes's and marched on, starin ahead.

Well, you don't need me tae come too.

Agnes caught up wi me, grabbin at ma airm.

Ah cannae go masel.

How no?

15   *Ah just cannae. Anyway, he's bringin his pal. If you don't go, ah cannae go. Come on, Mary, be a pal.*

The boys are waitin for us inside the foyer of the picture hoose. Jimmy McKeown is a year aulder than us, wi a broad nose, a bit bent tae the side, and straight dirty-fair hair in a side shed. The pal is staunin hauf behind him, a wee skinny laddie wi roond baby
20 cheeks and red lips like a lassie.

This is Shuggie, he's ma cousin.

This is Mary.

Hiya.

Will we go in?

25   *After yous, girls.*

They're polite, even though Jimmy is actin the big shot and the pal still hasnae opened his mooth. Agnes and me go first, intae the daurk picture hoose. Agnes leadin the way tae the back row where the chummy seats are. She sits doon in wan but when ah go tae sit next tae her she mutters *naw, you huvtae sit wae Shuggie* and shoves me ower tae the
30 next seat, where the airm rest forms a barrier between me and her. Ah feel Shuggie's knees pushin intae mines as he squeezes by me tae sit in the other hauf of the seat. Ah move as far ower tae the side nearest Agnes as ah can, but ah cannae help smellin the rough hairy smell of his sports jaicket under the sourness of the aftershave he must of plastered on his baby cheeks.

MARKS

Questions

19. By referring to the extract as a whole, explain how dialogue is used effectively to help develop the contrast in characterisation between Mary and Agnes. You should give **two** specific examples.

4

20. Look at lines 1—3. Explain how **two** examples of the writer's use of language convey the idea of the characters being in a rush.

4

21. Look at lines 6—11. Mary's reactions to Agnes's plan are described. In what **two** ways does the writer suggest Mary's annoyance?

2

22. Look at lines 17—20. Explain how Mary's discomfort is made clear in her description of either Jimmy or Shuggie.

2

23. By referring closely to this story and to **at least one** other story by Donovan, discuss the writer's use of narrative style.

8

OR

Text 3 — Prose

If you choose this text you may not write a critical essay on Prose in Section 2.

Read the extract below and then attempt the following questions.

The Cone-Gatherers by Robin Jenkins

In this extract, Roderick, the son of Lady Runcie-Campbell, has become stuck, while climbing a fir tree. As Lady Runcie-Campbell runs for help, a shot rings out . . .

From the silver fir to the Point took ten minutes; during them she seemed to travel to the furthest limits of her being, there to be baulked by not finding what she had hoped to find, and without which she could never return.

Behind her, always at that proper distance, ran Baird, a big red-eared solemn man, who
5 kept thinking what a good thing it was he had, after all, taken Manson with him to the tree. The lady had promised to reward Bob; but it was a recognised rule of the world that if a subordinate was rewarded, his master must be rewarded also, to maintain stations, and of course, more handsomely according to his higher degree. In the war, for instance, there were different medals for privates and officers, although they fought in
10 the same battles.

From a bank of whins and bracken she looked down on the promontory. Never had the loch been so potently beautiful: it was as vast, bright, and as detailed as a dream; and there seemed to be a wonderful interpretation, if it could only be known. A warship steamed down from the loch. So intimate a part of the dream was it, she seemed, during
15 those few moments of suspense upon the bank, to know all its crew and what was to be each man's fate in the sea towards which it was bound. There too, dream-like were the pines, her favourite trees, making against sea and sky what had always struck her as Scottish gestures, recalling the eerie tormented tragic grandeur of the old native ballads. Gulls, as prodigal of time and sky as she must be parsimonious, flew and shrieked high
20 over them.

She could not see any men; they must be hidden by the trees. But as she began to go down the bank, tearing her clothes on the whins and splintering the bracken, she heard the report of a gun, followed by a scream, and then by the quickened wails of the gulls.

As she raced among the pines, making for that gunshot, she prayed that Duror in his
25 madness had not hurt the cone-gatherers, not for their sakes, nor for his, nor for his wife's, but for her son's.

She saw Duror before she saw them. He was walking away among the pine trees with so infinite a desolation in his every step that it was this memory of him, rather than that of the little hunchback dangling from the tree, or that of his brother, climbing so frenziedly
30 up into it, which was to torment her sleep for months.

She forced herself to go over to the tree. It was the strap of his bag which had caught on a branch. He hung therefore in twisted fashion, and kept swinging. His arms were loose and dangled in macabre gestures of supplication. Though he smiled, he was dead.

MARKS

Questions

24. Read lines 1—3

   How does the writer convey the anxiety of Lady Runcie-Campbell as she runs to the Point?

   2

25. Read lines 4—10

   Summarise the thoughts going through Baird's mind as he runs behind Lady Runcie-Campbell.

   2

26. Read lines 11—20

   What does the writer's word choice convey about the setting?

   4

27. Read lines 21—23

   Quote the expressions which convey the difficulty Lady Runcie-Campbell had as she tried to reach the trees.

   2

28. Read lines 24—30

   What is surprising about Duror's reaction to Calum's death?

   2

29. With close reference to this extract and to elsewhere in the novel, discuss how the theme of death is explored.

   8

OR

Text 4 — Prose

If you choose this text you may not write a critical essay on Prose in Section 2.

Read the extract below and then attempt the following questions.

The Testament of Gideon Mack by James Robertson

'On ane o' their first walks in that gloomy place, she an' her maid had stumbled upon a
hidden path that led doun an' doun into the verra' he'rt o' the chasm. An' there they had
come across a black-avised gentleman, dressed in the finest cla'es, danderin' aside the
breengin' torrent an' smokin' his pipe as if he did it every day o' his life. He greeted
5   them, but they couldna hear a word, sae he led them into a cavern whaur the water ran
slow an' silent an' black as tar. There was a table an' chair made o' iron fixed into the
rock, wi' a chain attached to the chair, an' twa great slaverin' hounds sleepin' i' the
mooth o' the cave. An' faur, faur ben, they thocht they could see the faint licht o' a
bleezin' fire, an' even imagined they could hear voices, but that surely couldna be!

10 'Jean was gey fear'd, but the stranger spak' wi a gentle voice, an' speired efter the
leddy's health in her ain native tongue. "You are sad, and far from home," he said, "but I
have the power to transport you there, where you may be happy again." An' the leddy o'
Keldo confessed to Dod Eadie that, tho' she had merriet the laird, she had done it for
siller, no' for love, an' that she had anither lover in her ain land that she green'd to see.
15 She had jaloused by noo wha the gentleman o' the cavern micht be, but she didna care.
She said that she wad dearly like to be joined wi' her lover aince mair. "That may be
done in an instant," said the gentleman, "but your companion must wait for your return
at the head of the path." The maid pleaded wi' her no' to bargain wi' sic' a frichtsome
craitur', but her mistress ordered her to withdraw an' attend her at the path heid. Syne
20 the man sent the leddy o' Keldo owre the sea, by what means she never related to Dod,
an' she was reunited wi' her lover. When she cam' back, tho' she felt she had been awa'
for days, only an 'oor had passed. "Whenever you wish it," the stranger said, "I can
arrange for you to make that journey, but there is a price, and that is that you sign a
bond assigning your soul to me." He had the document a' drawn up, an' a pen ready for
25 her, on the iron table. Eagerly she sat doun to sign, but there was nae ink. The De'il—
for ye may be sure it was he—produced a pocket-knife frae his coat. "Since you will
supply the soul, you may supply the ink also," he said, an' nicked her airm wi' the blade
sae that the blude trickled oot. She dipped the pen in the wound an' bent to sign, but
again she hesitated. "It is a fair bargain," she said, "but I would fain make another with
30 you. I pledge to settle the account with a human soul, but let the name be blank. Either,
when you redeem the pledge, it will be mine, or it will belong to one far more innocent
than I." By this she had Jean in mind, an' the De'il, kennin' her meanin' wi' a canny look
agreed to her proposal. Whan Dod heard this, he cried oot, "An' had ye nae he'rt that ye
could sign awa' my dear Jean for the sake o' your ain sinfu', selfish ways?" "Alas, that I
35 had not!" lamented the leddy, "for I was consumed with my own desires, and thought
that I would find some way to outwit him ere the time of reckoning came. And when he
claimed her some weeks after, I tried to prevent him taking her, and wrestled with him at
the mouth of that horrid cave, but he was too strong and dragged her beyond the dripping
teeth of his hounds where I could not reach her. I pleaded with him, and took from my
40 wrist a gold bracelet and threw it over the hounds to him, and said if he would only
release her he would have all the gold he desired. But he laughed at me for a fool, saying
that he had more gold than he could wish for, and that it was nothing compared with the
two souls he had gained—for, he said, by my deeds I was surely bound for his kingdom in

MARKS

45 any event. And he kicked the bracelet from him as if it were but worthless trash." An' the mistress flung hersel' at the feet o' Dod Eadie, an' sobbed for what she had done, an' begged his forgiveness, an' tauld him that if he wad gang wi' her, she wad plead again wi' the De'il for the lass's release, an' if need be wad offer hersel' in her place, an' Dod wad ha'e Jean back an' lead her to safety.'

ane: one;   *black-avised*: dark-featured;   *cla'es*: clothes;   *danderin'*: strolling; *breengin'*: rushing;   *faur ben*: deep within;   *gey fear'd*: very afraid;   *siller*: money; *green'd*: yearned;   *jaloused*: guessed;   *craitur'*: creature.

Questions

30. Using your own words, summarise the story told here of the mistress and Jean, making at least **four** key points.

4

31. Using **two** specific examples from lines 1—9, show how the description of the cave and/or the gentleman help to create a menacing atmosphere.

4

32. Identify two aspects of the mistress's character, as described in this extract. Give **two** examples to support your impressions.

4

33. Referring to this extract and to elsewhere in the novel, discuss the writer's use of narrative style.

8

OR

Text 5 — Prose

If you choose this text you may not write a critical essay on Prose in Section 2.

Read the extract below and then attempt the following questions.

***Kidnapped* by Robert Louis Stevenson**

In this extract, which is from Chapter 23 of the novel, David Balfour and Alan Breck Stewart are with Cluny Macpherson in 'Cluny's Cage'.

All the while Cluny entertained us with stories of Prince Charlie's stay in the Cage, giving us the very words of the speakers, and rising from his place to show us where they stood. By these, I gathered the Prince was a gracious, spirited boy, like the son of a race of polite kings, but not so wise as Solomon. I gathered, too, that while he was in the Cage,
5 he was often drunk; so the fault that has since, by all accounts, made such a wreck of him, had even then begun to show itself.

We were no sooner done eating than Cluny brought out an old, thumbed, greasy pack of cards, such as you may find in a mean inn; and his eyes brightened in his face as he proposed that we should fall to playing.

10 Now this was one of the things I had been brought up to eschew like disgrace; it being held by my father neither the part of a Christian nor yet of a gentleman to set his own livelihood and fish for that of others, on the cast of painted pasteboard. To be sure, I might have pleaded my fatigue, which was excuse enough; but I thought it behoved that I should bear a testimony. I must have got very red in the face, but I spoke steadily, and
15 told them I had no call to be a judge of others, but for my own part, it was a matter in which I had no clearness.

Cluny stopped mingling the cards. 'What in deil's name is this?' says he. 'What kind of Whiggish, canting talk is this, for the house of Cluny Macpherson?'

'I will put my hand in the fire for Mr. Balfour,' says Alan. 'He is an honest and a mettle
20 gentleman, and I would have ye bear in mind who says it. I bear a king's name,' says he, cocking his hat; 'and I and any that I call friend are company for the best. But the gentleman is tired, and should sleep; if he has no mind to the cartes, it will never hinder you and me. And I'm fit and willing, sir, to play ye any game that ye can name.'

'Sir,' says Cluny, 'in this poor house of mine I would have you to ken that any gentleman
25 may follow his pleasure. If your friend would like to stand on his head, he is welcome. And if either he, or you, or any other man, is not precisely satisfied, I will be proud to step outside with him.'

I had no will that these two friends should cut their throats for my sake.

'Sir,' said I, 'I am very wearied, as Alan says; and what's more, as you are a man that
30 likely has sons of your own, I may tell you it was a promise to my father.'

'Say nae mair, say nae mair,' said Cluny, and pointed me to a bed of heather in a corner of the Cage. For all that he was displeased enough, looked at me askance, and grumbled when he looked. And indeed it must be owned that both my scruples and the words in which I declared them, smacked somewhat of the Covenanter, and were little in their
35 place among wild Highland Jacobites.

MARKS

Questions

34. Look at paragraph 1 (lines 1—6).

In your own words, what are David's initial contrasting impressions of Cluny Macpherson?   **2**

35. Look at paragraph 3 (lines 10—16).

What is David's response to Cluny's suggestion to play cards and how does the author's language emphasise this response?   **3**

36. Look at lines 17—27.

(a) With reference to the author's use of **sentence structure**, explain in detail Cluny's **tone** in responding to David's earlier comments on the playing of cards.   **3**

(b) In response to Cluny, Alan says: "I will put my hand in the fire for Mr Balfour." (line 19)

Identify the technique being used here and explain in detail what Alan means by it.   **2**

37. Look at lines 28—35.

In your own words as far as possible, how does David excuse his attitude towards Alan and Cluny playing cards?   **2**

38. With close reference to this extract and elsewhere in the novel, discuss how the relationship between Alan and David could be considered 'complex'.   **8**

PART C — SCOTTISH TEXT — POETRY

Text 1 — Poetry

If you choose this text you may not write a critical essay on Poetry in Section 2.

Read the poem below and then attempt the following questions.

Havisham by Carol Ann Duffy

Beloved sweetheart bastard. Not a day since then
I haven't wished him dead. Prayed for it
so hard I've dark green pebbles for eyes,
ropes on the back of my hands I could strangle with.

5 Spinster. I stink and remember. Whole days
in bed cawing Nooooo at the wall; the dress
yellowing, trembling if I open the wardrobe;
the slewed mirror, full-length, her, myself, who did this

to me? Puce curses that are sounds not words.
10 Some nights better, the lost body over me,
my fluent tongue in its mouth in its ear
then down till I suddenly bite awake. Love's

hate behind a white veil; a red balloon bursting
in my face. Bang. I stabbed at a wedding cake.
15 Give me a male corpse for a long slow honeymoon.
Don't think it's only the heart that b-b-b-breaks.

MARKS

Questions

39. Many of the main concerns or ideas of the poem come across clearly in the first stanza.

    (a) Identify **two** of these main concerns or ideas.   2

    (b) Show how **one** example of the poet's use of language in stanza one helps to clarify or illustrate her meaning.   2

40. Show how **one** example of the poet's language in lines 5—9 highlights Havisham's distressed state during the day.   2

41. Show how **one** example of the poet's use of language in lines 10—12 highlights the nature of Havisham's dreams at night.   2

42. How effective do you find any **two** aspects of the final stanza as a conclusion to the poem?

    Your answer might deal with ideas and/or language.   4

43. With close textual reference, show how the ideas and/or language used when presenting the theme of love in this poem are similar and/or different to the way love is explored in another poem or poems by Duffy.   8

OR

Text 2 — Poetry

If you choose this text you may not write a critical essay on Poetry in Section 2.

Read the poem below and then attempt the following questions.

Bed **by Jackie Kay**

She is that guid to me so she is
An Am a burden tae her, I know Am ur.
Stuck here in this big blastit bed
Year in, year oot, ony saint wuid complain.

5   There's things she has tae dae fir me
A' wish she didnae huv tae dae.
Am her wean noo, wey ma great tent o' nappy,
Am champed egg in a cup, an mashed tattie.

Aw the treats A' used tae gie her,
10 She's gieing me. A' dinny ken whit happened.
We dinny talk any mair. Whether it's jist
The blethers ha been plucked oot o' us

Am here like some skinny chicken,
Ma skin aw bubbles and dots and spots,
15 Loose flap noo (an yet as a young wuman
A'took pride in ma guid smooth skin.)

Aw A' dae is sit an look oot this windae.
A've seen hale generations graw up
an simmer doon fray this same windae –
20 That's no seen a lick o' paint fir donkeys.

The Kerrs have disappeared, but the last
Campbells ur still here so Am telt –
Tho' hauf the time A' dinny believe her:
A've no seen ony Campbell in a lang time.

25 My dochter says 'Awright mother?'
Haunds me a thin broth or puried neep
An A say 'Aye fine,' an canny help
The great heaving sigh that comes oot

MARKS

My auld loose lips, nor ma crabbit tut,

30 Nor ma froon when A' pu' ma cardie tight

Aroon ma shooders fir the night drawin in.

Am jist biding time so am ur.

Time is whit A' hauld between

The soft bits o' ma thumbs,

35 The skeleton underneath ma night goon;

Aw the while the glaring selfish moon

Lights up this drab wee prison.

A'll be gone and how wull she feel?

No that Am saying A' want her guilty.

40 No that Am saying Am no grateful.

Questions

44. Look at the poem as a **whole** and identify **four** of the main ideas contained in the poem.   4

45. By referring to lines 1—20, show how word choice and sentence structure give a description of the speaker's helplessness/reliance on others.   4

46. By referring to lines 16—40, explain **one** thing that we learn about:

    (a) the community the speaker lives in   2

    (b) the speaker's attitude to her life at this time.   2

47. Jackie Kay often explores relationships in her poems. Refer briefly to the central relationship in this poem and go on to discuss a central relationship in **at least one** other poem by Jackie Kay.   8

OR

Text 3 — Poetry

If you choose this text you may not write a critical essay on Poetry in Section 2.

Read the poem below and then attempt the following questions.

Aunt Julia **by Norman MacCaig**

Aunt Julia spoke Gaelic
very loud and very fast.
I could not answer her —
I could not understand her.

5 She wore men's boots
when she wore any.
— I can see her strong foot,
stained with peat,
paddling with the treadle of the spinning wheel
10 while her right hand drew yarn
marvellously out of the air.

Hers was the only house
where I've lain at night
in a box bed, listening to
15 crickets being friendly.

She was buckets
and water flouncing into them.
She was winds pouring wetly
round house-ends.
20 She was brown eggs, black skirts
and a keeper of threepenny bits
in a teapot.

Aunt Julia spoke Gaelic
very loud and very fast.
25 By the time I had learned
a little, she lay
silenced in the absolute black
of a sandy grave
at Luskentyre.

MARKS

30 But I hear her still, welcoming me

with a seagull's voice

across a hundred yards

of peatscrapes and lazybeds

and getting angry, getting angry

35 with so many questions

unanswered.

Questions

48. By referring to **one** technique, show how the first stanza is an effective opening to the poem.

2

49. In stanza two, show how MacCaig uses language to convey the memorable aspects of Aunt Julia's personality.

4

50. Show how any **one** example of the poet's use of language in stanza four contributes to his description of Aunt Julia.

2

51. By referring to the last stanza, show how MacCaig creates a sense of regret.

4

52. MacCaig often observes people or places in his poetry. Referring closely to this poem and to **at least one** other poem by MacCaig, show how MacCaig uses observation of people or places in his poems.

8

OR

Text 4 — Poetry

If you choose this text you may not write a critical essay on Poetry in Section 2.

Read the poem below and then attempt the following questions.

Trio **by Edwin Morgan**

Coming up Buchanan Street, quickly, on a sharp winter evening
a young man and two girls, under the Christmas lights –
The young man carries a new guitar in his arms,
the girl on the inside carries a very young baby,
5 and the girl on the outside carries a chihuahua.
And the three of them are laughing, their breath rises
in a cloud of happiness, and as they pass
the boy says, 'Wait till he sees this but!'
The chihuahua has a tiny Royal Stewart tartan coat like a teapot-
10   holder,
the baby in its white shawl is all bright eyes and mouth like favours
    in a fresh sweet cake,
the guitar swells out under its milky plastic cover, tied at the neck
    with silver tinsel tape and a brisk sprig of mistletoe.
15 Orphean sprig! Melting baby! Warm chihuahua!
The vale of tears is powerless before you.
Whether Christ is born, or is not born, you
put paid to fate, it abdicates
                  under the Christmas lights.
20 Monsters of the year
  go blank, are scattered back,
  can't bear this march of three.

And the three have passed, vanished in the crowd
(yet not vanished, for in their arms they wind
25 the life of men and beasts, and music,
laughter ringing them round like a guard)
at the end of this winter's day.

MARKS

Questions

53. Look at lines 1—2. Show how the poet's use of language effectively brings the scene to life.   **2**

54. Examine **three** examples of how the poet uses language to create a positive atmosphere in lines 6—14.   **6**

55. (a) Identify **two** of the central concerns of the poem.   **2**

    (b) How effective do you find any aspect of lines 15—27 in enforcing either of these two concerns? You may refer to ideas and/or language.   **2**

56. With close textual reference, discuss in what ways this poem is similar to another poem or poems by Morgan you have studied. You may refer to ideas and/or language in your answer.   **8**

[END OF SECTION 1]

SECTION 2 — CRITICAL ESSAY — 20 marks

Attempt ONE question from this Section of the paper choosing from the following genres — Drama, Prose, Poetry, Film and Television Drama, or Language.

You may use a Scottish text but NOT the one you used in Section 1.

Your essay should be on a different GENRE to the one you chose in Section 1.

You should spend about 45 minutes on the essay.

DRAMA

Answers to questions on Drama should refer to the text and to such relevant features as characterisation, key scene(s), structure, climax, theme, plot, conflict, setting . . .

1. Choose a play which you feel has a turning-point.

   Describe briefly what happens at this turning point and then, by referring to appropriate techniques, go on to explain how it makes an impact on the play as a whole.

2. Choose a play in which the playwright presents a flawed character who you feel is more worthy of our sympathy than criticism.

   By referring to appropriate techniques, show how the character's flawed nature is revealed, then explain how, despite this, we are led to feel sympathy for her/him.

PROSE

Answers to questions on Prose should refer to the text and to such relevant features as characterisation, setting, language, key incident(s), climax, turning point, plot, structure, narrative technique, theme, ideas, description . . .

3. Choose a novel **or** a short story **or** a work of non-fiction which explores an important theme.

   By referring to appropriate techniques, show how the author has explored this theme.

4. Choose a novel **or** a short story in which the author creates a fascinating character.

   By referring to appropriate techniques, show how the author has created this character and why you found him/her so fascinating.

POETRY

Answers to questions on Poetry should refer to the text and to such relevant features as word choice, tone, imagery, structure, content, rhythm, rhyme, theme, sound, ideas . . .

5. Choose a poem which made a lasting impression on you.

   Explain briefly what the poem is about, then, by referring to appropriate techniques, show how the poem has made this lasting impression.

6. Choose a poem which features an encounter or an incident.

   By referring to appropriate techniques, show how the poet's development of the encounter or incident leads you to a deeper understanding of the poem's central concerns.

FILM AND TELEVISION DRAMA

Answers to questions on Film and Television Drama should refer to the text and to such relevant features as use of camera, key sequence, characterisation, mise-en-scène, editing, setting, music/sound, special effects, plot, dialogue . . .

7. Choose a scene or sequence from a film **or** television drama* which had an impact on you.

   Briefly describe the events which led to this scene or sequence, then, by referring to appropriate techniques, go on to show how this impact was created.

8. Choose a film or television drama which belongs to a particular genre (eg crime, adventure, romance, soap opera, sit-com, thriller...)

   By referring to appropriate techniques, explain how the film or television makers have used features of this genre effectively.

* "television drama" includes a single play, a series or a serial.

LANGUAGE

> *Answers to questions on Language should refer to the text and to such relevant features as register, accent, dialect, slang, jargon, vocabulary, tone, abbreviation . . .*

9. Choose a print or non-print text which aims to persuade people.

   By referring to specific examples from your chosen text, show how persuasive techniques are used to engage the reader/viewer.

10. Consider a form of communication used by a particular group of people.

   By referring to appropriate techniques such as distinctive vocabulary or grammatical constructions, show how the group's language is different from that used by the general population and discuss the advantages to the group of using its specific language.

[END OF SECTION 2]

[END OF SPECIMEN QUESTION PAPER]

Acknowledgement of Copyright

Section 1 Question 1   Extract is taken from *"Tally's Blood"* by Ann Marie di Mambro, ISBN 9781471808401. Published by Hodder Education. Reproduced by permission of Hodder Education.

Section 1 Question 2   Extract is taken from *"Bold Girls"* by Rona Munro, ISBN 9780340655276. Published by Hodder Education. Reproduced by permission of Hodder Education.

Section 1 Question 3   Extract is taken from *"Sailmaker Plus"* by Alan Spence, ISBN 9780340973035. Published by Hodder Education. Reproduced by permission of Hodder Education.

Section 1 Question 4   Extract is taken from *"Telegram"* by Iain Crichton Smith from The Red Door, The Complete English Stories 1949-1976, ISBN 1841581607. Published by Birlinn. Reproduced by permission of Birlinn.

Section 1 Question 5   Extract is taken from *"A Chitterin' Bite"* by Anne Donovan from Hieroglyphics and Other Stories, ISBN 9781841955193. Published by Canongate Books Ltd. Reproduced by permission of Canongate Books Ltd.

Section 1 Question 6   Extract is taken from *"The Cone Gatherers"* by Robin Jenkins, ISBN 9781841959894. Published by Canongate Books Ltd. Reproduced by permission of Canongate Books Ltd.

Section 1 Question 7   Extract is taken from *"The Testament of Gideon Mack"* by James Robertson, ISBN 9780141049663. Published by Penguin Books Ltd. Reproduced by permission of Penguin Books Ltd.

Section 1 Question 8   Extract is taken from *"Kidnapped"* by Robert Louis Stevenson. Public Domain.

Section 1 Question 9   Poem, *"Havisham"* by Carol Ann Duffy, is taken from New Selected Poems 1984-2004, ISBN 9780330433945. Published by Picador. Reproduced by permission of Pan Macmillan.

Section 1 Question 10   Poem, *"Bed"* by Jackie Kay, is taken from Darling: New & Selected Poems, ISBN 9781852247775. Published by Bloodaxe Books, 2007. Reproduced by permission of Bloodaxe Books.

Section 1 Question 11   Poem, *"Aunt Julia"* by Norman MacCaig, is taken from The Poems of Norman MacCaig (edited by Ewan MacCaig), ISBN 9781846971365. Published by Polygon. Reproduced by permission of Birlinn.

Section 1 Question 12   Poem, *"Trio"* by Edwin Morgan, is taken from Edwin Morgan New Selected Poems, ISBN 1857544595. Published by Carcanet Press Ltd. Reproduced by permission of Carcanet Press Ltd.

Model Paper 1

Whilst this Model Practice Paper has been specially commissioned by Hodder Gibson for use as practice for the National 5 exams, the key reference documents remain the SQA Specimen Paper 2013 and the SQA Past Paper 2014.

HODDER
GIBSON
LEARN MORE

National Qualifications
MODEL PAPER 1

English
Reading for Understanding, Analysis and Evaluation

Duration — 1 hour

Total marks — 30

When you are told to do so, open the booklet, read the passage and attempt all the questions, using your own words as far as possible.

Before attempting the questions you must check that your answer booklet is for the same subject and level as this question paper.

On the answer booklet, you must clearly identify the question number you are attempting.

Use **blue** or **black** ink.

Before leaving the examination room you must give your answer booklet to the Invigilator. If you do not, you may lose all the marks for this paper.

SUPERSTITION

In this passage, the writer explores how superstition can both help and hinder us.

Tennis players are a funny bunch. Have you noticed how they always ask for three balls instead of two; how they bounce the ball the same number of times before serving, as if any deviation from their routine might bring the world collapsing on their heads?

5   But the superstitions and rituals so beloved by the world's top players are not confined to the court. They take even more bizarre twists when the poor dears get home after their matches. Goran Ivanisevic got it into his head that if he won a match he had to repeat everything he did the previous day, such as eating the same food at the same restaurant, talking to the same people and watching the same TV programmes. One year this meant that he had to watch Teletubbies every morning during his Wimbledon campaign. "Sometimes it got very boring," he
10 said.

Could it be that these multifarious superstitions tell us something of deeper importance not only about humanity but about other species on the planet?

The answer, I think, is to be found in the world of pigeon. Yes, really. These feathered fellows, you see, are the tennis players of the bird world. Don't take my word for it: that was the
15 opinion of B. F. Skinner, the man widely regarded as the father of modern psychology.

Skinner's view was based on a groundbreaking experiment that he carried out in 1947 in which he placed some hungry pigeons in a cage attached to an automatic mechanism that delivered food "at regular intervals with no reference whatsoever to the bird's behaviour". He discovered that the pigeons associated the delivery of the food with whatever chance actions they happened to be
20 performing at the moment it was first delivered. So what did the pigeons do? They kept performing the same actions, even though they had no effect whatsoever on the release of food.

I know, I know. This is nothing compared with the weird behaviour that goes on at Wimbledon, but do you see the connection? The pigeons were acting as if they could influence the mechanism delivering the Trill in just the same way that Ivanisevic thought that he could
25 influence the outcome of his next match by watching Teletubbies. To put it a tad formally, they both witnessed a random connection between a particular kind of behaviour and a desired outcome, and then (wrongly) inferred that one caused the other.

But did Ivanisevic really believe that his superstitions were effective or was he just having us on? Well, let's hear from the man himself — this is what he said when asked if he had ever
30 abandoned a ritual when it stopped working: "I didn't. They do work. I won Wimbledon." So, he really did believe. And what of the pigeons? They were, unfortunately, unavailable for interview.

Even cricketers, perhaps the brightest and most sensible sportsmen of all (well, that's what they tell us), are not immune to superstition. Jack Russell, the former England wicketkeeper, was among the most notorious, refusing to change his hat or wicketkeeping pads throughout his
35 career, even though they became threadbare and smelly, something that really got up the noses of his team-mates.

But this raises another, deeper question: why do so many of us maintain rituals of various kinds when they have no real connection with the desired outcome? Or, to put it another way, why is superstitious behaviour so widespread, not just within our species but beyond, when it seems to
40 confer no tangible benefits? It's here that things get really interesting (and just a little complex). And, as with most interesting things, the answer is to be found in deep evolutionary history.

Imagine a caveman going to pick some berries from some bushes near his rocky abode. He hears some rustling in the bushes and wrongly infers that there is a lion lurking in there and scarpers.
45 He even gets a little superstitious about those bushes and gives them a wide berth in future. Is this superstition a problem to our caveman? Well, not if there are plenty other berry-bearing bushes from which to get his five-a-day.

But suppose that there really is a lion living in those bushes. The caveman's behaviour now looks not only sensible but life-saving. So, a tendency to perceive connections that do not actually
50 exist can confer huge evolutionary benefits, providing a cocoon of safety in a turbulent and dangerous world. The only proviso (according to some devilishly complicated mathematics known as game theory) is this: your superstitions must not impose too much of a burden on those occasions when they are without foundation.

And this is almost precisely what superstitions look like in the modern world. Some believe in
55 horoscopes, but few allow them to dictate their behaviour; some like to wear the same lucky shoes to every job interview, but it is not as if wearing a different pair would improve their chances of success; some like to bounce the ball precisely seven times before serving at tennis, but although they are wrong to suppose that this ball-bouncing is implicated in their success, it does not harm their prospects.

60 It is only when a superstition begins to compromise our deeper goals and aspirations that we have moved along the spectrum of irrationality far enough to risk a diagnosis of obsessive compulsive disorder. Take Kolo Touré, the former Arsenal defender who insists on being the last player to leave the dressing room after the half-time break. No real problem, you might think, except that when William Gallas, his team-mate, was injured and needed treatment at half-time
65 during a match, Touré stayed in the dressing room until Gallas had been treated, forcing Arsenal to start the second half with only nine players.

When a superstition that is supposed to help you actually hinders you, it is probably time to kick the ritual into touch. With a rabbit's foot, obviously.

Adapted from an article by Matthew Syed in The Times.

MARKS

Questions

1. In line 14, the writer says that pigeons "are the tennis players of the bird world". Referring to key ideas in lines 1–27, explain what he means by this.   **4**

2. Look at lines 28–36.

    (a) What impression does the writer create of Goran Ivanisevic in these lines?   **2**

    (b) How does the writer convey surprise at the behaviour of Jack Russell?   **2**

3. Explain **in your own words** what key points the writer is illustrating by referring to the caveman (lines 43–53).   **4**

4. Describe the key features of the **sentence structure** in lines 54–59 and explain how it helps to convey the writer's main point.   **4**

5. Look at lines 60–68.

    (a) Explain how effective you find the word "spectrum" (line 61) as an **image** or **metaphor** to illustrate people's "irrationality".   **2**

    (b) Why does the writer include the anecdote about the footballer Kolo Touré (lines 62–66)?   **2**

    (c) How effective do you find the tone of the last paragraph (lines 67–68) as a conclusion to the passage?   **2**

6. A common feature of the writer's style in this passage is to use words or expressions which are unexpected in order to create a light-hearted tone. Find **two** examples of this from lines 1–47 and explain what is unexpected about each.   **4**

7. Referring to the whole article, list **in your own words** the key points the writer makes about superstitions.   **4**

[END OF MODEL PRACTICE PAPER]

Page four

National Qualifications
MODEL PAPER 1

English
Critical Reading

Duration — 1 hour and 30 minutes

Total marks — 40

SECTION 1 — Scottish Text — 20 marks

Read an extract from a Scottish text you have previously studied and attempt the questions.

Choose ONE text from either

Part A — Drama   Pages 2–7
or
Part B — Prose   Pages 8–17
or
Part C — Poetry   Pages 18–25

Attempt ALL the questions for your chosen text.

SECTION 2 — Critical Essay — 20 marks

Write ONE critical essay on previously studied text from Drama, Prose, Poetry, Film and Television Drama, or Language.

Your answer must be on a different genre from that chosen in Section 1.

You should spend approximately 45 minutes on each Section.

Before attempting the questions you must check that your answer booklet is for the same subject and level as this question paper.

On the answer booklet, you must clearly identify the question number you are attempting.

Use **blue** or **black** ink.

Before leaving the examination room you must give your answer booklet to the Invigilator. If you do not you may lose all the marks for this paper.

SECTION 1 — SCOTTISH TEXT — 20 marks

PART A — SCOTTISH TEXT — DRAMA

Text 1 — Drama

If you choose this text you may not attempt a question on Drama in Section 2.

Read the extract below and then attempt the following questions.

Bold Girls **by Rona Munro**

This extract is from Act One.

Deirdre appears in Marie's house for the first time.

Deirdre comes into the room. She stands uncertain in the centre of the room.

Marie enters behind her

The three older women just stare at Deirdre.

DEIRDRE: Can I stay here till I'm dry, Mrs? They won't let me up the road.

5 *There is a pause then Marie finally stirs*

MARIE: You better sit down by the fire *(She switches on the TV)*

Deirdre sits by the fire

Nora, Marie and Cassie slowly sit as well, watching her

NORA: I don't know your face.

10 *Deirdre says nothing. She doesn't look up from the fire*

                Well where are you from?

Deirdre jerks her head without turning

                Where?

DEIRDRE: *(sullen, quietly)* Back of the school there.

15 NORA: What's that?

DEIRDRE: *(loudly)* Back of the school there.

NORA: Those houses next the off-licence?

Deirdre nods

                I know where you are. So what happened to you then?

20 *Deirdre shrugs. She looks up and catches Cassie's eye*

Cassie turns quickly to look at the TV

MARIE: Will you take a cup of tea, love?

Deirdre nods

Marie goes to make it

25 *Nora stares at Deirdre a while longer, then turns to Cassie*

NORA: So Cassie, looks like that wee brother of yours will miss his tea altogether?

CASSIE: *(with her eyes on the TV)* Looks like he might.

NORA: I hope he's the sense to stay in town.

MARKS

CASSIE: Sure he'll phone next door, let us know what's happening.

30 NORA: Aye he's a good boy.

There is a pause while everyone watches the TV in an uncomfortable silence

Marie brings Deirdre the tea and some biscuits. Deirdre takes it without saying anything, starts to eat and drink furtively and ravenously. Cassie and Marie exchange glances over her head

35 MARIE: Turn the sound up on that will you, Nora?

Questions

1. By referring to the whole extract, identify **four** ways in which Deirdre's behaviour makes her appear strange.   **4**

2. Describe the way each of the three older women treats Deirdre. Support your answers with reference to the text.   **6**

3. Why do you think Marie asks Nora to turn up the sound on the TV? (line 35)   **2**

4. By referring to this extract and to the play as a whole, discuss the role of Deirdre in the play.   **8**

OR

Text 2 — Drama

If you choose this text you may not attempt a question on Drama in Section 2.

Read the extract below and then attempt the following questions.

Sailmaker by Alan Spence

This extract is from the closing moments of Act One.

(DAVIE *and* BILLY *enter, opposite sides of stage*)

BILLY: What's up wi your face?

(DAVIE *shakes head*)

          What's the matter?

5 DAVIE: Ah just got ma jotters. Week's notice.

    BILLY: Jesus Christ! What for?

    DAVIE: Ach! They're saying the book's a dead loss. They're gonnae shut it awthegether. Put the sheriff's officers on tae the folk that still owe money.

    BILLY: Bastards.

10 DAVIE: Getting that doin just finished it. Losin the money an the ledgers an everythin.

    BILLY: But that wasnae your fault!

    DAVIE: Try tellin *them* that! So that's me. Scrubbed. Again. Laid off. Redundant. Services no longer required. Just like that. Ah don't know. Work aw yer days an what've ye got tae show for it? Turn roon an kick ye in the teeth. Ah mean, what *have* ye got
15   when ye come right down tae it. Nothin.

    BILLY: Ah might be able to get ye a start in our place. Cannae promise mind ye. An if there was anything it wouldnae be much. Maybe doin yer sweeper up or that.

    DAVIE: Anythin's better than nothin.

    BILLY: An once yer in the place, ye never know. Somethin better might come up.

20 DAVIE: *(Dead)* Aye.

    BILLY: Likes ae a storeman's job or that.

    DAVIE: Aye.

    BILLY: We never died a winter yet, eh?

(DAVIE *nods.* BILLY *exits*)

25 DAVIE: Scrubbed. Get yer jacket on. Pick up yer cards. On yer way pal! Out the door.

(ALEC *is playing with yacht, positions fid like bowsprit, bow like mast, tries to make 'sail' with cellophane, can't hold all the separate bits, drops them. DAVIE comes in behind him*)

    DAVIE: Bit of bad news son.

(*Pause*)

30   Ah've lost ma job. They gave me ma books.

    ALEC: What'll we dae?

MARKS

DAVIE: Billy says he might be able to fix me up wi something. Wouldnae be much. (*Shrugs*)
           Better than nothing. Ach, that was a lousy job anyway. Ah'm better off out ae it.
           Whatever happens.

35   Place is a right mess eh. Amazin how it gets on top of ye.

ALEC: Ah'll shove this in the Glory Hole. Out the road.

(*Folds up cellophane, puts tools in bag and picks up bow, yacht, carries the lot and exits*)

DAVIE: Ach aye. No to worry. Never died a winter yet.

Questions

5. Summarise what is said between Davie and Billy in lines 1–23. Make at least **four** key points.   4

6. Explain how the sentence structure of lines 12–15 help the audience to understand how Davie is feeling.   2

7. Explain how the dialogue in lines 16–23 emphasises the difference between the two characters.   2

8. Explain in detail what is revealed about Davie's personality in lines 32–38.   4

9. By referring to this extract and to elsewhere in the play, show how the playwright presents the character of Davie.   8

OR

Text 3 — Drama

If you choose this text you may not attempt a question on Drama in Section 2.

Read the extract below and then attempt the following questions.

Tally's Blood by Ann Marie di Mambro

This extract is from Act One, Scene Two. It is 1939. Lucia is five years old.

	MASSIMO:	Listen, Rosie, I thought you went to Glasgow to buy yourself a new coat.
	ROSINELLA:	Oh, but see when I saw that wee dress I just had to get her it. My heart's breaking for that wee lassie these days.
	MASSIMO:	She's just a wean. She'll no understand.
5	ROSINELLA:	But she's lovely in it, isn't she?
	MASSIMO:	Don't get me wrong. I don't grudge the wean a frock. God forbid. It's just you I'm worried about. Last year when I gave you money for a coat you bought jumpers to send to Italy.
	ROSINELLA:	So?

10 *Massimo smiles with great affection, squeezes her cheek between his thumb and forefinger.*

	MASSIMO:	So what have I to do with you, you daft wee besom, you?

Lucia comes back carrying her schoolbag: Massimo takes it from her.

	MASSIMO:	Oh, is this what I got? Let me see. Oh, that's great, so it is. Just what I was needing for bringing home the tatties. Oh here, it's awfy wee. You better just take
15		it, Lucia.

He pretends to put it on: Lucia giggles.

	LUCIA:	Uncle Massimo, you're awful silly.
	ROSINELLA:	Now away you go, Lucia, and take off your lovely dress.
	LUCIA:	*(Mood changing/petulant)* I want to keep it on.
20	ROSINELLA:	*(Coaxing)* You need to take it off, love.
	LUCIA:	No.
	MASSIMO:	Keep it nice for something special.
	LUCIA:	No.
	ROSINELLA:	If you take it off now I'll let you wear it to mass this Sunday.
25	LUCIA:	I want to keep it on.
	ROSINELLA:	Come on, hen.
	LUCIA:	I'm keeping it on, I says.
	MASSIMO:	You better no let her away with that.
	ROSINELLA:	Come on, darling, we'll get you changed.
30	LUCIA:	*(Starting to shout)* No, no, no.
	ROSINELLA:	*(Voice raised but pleading)* Now Lucia!

Massimo glances over shoulder in direction of front shop.

MARKS

	LUCIA:	I don't want to. I don't want to.

35 MASSIMO: Sshh! You two. I've got customers out there. *(To Lucia)* Do what your Auntie Rosinella tells you, darling, there's a good girl.

Rosinella takes Lucia's arm to lead her away.

ROSINELLA: Come on, Lucia.

Lucia starts to scream and pull back.

LUCIA: No, no, no, leave me alone, I want to keep it on. I want to keep it on.
40   No – no – no –

Rosinella and Massimo look helplessly at each other. Massimo also keeps glancing in direction of shop, anxious to get back.

ROSINELLA: *(Appealing)* Massimo.

MASSIMO: Maybe you're being too hard on her.

45 ROSINELLA: Me?

MASSIMO: Why no let her keep it on for a wee while, eh?

ROSINELLA: Just a wee while, then, OK.

Lucia controls her sobs (she's won).

LUCIA: Okay.

Questions

10. Summarise what happens in this extract. Make at least three key points.   **3**

11. What does the audience learn about Rosinella's character from lines 1–9?   **2**

12. By referring in detail to lines 19–49, explain how the playwright makes Lucia's behaviour typical of a young child.   **4**

13. At this stage in the play the characters have only been in Scotland for three years, but their speech shows clear signs of Scottish words and phrases. Quote three examples of this from anywhere in the extract.   **3**

14. The extract looks at the relationship between Lucia and her aunt and uncle. With close reference to this extract and elsewhere in the play, explain how their relationship is portrayed.   **8**

PART B — SCOTTISH TEXT — PROSE

Text 1 — Prose

If you choose this text you may not attempt a question on Prose in Section 2.

Read the extract below and then attempt the following questions.

The Cone-Gatherers by Robin Jenkins

This extract is from Chapter 11. Calum and Neil are in a tree when a storm begins and they climb down to seek shelter.

The brothers crept slowly downward. Every time lightning flashed and thunder crashed they thought their tree had been shattered, and clung, helpless as woodlice, waiting to be hurled to the ground with the fragments. The tree itself seemed to be terrified; every branch, every twig, heaved and slithered. At times it seemed to have torn its roots in its terror and to be dangling in
5 the air.

At last they reached the ground. At once Neil flung his bag of cones down and snatched up his knapsack. He shouted to Calum to do likewise.

"We'd never get to the hut alive," he gasped. "We'd get killed among the trees. Forby, it's too far away. We're going to the beach hut."

10 "But we're not allowed, Neil."

Neil clutched his brother and spoke to him as calmly as he could.

"I ken it's not allowed, Calum," he said. "I ken we gave our promise to Mr. Tulloch not to get into any more trouble. But look at the rain. We're soaked already. I've got rheumatics, and you ken your chest is weak. If we shelter under a tree it might get struck by lightning and we'd
15 be killed. In three minutes we can reach the beach hut."

"But we promised, Neil. The lady will be angry again."

"Do you want me then to be a useless cripple for the rest of my days? What if she is angry? All she can do is tell us to leave her wood, and I'll be glad to go. I don't want you to do what you think is wrong, Calum; but sometimes we've got to choose between two things, neither of them
20 to our liking. We'll do no harm. We'll leave the place as we find it. Nobody will ever ken we've been in it. What do you say then?"

Calum nodded unhappily.

"I think maybe we should go," he said.

"All right then. We'd better run for it. But didn't I tell you to drop your cone bag?"

25 "They'll get all wet, Neil."

Neil stood gaping; he saw the rain streaming down the green grime on his brother's face; beyond Calum was the wood shrouded in wet.

"They'll get wet," he heard himself repeating.

"Aye, that's right, Neil. Mind what Mr. Tulloch said, if they get wet they're spoiled."

30 It was no use being bitter or angry or sarcastic.

"Is there never to be any sun again then," cried Neil, "to dry them?"

Calum looked up at the sky.

"I think so, Neil," he murmured.

MARKS

Questions

15. Explain **two** ways in which the writer's use of language in lines 1–5 conveys the violence of the storm.   **4**

16. Look at lines 6–10. Show how the writer's word choice makes clear how impatient Neil is. Refer to **two** examples.   **2**

17. Using your own words as far as possible, summarise the key points in Neil's argument to persuade Calum to go to the beach hut (lines 12–21). Make at least **four** key points.   **4**

18. How does the writer make Calum seem childlike in lines 25–34?   **2**

19. By referring to this extract and to elsewhere in the novel, discuss the relationship between Calum and Neil.   **8**

OR

Text 2 — Prose

If you choose this text you may not attempt a question on Prose in Section 2.

Read the extract below and then attempt the following questions.

The Testament of Gideon Mack by James Robertson

This extract is from Chapter 25. Gideon is visiting Catherine Craigie for the first time. He has rung the bell twice, but nothing has happened...

"Just come in, for heaven's sake. It's not locked."

I leaned forward to open the door and noticed a handwritten card taped to wall of the vestibule: *Please ring and enter. If locked go away.*

"Can't you read?" the voice said as I let myself in.

5   "Sorry," I said, "I only just saw it. I'm sorry if I've interrupted you."

"You shouldn't have rung the bell if you didn't want to interrupt me," Miss Craigie said. "I don't sit around waiting for visitors all day, you know. Oh, it's you."

She said these last words not apologetically but with added distaste. It was dark in the hallway, and I could not make out the expression on her face, but the tone of voice told
10   me all I needed to know. I'd been well warned by various members of my flock: Catherine Craigie thought that the Kirk, by and large, had been, was and always would be a scabrous outbreak on the flesh of Scotland.

I was wearing my dog collar – I was planning to make some other calls that evening – and assumed that this was the cause of her aggravation. I tapped it with my forefinger.

15   "It doesn't make you a bad person," I said.

"Hmph," she retorted. "It doesn't make you a good one either. What do you want?"

"I've come to say hello, Miss Craigie. I've been here nearly four years and I feel we should have met by now." This didn't seem to impress her. "And I want to ask you some questions about the standing stones. I've been reading your book."

20   "Well, it's all in there, so I don't see why you need to come bothering me if you haven't taken the trouble to read it properly."

"Supplementary questions," I said. "Arising out of what I've read."

"I know what a supplementary question is," she said. "Such as?"

I'd had the forethought to compose something beforehand.

25   "Well, it seems to me, in all this debate about pre-Christian and Christianised Picts, that we forget that they were under pressure from two rival Christianities, the Celtic and the Roman – the Scots in the west and the Northumbrians in the south. And I wondered what bearing that might have had on the symbols on the stones."

During this speech her head inclined toward me like a bird's listening for danger, or for a
30   worm. Later, I realised that this stance was in part due to her illness, which prevented her from moving her neck very much. She was standing halfway down the hallway, holding on to a tall wooden plant-stand positioned in the middle of a large rug. There was no plant on the plant-stand and it took me a moment to understand the reason for its location: the lay-out of the hall, from the front door to the foot of the stairs and on towards the back
35   lobby, was a kind of domestic rock-face, with hand-holds and rest points along the way, some pre-existing and some strategically placed: the plant-stand, a chair, a table, a stool, a shelf, the banister end, radiators. This horizontal climbing-wall was how Miss Craigie managed to get around her house.

MARKS

Questions

20. By referring closely to lines 1–12, show how the writer presents Miss Craigie as an intimidating character.   **4**

21. Show how the dialogue in lines 13–23 conveys the friction between Gideon and Miss Craigie.   **4**

22. Show how the writer's **sentence structure** and **imagery** help to describe the layout of Miss Craigie's hallway in lines 31–38.   **4**

23. By referring to the extract and to elsewhere in the novel, discuss the relationship between Gideon and Miss Craigie.   **8**

OR

Text 3 — Prose

If you choose this text you may not attempt a question on Prose in Section 2.

Read the extract below and then attempt the following questions.

Kidnapped by Robert Louis Stevenson

This extract is from Chapter 19 – "The House of Fear". David and Alan arrive at the home of James Stewart of the Glens.

At last, about half-past ten of the clock, we came to the top of a brae, and saw lights below us. It seemed a house door stood open and let out a beam of fire and candle-light; and all round the house and steading five or six persons were moving hurriedly about, each carrying a lighted brand.

5 "James must have tint his wits," said Alan. "If this was the soldiers instead of you and me, he would be in a bonny mess. But I dare say he'll have a sentry on the road, and he would ken well enough no soldiers would find the way that we came."

Hereupon he whistled three times, in a particular manner. It was strange to see how, at the first sound of it, all the moving torches came to a stand, as if the bearers were affrighted; and 10 how, at the third, the bustle began again as before.

Having thus set folks' minds at rest, we came down the brae, and were met at the yard gate (for this place was like a well-doing farm) by a tall, handsome man of more than fifty, who cried out to Alan in the Gaelic.

"James Stewart," said Alan, "I will ask ye to speak in Scotch, for here is a young gentleman 15 with me that has nane of the other. This is him," he added, putting his arm through mine, "a young gentleman of the Lowlands, and a laird in his country too, but I am thinking it will be the better for his health if we give his name the go-by."

James of the Glens turned to me for a moment, and greeted me courteously enough; the next he had turned to Alan.

20 "This has been a dreadful accident," he cried. "It will bring trouble on the country." And he wrung his hands.

"Hoots!" said Alan, "ye must take the sour with the sweet, man. Colin Roy is dead, and be thankful for that!"

"Ay," said James, "and by my troth, I wish he was alive again! It's all very fine to blow and 25 boast beforehand; but now it's done, Alan; and who's to bear the wyte of it? The accident fell out in Appin – mind ye that, Alan; it's Appin that must pay; and I am a man that has a family."

While this was going on I looked about me at the servants. Some were on ladders, digging in the thatch of the house or the farm buildings, from which they brought out guns, swords, and 30 different weapons of war; others carried them away; and by the sound of mattock blows from somewhere farther down the brae, I suppose they buried them. Though they were all so busy, there prevailed no kind of order in their efforts; men struggled together for the same gun and ran into each other with their burning torches; and James was continually turning about from his talk with Alan, to cry out orders which were apparently never understood. 35 The faces in the torchlight were like those of people overborne with hurry and panic; and though none spoke above his breath, their speech sounded both anxious and angry.

MARKS

Questions

24. Look at lines 1–7.

    Why does Alan think that "James must have tint his wits"? 2

25. What impression of David is Alan trying to create when he introduces him to James Stewart? Support your answer with reference to lines 14–17. 2

26. By referring to lines 20–27, explain in your own words the differing reactions of Alan and James to the "accident". 4

27. Show how the writer creates a sense of panic in lines 28–36. 4

28. With reference to this extract and to elsewhere in the novel, discuss the characterisation of Alan Breck. 8

OR

Text 4 — Prose

If you choose this text you may not attempt a question on Prose in Section 2.

Read the extract below and then attempt the following questions.

Mother and Son by Iain Crichton Smith

In the bed was a woman. She was sleeping, her mouth tightly shut and prim and anaemic. There was a bitter smile on her lips as if fixed there; just as you sometimes see the insurance man coming to the door with the same smile each day, the same brilliant smile which never falls away till he's gone into the anonymity of the streets. The forehead was
5 not very high and not low, though its wrinkles gave it an expression of concentration as if the woman were wrestling with some terrible witch's idea in dreams.

The man looked at her for a moment, then fumbled for his matches again and began to light a fire. The sticks fell out of place and he cursed vindictively and helplessly. For a moment he sat squatting on his haunches staring into the fire, as if he were thinking of
10 some state of innocence, some state to which he could not return: a reminiscent smile dimpled his cheeks and showed in eyes which immediately became still and dangerous again.

The clock struck five wheezingly and, at the first chime, the woman woke up. She started as she saw the figure crouched over the fire and then subsided: "It's only you." There was
15 relief in the voice, but there was a curious hint of contempt or acceptance. He still sat staring into the fire and answered dully: "Yes, it's only me!" He couldn't be said to speak the words: they fell away from him as sometimes happens when one is in a deep reverie where every question is met by its answer almost instinctively.

"Well, what's the matter with you!" she snapped pettishly, "sitting there moping with the
20 tea to be made. I sometimes don't know why we christened you John" – with a sigh. "My father was never like you. He was a man who knew his business."

"All right, *all* right," he said despairingly. "Can't you get a new record for your gramophone. I've heard all that before," as if he were conscious of the inadequacy of this familiar retort – he added: "hundreds of times." But she wasn't to be stopped.

25 "I can't understand what has come over you lately. You keep mooning about the house, pacing up and down with your hands in your pockets. Do you know what's going to happen to you, you'll be taken to the asylum. That's where you'll go. Your father's people had something wrong with their heads, it was in your family but not in ours."

MARKS

Questions

29. Explain two ways the writer creates an unpleasant impression of the mother in lines 1–6.   **4**

30. Show how the man's reaction is made clear in lines 7–12.   **2**

31. Look at lines 13–18. Describe in your own words the way the son replies to his mother's comment.   **2**

32. By referring closely to lines 19–28, show how the hostility between mother and son is made clear to the reader.   **4**

33. By referring to this story and to at least one other by Iain Crichton Smith, discuss how he explores conflict between characters.   **8**

OR

Text 5 — Prose

If you choose this text you may not attempt a question on Prose in Section 2.

Read the extract below and then attempt the following questions.

Zimmerobics **by Anne Donovan**

And there's this constant feeling of awareness in every part of my body; jaggy pains in my elbows and knees, vertebrae grinding against one another, bits that used to fit together smoothly now clicking and clunking like the central heating boiler starting up. I did once try to explain it to Catherine.

5 "It's like the shows, those games where you get a circle on a stick and you have to feed it along a twisted wire, very carefully without touching it and, if you touch the wire a bell rings."

"Uh-huh." She is busy rearranging ornaments on the mantelpiece.

"It's like that. I have to do everything really slowly and carefully, otherwise it hurts."

10 Catherine gave me one of her looks and said I should take more interest in things. She knows I can't knit any more and reading tires me but she's always trying to get me to put photographs in albums or watch the TV.

"*Top Hat*'s on TV this afternoon," she said as she was getting ready to leave. "Fred Astaire and Ginger Rogers."

15 "Oh, is it?"

"It starts at two-thirty and it's all set for you. I'm away for the two o'clock bus. See you on Friday."

I didn't watch the film. I'd rather sit and daydream out of the window, lost inside my own head. Catherine can't understand as it's not in her nature to daydream or dawdle or drift.
20 She's like an office stapler, precisely snapping shut, securing papers in the correct order forever. She never lets anything go. When she returned on Friday the first thing she said to me was:

"Did you enjoy the film?"

I was caught off my guard.

25 "The film?"

"*Top Hat* – you didn't watch it, did you? I knew you wouldn't. I don't know why I bother. You've no interest in anything outside yourself. You never even bother to go along to the dayroom. There's three ladies sitting there now, having a wee chat. You could go and meet people."

30 Catherine always pronounces "meet" as if it were printed in capital letters. This was one of her favourite monologues, that I should MEET people in the dayroom. I knew I could shuffle along there with my Zimmer but I could never be bothered. There was bingo on Mondays and a drink on Saturday nights but I never went to either. She thinks I'm a snob, that I think I'm better that these women but it's not that; it's just, I'd rather sit here.

MARKS

Questions

34. Look at lines 1–4. By referring to two examples of the writer's use of language, show how she conveys the narrator's physical discomfort.   **4**

35. What impressions of Catherine's personality can be seen in lines 5–17? Support your points with textual reference.   **4**

36. Show how, in lines 18–34, the writer conveys the contrast between the narrator and her niece.   **4**

37. By referring to this story and to **at least one other story** by Anne Donovan, discuss the way she explores conflict between characters.   **8**

PART C — SCOTTISH TEXT — POETRY

Text 1 — Poetry

If you choose this text you may not attempt a question on Poetry in Section 2.

Read the poem below and then attempt the following questions.

Originally by Carol Ann Duffy

We came from our own country in a red room
which fell through the fields, our mother singing
our father's name to the turn of the wheels.
My brothers cried, one of them bawling *Home*,
5 *Home*, as the miles rushed back to the city,
the street, the house, the vacant rooms
where we didn't live any more. I stared
at the eyes of a blind toy, holding its paw.

All childhood is an emigration. Some are slow,
10 leaving you standing, resigned, up an avenue
where no one you know stays. Others are sudden.
Your accent wrong. Corners, which seem familiar,
leading to unimagined, pebble-dashed estates, big boys
eating worms and shouting words you don't understand.
15 My parents' anxiety stirred like a loose tooth
in my head. *I want our own country*, I said.

But then you forget, or don't recall, or change,
and, seeing your brother swallow a slug, feel only
a skelf of shame. I remember my tongue
20 shedding its skin like a snake, my voice
in the classroom sounding just like the rest. Do I only think
I lost a river, culture, speech, sense of first space
and the right place? Now, *Where do you come from?*
strangers ask. *Originally?* And I hesitate.

MARKS

Questions

38. Summarise the key things that happen to the speaker of this poem. Make at least **three** points.   **3**

39. "All childhood is an emigration." (line 9)

    (a) Explain briefly what the poet means by this.   **1**

    (b) Referring closely to lines 9–14, show how the poet's use of language makes a clear distinction between "slow" and "sudden" emigration.   **4**

40. By referring closely to lines 17–24, show how the poet conveys the speaker's feelings of uncertainty.   **4**

41. By referring to **at least one** other poem by Carol Ann Duffy, discuss in what ways *Originally* is similar and/or dissimilar to other poetry by her. You may refer to language and/or ideas in your answer.   **8**

OR

Text 2 — Poetry

If you choose this text you may not attempt a question on Poetry in Section 2.

Read the extract below and then attempt the following questions.

Hyena **by Edwin Morgan**

I am waiting for you.
I have been travelling all morning through the bush
and not eaten.
I am lying at the edge of the bush
5 on a dusty path that leads from the burnt-out kraal.
I am panting, it is midday, I found no water-hole.
I am very fierce without food and although my eyes
are screwed to slits against the sun
you must believe I am prepared to spring.

10 What do you think of me?
I have a rough coat like Africa.
I am crafty with dark spots
like the bush-tufted plains of Africa.
I sprawl as a shaggy bundle of gathered energy
15 like Africa sprawling in its waters.
I trot, I lope, I slaver, I am a ranger.
I hunch my shoulders. I eat the dead.

Do you like my song?
When the moon pours hard and cold on the veldt
20 I sing, and I am the slave of darkness.
Over the stone walls and the mud walls and the ruined places
and the owls, the moonlight falls.
I sniff a broken drum. I bristle. My pelt is silver.
I howl my song to the moon – up it goes.
25 Would you meet me there in the waste places?

MARKS

Questions

42. Look at lines 1–9. By referring to two poetic techniques, show how the poet makes the hyena sound threating in these lines.   4

43. Look at lines 10–17.

    (a) All the similes in these lines refer to "Africa". Why do you think the poet does this?   2

    (b) Show how the sentence structure in lines 16–17 enhances the poet's description of the hyena.   2

44. Explain in detail how the poet conveys the harshness of the hyena's world in lines 18–25.   4

45. By referring to this poem and to **at least one** other poem by Edwin Morgan, discuss the view he presents of the natural world.   8

OR

Text 3 — Poetry

If you choose this text you may not attempt a question on Poetry in Section 2.

Read the poem below and then attempt the following questions.

Assisi **by Norman MacCaig**

The dwarf with his hands on backwards
sat, slumped like a half-filled sack
on tiny twisted legs from which
sawdust might run,
5 outside the three tiers of churches built
in honour of St Francis, brother
of the poor, talker with birds, over whom
he had the advantage
of not being dead yet.

10 A priest explained
how clever it was of Giotto
to make his frescoes tell stories
that would reveal to the illiterate the goodness
of God and the suffering
15 of His Son. I understood
the explanation and
the cleverness.

A rush of tourists, clucking contentedly,
fluttered after him as he scattered
20 the grain of the Word. It was they who had passed
the ruined temple outside, whose eyes
wept pus, whose back was higher
than his head, whose lopsided mouth
said *Grazie* in a voice as sweet
25 as a child's when she speaks to her mother
or a bird's when it spoke
to St Francis.

MARKS

Questions

46. For each of the following, show how any one example of the poet's use of language contributes to his description of:

    (a) the dwarf

    (b) the church

    (c) the tourists   6

47. What is the poet's attitude to the priest? Justify your answer with close reference to lines 10–20.   3

48. Look at lines 24–27. Do you think this is an effective way to end the poem? Justify your answer by referring to these lines and to the poem as a whole.   3

49. Referring to this poem and to **at least one** other poem by Norman MacCaig, discuss how he creates feelings of sympathy in the reader.   8

OR

Text 4 — Poetry

If you choose this text you may not attempt a question on Poetry in Section 2.

Read the extract below and then attempt the following questions.

My Grandmother's Houses **by Jackie Kay**

By the time I am seven we are almost the same height.
She still walks faster, rushing me down the High Street
till we get to her cleaning house. The hall is huge.
Rooms lead off like an octopus's arms.
5 I sit in a room with a grand piano, top open –
a one-winged creature, whilst my gran polishes
for hours. Finally bored I start to pick some notes,
oh can you wash a sailor's shirt oh can you wash and clean
till my gran comes running, duster in hand.
10 I told you don't touch anything. The woman comes too;
the posh one all smiles that make goosepimples
run up my arms. Would you like to sing me a song?
Someone's crying my Lord Kumbaya. Lovely, she says,
beautiful child, skin the colour of café au lait.
15 "Café oh what? Hope she's not being any bother."
Not at all. Not at all. You just get back to your work.
On the way back to her high rise I see her
like the hunchback of Notre Dame. Everytime I crouch
over a comic she slaps me. Sit up straight.

MARKS

Questions

50. Identify **four** aspects of the grandmother's personality that emerge from the extract. 4

51. Choose **one** example of imagery from lines 4–7 and explain what it suggests about what is being described. 2

52. By referring closely to lines 10–16, describe how the poet conveys the personality of "the woman". 6

53. By referring to *My Grandmother's Houses* and to **at least one** other poem by Jackie Kay, discuss how she creates vivid impressions of people. 8

[END OF SECTION 1]

SECTION 2 — CRITICAL ESSAY — 20 marks

Attempt ONE question from this section of the paper from ONE of the Parts A-E.

You may use a Scottish text but <u>not</u> the one used in Section 1.

Your essay should be on a different <u>genre</u> to the one used in Section 1.

Write the number of your chosen question in the margin of your answer.

You should spend about 45 minutes on the essay.

DRAMA

Answers to questions in this part should refer to the text and to such relevant features as characterisation, key scene(s), structure, climax, theme, plot, conflict, setting . . .

1. Choose a play in which there is conflict between two characters in a family **or** a group.

   Show how the conflict occurs and then, by referring to appropriate techniques, explain how it affects the characters and the events of the play.

2. Choose a play in which a main character's actions have a significant effect on the rest of the play.

   By referring to appropriate techniques, show how this character's actions have affected the other characters **and/or** the outcome of the play.

PROSE

Answers to questions in this part should refer to the text and to such relevant features as characterisation, setting, language, key incident(s), climax, turning point, plot, structure, narrative technique, theme, ideas, description . . .

3. Choose a novel **or** short story in which you feel sympathy with one of the main characters because of the difficulties or injustice or hardships she or he has to face.

   Describe the problems the character faces and, by referring to appropriate techniques, show how you are made to feel sympathy for her or him.

4. Choose a novel **or** a short story **or** a work of non-fiction in which the writer uses a memorable style/voice/narrative technique.

   By referring to appropriate techniques, explain in detail how features of the writing style/voice/narrative technique contribute to the effectiveness of the text.

POETRY

> *Answers to questions in this part should refer to the text and to such relevant features as word choice, tone, imagery, structure, content, rhythm, rhyme, theme, sound, ideas . . .*

5. Choose a poem which describes a person's experience.

   By referring to appropriate techniques, explain how the description of the experience makes the poem more interesting.

6. Choose a poem which has as one of its central concerns a personal, social or religious issue.

   By referring to appropriate techniques, show how the poem increases your understanding of the issue.

FILM AND TV DRAMA

> *Answers to questions in this part should refer to the text and to such relevant features as use of camera, key sequence, characterisation, mise-en-scène, editing, setting, music/ sound, special effects, plot, dialogue . . .*

7. Choose a film or TV drama* which has a character who could be described as a hero or as a villain.

   By referring to appropriate techniques, explain how the character is introduced and then developed throughout the film or TV drama.

8. Choose a sequence from a film which is important both to the atmosphere and to the plot of the film.

   By referring to appropriate techniques, show how atmosphere is created in the sequence and go on to show how the sequence and the atmosphere are important to the film as a whole.

* "TV drama" includes a single play, a series or a serial.

LANGUAGE STUDY

> *Answers to questions in this part should refer to the text and to such relevant features as register, accent, dialect, slang, jargon, vocabulary, tone, abbreviation . . .*

9. Consider the differences between written language and an aspect of spoken language which you have studied.

   By referring to specific examples and to appropriate features of language, explain the similarities and differences between the two forms of language you have studied.

10. Consider the language of advertising.

   In any one advertisement identify the ways in which language is used successfully. By referring to specific examples and to appropriate features of language, explain what it is about these usages which make them effective.

[END OF SECTION 2]

[END OF MODEL PRACTICE PAPER]

Page three

Model Paper 2

Whilst this Model Practice Paper has been specially commissioned by Hodder Gibson for use as practice for the National 5 exams, the key reference documents remain the SQA Specimen Paper 2013 and the SQA Past Paper 2014.

National Qualifications
MODEL PAPER 2

English
Reading for Understanding, Analysis and Evaluation

Duration — 1 hour

Total marks — 30

When you are told to do so, open the booklet, read the passage and attempt all the questions, using your own words as far as possible.

Before attempting the questions you must check that your answer booklet is for the same subject and level as this question paper.

On the answer booklet, you must clearly identify the question number you are attempting.

Use **blue** or **black** ink.

Before leaving the examination room you must give your answer booklet to the Invigilator.
If you do not, you may lose all the marks for this paper.

The gr8 db8

Recently, a newspaper article headed "I h8 txt msgs: how texting is wrecking our language" argued that texters are "vandals who are doing to our language what Genghis Khan did to his neighbours 800 years ago. They are destroying it: pillaging our punctuation; savaging our sentences."

As a new variety of language, texting has been condemned as "textese", "slanguage", a "digital
5   virus, "bleak, bald, sad shorthand", "drab shrinktalk which masks dyslexia, poor spelling and mental laziness".

Ever since the arrival of printing — thought to be the invention of the devil because it would put false opinions into people's minds — people have been arguing that new   technology   would   have disastrous consequences for language. Scares accompanied the introduction of the telegraph, the
10   telephone, and broadcasting. But has there ever been a linguistic phenomenon that has aroused such curiosity, suspicion, fear, confusion, antagonism, fascination, excitement and enthusiasm all at once as texting?

People think that the written language seen on mobile phone screens is new and alien, but all the popular beliefs about texting are wrong. Its distinctiveness is not a new phenomenon, nor is
15   its use restricted to the young. There is increasing evidence that it helps rather than hinders literacy. Texting has added a new dimension to language use, but its long-term impact is negligible.

Research has made it clear that the early media hysteria about the novelty (and thus the dangers) of text messaging was misplaced. People seem to have swallowed whole the stories
20   that youngsters use nothing but abbreviations when they text, such as the reports that a teenager had written an essay so full of textspeak that her teacher was unable to understand it. An extract was posted online, and quoted incessantly, but, as no one was ever able to track down the entire essay, it was probably a hoax.

There are several distinctive features of the way texts are written that combine to give the
25   impression of novelty, but people have been initialising common phrases for ages. IOU is known from 1618. There is no real difference between a modern kid's "lol" ("laughing out loud") and an earlier generation's "SWALK" ("sealed with a loving kiss").

English has had abbreviated words ever since it began to be written down. Words such as exam, vet, fridge and bus are so familiar that they have effectively become new words. When some of
30   these abbreviated forms first came into use, they also attracted criticism. In 1711, for example, Joseph Addison complained about the way words were being "miserably curtailed" — he mentioned pos (itive) and incog (nito).

Texters use deviant spellings — and they know they are deviant. But they are by no means the first to use such nonstandard forms as "cos" for "because" or "wot" for "what". Several of
35   these are so much part of English literary tradition that they have been given entries in the Oxford English Dictionary. "Cos" is there from 1828 and "wot" from 1829. Many can be found in the way dialect is written by such writers as Charles Dickens, Mark Twain, Walter Scott and D.H. Lawrence.

Sending a message on a mobile phone is not the most natural of ways to communicate. The
40   keypad isn't linguistically sensible. No one took letter-frequency considerations into account when designing it. For example, key 7 on my mobile contains four symbols, pqrs. It takes four key-presses to access the letter s, and yet s is one of the most frequently occurring letters in English. It is twice as easy to input q, which is one of the least frequently occurring letters. It should be the other way round. So any strategy that reduces the time and awkwardness of
45   inputting graphic symbols is bound to be attractive.

Abbreviations were used as a natural, intuitive response to a technological problem. And they appeared in next to no time. Texters simply transferred (and then embellished) what they had encountered in other settings. We have all left notes in which we have replaced "and" with "&", "three" with "3", and so on.

50 But the need to save time and energy is by no means the whole story of texting. When we look at some texts, they are linguistically quite complex. There are an extraordinary number of ways in which people play with language — creating riddles, solving crosswords, playing Scrabble, inventing new words. Professional writers do the same — providing catchy copy for advertising slogans, thinking up puns in newspaper headlines, and writing poems, novels and plays. Children
55 quickly learn that one of the most enjoyable things you can do with language is to play with its sounds, words, grammar — and spelling.

An extraordinary number of doom-laden prophecies have been made about the supposed linguistic evils unleashed by texting. Sadly, its creative potential has been virtually ignored. But children could not be good at texting if they had not already developed considerable literacy
60 awareness. Before you can write and play with abbreviated forms, you need to have a sense of how the sounds of your language relate to the letters. You need to know that there are such things as alternative spellings. If you are aware that your texting behaviour is different, you must have already realized that there is such a thing as a standard.

Some people dislike texting. Some are bemused by it. But it is merely the latest manifestation
65 of the human ability to be linguistically creative and to adapt language to suit the demands of diverse settings. There is no disaster pending. We will not see a new generation of adults growing up unable to write proper English. The language as a whole will not decline. In texting what we are seeing, in a small way, is language in evolution.

Adapted from an article by David Crystal in The Guardian.

Questions

1. Choose any **two** examples of the language used to criticise texting in lines 1–6 and explain why each is effective in conveying disapproval.   **4**

2. Look at lines 7–12.

   (a) What difference does the writer identify between the reaction to texting and the reaction to other new technologies?   **2**

   (b) Explain one way in which the writer's use of language in these lines conveys his surprise at the reaction to texting.   **2**

3. In lines 13–14 the writer says: "... all the popular beliefs about texting are wrong". **Explain in your own words** the evidence he provides for this in the rest of the paragraph.   **3**

4. Show how any **two** examples of the writer's word choice in lines 18–23 make clear his belief that the critics of texting are in the wrong.   **4**

5. Explain briefly how, in lines 24–38, the writer makes texting appear respectable.   **3**

6. Explain the function of each of the three dashes used in lines 50–56.   **3**

7. Show how any **two** examples of the writer's use of language in the last paragraph (lines 64–68) create a reassuring tone.   **4**

8. Referring to lines 24–63, summarise **in your own words** the key reasons not to worry about texting.   **5**

[END OF MODEL PRACTICE PAPER]

National
Qualifications
MODEL PAPER 2

English
Critical Reading

Duration — 1 hour and 30 minutes

Total marks — 40

SECTION 1 — Scottish Text — 20 marks

Read an extract from a Scottish text you have previously studied and attempt the questions.

Choose ONE text from either

Part A — Drama   Pages 2–9
or
Part B — Prose   Pages 10–19
or
Part C — Poetry   Pages 20–26

Attempt ALL the questions for your chosen text.

SECTION 2 — Critical Essay — 20 marks

Write ONE critical essay on previously studied text from Drama, Prose, Poetry, Film and Television Drama, or Language.

Your answer must be on a different genre from that chosen in Section 1.

You should spend approximately 45 minutes on each Section.

Before attempting the questions you must check that your answer booklet is for the same subject and level as this question paper.

On the answer booklet, you must clearly identify the question number you are attempting.

Use **blue** or **black** ink.

Before leaving the examination room you must give your answer booklet to the Invigilator. If you do not you may lose all the marks for this paper.

SECTION 1 — SCOTTISH TEXT — 20 marks

PART A — SCOTTISH TEXT — DRAMA

Text 1 — Drama

If you choose this text you may not attempt a question on Drama in Section 2.

Read the extract below and then attempt the following questions.

Tally's Blood by Ann Marie di Mambro

This extract is from Act Two, Scene Two, in the back shop.

	ROSINELLA:	You like Silvio Palombo, don't you?
	LUCIA:	He's okay.
	ROSINELLA:	Nice looking boy too.
	LUCIA:	He's okay.
5	ROSINELLA:	Oh, come on, Lucia, you can't kid me on. I know you're daft for him. But I like the way you kind of stand back a bit – don't let him see you're too keen. Italian boys like that. Don't want him to get fed up waiting.
	LUCIA:	Auntie Rosinella…?
10	ROSINELLA:	He cannae keep his eyes off you. And if he's who you want, then it's not for me to stand in your way. But I told his mother. I made sure I told her. 'Mrs Palombo', I said, 'our Lucia's a lady. She's not been brought up to work in a shop, running after some man'. I tell you, Lucia, she liked me for that. They've got class that family.
	LUCIA:	Auntie Rosinella…?
15	ROSINELLA:	I hear them all the time. 'Ma lassie's an awfy good worker' – 'Ma lassie cleaned four chickens' – I promised myself – my Lucia's to marry a man that really loves HER – no to put her in a shop and make her work. How much you got there?
	LUCIA:	Three pounds, seven and tenpence ha'penny.
20	ROSINELLA:	That's what I want for you – a good life – with a good Italian man – here.
	LUCIA:	Auntie Rosinella…?
	ROSINELLA:	You see the way the Italians are getting on now, eh? Beginning to make a wee bit money? Because they're prepared to WORK that's why. I don't know anybody works so hard as the Italian men.
25		*Hughie in with pail and mop.*
	HUGHIE:	That's the tables cleared and the front shop mopped, Mrs Pedreschi, and the chip pan cleaned out. Is the milk boiled?
	ROSINELLA:	Should be.
30		*She turns attention back to Lucia, Hughie lifts pot from stove and pours contents into two pails; he covers them and sets them aside, working like a Trojan.*
	ROSINELLA:	And the way they love their families. Nobody loves their families like the Italians! You want to stay for a wee bit pasta, Hughie? It's your favourite – Rigatoni.

| 35 | HUGHIE: | No thanks, Mrs Pedreschi. I better get up the road. Bridget's going out and I don't like my mammy left on her own. |

35 HUGHIE: No thanks, Mrs Pedreschi. I better get up the road. Bridget's going out and I don't like my mammy left on her own.

ROSINELLA: Bridget's going out is she? Don't tell me she's winching?

HUGHIE: No. Her and Davie are going up to Charmaine's the night – to go over all the arrangements. My mammy's no up to it.

40 ROSINELLA: That's right. When's the wedding now?

HUGHIE: Saturday.

ROSINELLA: Is he no getting married a wee bit quick, your brother?

Hughie shrugs, a bit embarrassed: Lucia mortified at Rosinella.

ROSINELLA: And where are they going to stay?

45 HUGHIE: At Charmaine's.

ROSINELLA: It's funny that, isn't it? But that's the way they do it here. In Italy, the girl must go to her husband's house. That's why you must have land if you've got sons.

Massimo in.

50   So that'll be your mammy left with her eldest and her youngest, eh? I don't see your Bridget ever marrying, do you? You see, Lucia, there's a lot of women Bridget's age no' married. The war killed that many young men. I'm right there, aren't I, Massimo?

MASSIMO: You got those pails ready, son?

55 HUGHIE: I'll bring them through.

MASSIMO: And give's a hand to put these shutters up before you go.

Hughie and Massimo out: Rosinella watches him go.

ROSINELLA: I'm right about that Davie, amn't I, Lucia? Give it five or six months, Hughie'll be telling us he's an uncle again. Mind you, I suppose
60   his mother must feel it, right enough. Can you find me a wee envelope hen, a wee poke or something? What was I saying... ah, yes... See what I mean about Italian men? Just take that brother of Hughie's. Getting married on a Saturday. Give him two or three days and he'll be out DRINKING with his pals.

65   *Rosinella shushes up when Hughie comes in, followed by Massimo: all locked up. Massimo takes off his apron, reaches for a bottle of wine.*

MASSIMO: Thanks, Hughie, son. You want a wee glass of wine?

HUGHIE: I better not, Mr Pedreschi. I better get up the road.

MARKS

Questions

1. Read lines 1–19.

    (a) Show how the playwright makes the audience aware of **two** aspects of Rosinella's character.   **4**

    (b) How is the audience made aware of Lucia's lack of interest in what her aunt is saying?   **2**

2. In lines 20–68 Rosinella displays a number of prejudices. Explain how the playwright makes the audience aware of how silly her prejudices are. Refer to at least three different prejudices.   **6**

3. Referring to the extract and elsewhere in the play, discuss the role of Hughie in the play as a whole.   **8**

OR

Text 2 — Drama

If you choose this text you may not attempt a question on Drama in Section 2.

Read the extract below and then attempt the following questions.

Bold Girls by Rona Munro

This extract is from Scene 2 in the Club. Cassie is dancing alone, and Nora persuades Marie to join her.

> *Marie crosses over and joins Cassie, who beams, applauding her. Marie starts shuffling cautiously from foot to foot.*

CASSIE: I'm telling you this is a great diet Marie, you really feel the benefit of the gin.

MARIE: Well maybe you should go easy now Cassie.

5 CASSIE: Oh I'm a long way from being lockjawed

> *Nora is beckoning at them frantically.*

MARIE: Your mummy's asking us to come and sit down.

CASSIE: The song's just started.

> *Marie glances round nervously.*

10   What? Are they all watching us?

MARIE: They are.

CASSIE: Let them.

MARIE: (*with a shaky laugh*): Feel a bit like the last meat pie in the shop out here, Cassie.

CASSIE: Well let them stay hungry. They can just look and think what they like.

15 MARIE: Cassie, what's wrong?

CASSIE: Oh, I'm just bad, Marie, didn't you know?

MARIE: No. I never knew that.

CASSIE: You remember that wee girl in Turf Lodge, the one Martin couldn't get enough of? She was a decent wee girl. She's bad now. Ask my mummy.

20 MARIE: Have you had words?

CASSIE: He's out in less than a year, Marie.

MARIE: *Martin!?*

CASSIE: Joe.

MARIE: I know. It'll be all right Cassie.

25   *They stop dancing, they look at each other.*

MARIE: It'll be all right, Cassie.

CASSIE: I tell you Marie I can't stand the *smell* of him. The greasy, grinning, beer bellied smell of him. And he's winking away about all he's been dreaming of, wriggling his fat fingers over me like I'm a poke of chips – I
30   don't want him in the house in my *bed*, Marie.

MARIE: You'll cope.

CASSIE: Oh I'm just bad. I am.

MARIE: Don't. Don't say that about yourself.

CASSIE: I'll go crazy.

35 MARIE: I won't let you. You won't get a chance Cassie, I'll just be across the road, I won't let you go crazy. You just see what you'll get if you try it.

           Slowly Cassie smiles at her.

           (*Putting a hand on Cassie's arm*) Now will you come and sit down?

Questions

4. Show how the playwright contrasts the characters of Marie and Cassie through their language and their actions in lines 1–14.   4

5. Explain how the dialogue in lines 15–38 reveals aspects of the relationship between Marie and Cassie.   4

6. Referring closely to the language of lines 27–30 show how Cassie reveals her attitude to Joe.   4

7. Referring to the extract and elsewhere in the play, discuss the relationship between Marie and Cassie.   8

OR

Text 3 — Drama

If you choose this text you may not attempt a question on Drama in Section 2.

Read the extract below and then attempt the following questions.

Sailmaker **by Alan Spence**

This extract is from Act One.

> *(Enter DAVIE and BILLY, talking as they walk)*

DAVIE: Eh, Billy ... that coupla quid ah tapped off ye. Could it wait till next week?

BILLY: Aye sure.

DAVIE: Things are still a wee bit tight.

5 BILLY: What's the score?

DAVIE: Eh?

BILLY: Ye shouldnae be this skint. What is it?

DAVIE: Ah told ye. It's the job. Just hasnae been so great. No sellin enough. No collectin enough. No getting much over the basic.

10 BILLY: Aye, but ye should be able tae get by. Just the two ae ye.

DAVIE: It's no easy.

BILLY: Ye bevvyin?

DAVIE: Just a wee half when ah finish ma work. An by Christ ah need it.

15 BILLY: Ye bettin too heavy? Is that it?

DAVIE: *(Hesitates then decides to tell him)* It started a coupla months ago. Backed a favourite. Absolutely surefire certainty. Couldnae lose. But it was even money, so ah had tae put quite a whack on it. *(Slightly shamefaced)* Best part ae a week's wages.

20 BILLY: An it got beat?

DAVIE: Out the park. So ah made it up by borrowin off the bookie. He does his moneylender on the side. Charges interest.

BILLY: An every week ye miss the interest it goes up.

DAVIE: This is it. Now when ah pay him ah'm just clearing the interest. Ah'm no even
25 touchin the original amount ah borrowed. Ah must have paid him back two or three times over, an ah still owe him the full whack.

BILLY: Bastard, eh? Sicken ye. And he's a pape.

> *(DAVIE laughs)*

	DAVIE:	Still, aw ah need's a wee turn. Ah mean ma luck's got tae change sometime hasn't it? Law of averages.
30		

      BILLY: Whatever that is.

      DAVIE: Thing's have got tae get better.

      BILLY: It's a mug's game. The punter canny win.

      DAVIE: Got tae keep trying.

35   BILLY: Flingin it away!

             Look, don't get me wrong. Ah don't mind helping ye out, but I'm no exactly rollin in it maself.

      DAVIE: Ye'll get yer money back.

      BILLY: That's no what ah mean!

40   DAVIE: What am ah supposed tae dae? Get a job as a company director or something! Ah'll go doon tae the broo in the morning!

      BILLY: There must be some way tae get this bookie aff yer back for a start.

      DAVIE: Aye sure!

      BILLY: Ah mean, you've paid him.

45   DAVIE: Ah knew his terms.

      BILLY: It's no even legal.

      DAVIE: Neither is getting his heavies tae kick folk's heids in.

      BILLY: So maybe he's no the only wan that knows a few hard men.

      DAVIE: (*Sighs*) Whit a carry on, eh?

MARKS

Questions

8. Referring to the whole extract, explain why Davie is having money problems. Make at least four key points.   **4**

9. What does the audience learn in lines 1–14 about the character of Billy?   **2**

10. Why does Davie laugh (line 28)?   **2**

11. Look closely at lines 29–49. Referring closely to the text, explain how this dialogue shows clearly the difference in outlook between Davie and Billy.   **4**

12. Money problems and ways to escape them are an important theme in *Sailmaker*. With reference to the extract and to elsewhere in the play, disuss how this theme is explored.   **8**

PART B — SCOTTISH TEXT — PROSE

Text 1 — Prose

If you choose this text you may not attempt a question on Prose in Section 2.

Read the extract below and then attempt the following questions.

In Church by Iain Crichton Smith

"At the age of eighteen I was forced into the army to fight for what they call one's country. I did not know what this was since my gaze was always directed inward and not outward. I was put among men whom I despised and feared – they fornicated and drank and spat and lived filthily. Yet they were my comrades in arms.

5 "I was being shot at by strangers. I was up to my knees in green slime. I was harassed by rats. I entered trenches to find the dead buried in the walls. Once, however, on a clear starry night at Christmas time we had a truce. This lasted into the following day. We – Germans and English – showed each other our photographs, though I had none. We, that is, the others, played football. At the end of it a German officer came up to us and said:
10 'You had better get back to your dugouts: we are starting a barrage at 13.00 hours.' He consulted his watch and we went back to our trenches after he had shaken hands with each other.

"One day I could bear no more of the killing and I ran away. And I came here, Lord. And now I should like to say something to you, Lord. I was never foolish enough to think that
15 I understood your ways. Nevertheless I thought you were on the side of the good and the innocent. Now I no longer believe so. You may strike me dead with your lightning – I invite you to do so – but I think that will not happen. All these years, Lord, you have cheated me. You in your immense absence." He paused a moment as if savouring the phrase. "Your immense absence. As for me, I have been silent for a year without love,
20 without hope. I have lived like an animal, I who was willing to give my all to you. Lord, do you know what it is to be alone? For in order to live we need language and human beings.

"I think, Lord, that I hate you. I hate you for inventing the world and then abandoning it. I hate you because you have not intervened to save the world.

25 "I hate you because you are as indifferent as the generals. I hate you because of my weakness.

"I hate you, God, because of what you have done to mankind."

He stopped and looked at Colin as if he were asking him, Am I a good preacher or not?

"You have said," said Colin after a long time, "exactly what I would have said. "I have no
30 wish to ..."

"Betray me? But you are an officer. It is your duty. What else can you do?"

MARKS

Questions

13. Explain briefly what has led up to this moment in the story, and say what happens immediately after it.   **4**

14. How do any **two** examples of the writer's use of language in lines 1–4 make clear the speaker's dislike for the army?   **2**

15. Explain one way in which the writer uses contrast in lines 5–12 to emphasise the strangeness of the Christmas truce.   **2**

16. Explain your own words why the speaker is angry at God.   **4**

17. Referring to the extract and to **at least one** other story by Iain Crichton Smith, discuss how he makes the reader aware of the personality of a main character.   **8**

OR

Text 2 — Prose

If you choose this text you may not write a critical essay on Prose in Section 2.

Read the extract below and then attempt the following questions.

Away in a Manger by Anne Donovan

They turned the corner and the cauld evaporated. The square shimmerin wi light, brightness sharp against the gloomy street. Trees frosted wi light. Lights shaped intae circles and flowers, like the plastic jewellery sets wee lassies love. Lights switchin on and off in a mad rhythm ae their ain, tryin tae look like bells ringin and snow fallin. Reindeer
5 and Santas, holly, ivy, robins, all bleezin wi light. Amy gazed at them, eyes shinin.

"Haud ma haund tae get across this road. There's lots of motors here." Sandra pulled Amy close tae her. "They're lovely aren't they?"

"Uh huh." Amy nodded. "Can we walk right round the square?"

A tape of Christmas carols was playin on the sound system, fillin the air like a cracklin
10 heavenly choir. Sandra and Amy joined the other faimlies wanderin round.

"Look at they reindeer, Mark!"

"There's a star, Daddy!"

"Check the size a that tree!"

Amy stopped in front of the big Christmas tree in the square.

15 "Can we sit doon tae look at it, Mammy?"

"Naw, just keep walkin', pet. It's too cauld."

Anyway, nearly every bench was occupied. Newspapers neatly smoothed oot like bedclothes. Some folk were huddled under auld coats, tryin tae sleep their way intae oblivion while others sat upright, hauf-empty cans in their haunds, starin at passers-by.
20 Sandra minded when she was wee and her mammy'd brought her tae see the lights. There were folk on benches then, down-and-outs, faces shrunk wi drink and neglect, an auld cap lyin hauf-heartedly by their sides. But now the people who slept in the square werenae just auld drunks and it was hard tae pick them oot fae everyone else. That couple ower there wi their bags roond them, were they just havin a rest fae their Christmas shoppin,
25 watchin the lights? But who in their right minds would be sittin on a bench in George Square on this freezing cauld night if they had a hame tae go tae?

Amy tugged at her airm. "Ah know that song."

"Whit song?"

"That one." Amy pointed upwards. "Silent Night, Holy Night."

30 "Do you?"

"We learned it at school. Mrs Anderson was telling us aboot the baby Jesus and how there was nae room at the inn so he was born in a stable."

"Oh."

"It's no ma favourite, but."

35 "What's no your favourite?"

"Silent Night. Guess what ma favourite is?"

MARKS

"Don't know."

"Guess, Mammy, you have tae guess."

40 Sandra couldnae be bothered guessin but she knew there'd be nae peace tae she'd made some attempt and anyway, Amy'd get bored wi the "Guess what?" game quick enough.

"Little donkey?"

"Naw."

"O Little Town of Bethlehem?"

45 "Naw. Gie in?"

"OK."

"Away in a Manger. Ah've won!" Amy jumped up and doon. "Mammy, what's a manger?"

Questions

18. Show how the writer creates a mood of excitement in lines 1–10.   **4**

19. Why do you think lines 11–13 are included in the story at this point?   **2**

20. What difference does Sandra notice between the square now and what it was like when she went with her mother?   **2**

21. It what ways are lines 27–48 typical of an exchange between an excited child and a parent?   **4**

22. Referring to the extract and to **at least one** other story by Anne Donovan, discuss the way she explores parent/child relationships.   **8**

OR

Text 3 — Prose

If you choose this text you may not write a critical essay on Prose in Section 2.

Read the extract below and then attempt the following questions.

The Cone-Gatherers by Robin Jenkins

This extract is from Chapter Five. Calum and Neil are high in a tree; they hear Duror starting to climb towards them.

They heard the scrapes and thumps of his nailed boots on the rungs and then on the branches. A branch cracked suddenly. He exclaimed as if in anger, and paused for a full minute. When he resumed he climbed even more slowly than before. Soon he stopped. He was still a long way below.

5 They waited, but he did not start to climb again. For three or four minutes they waited. Still he remained motionless and silent. One of the dogs barked unhappily.

They thought that he must have climbed as high as he wished and now was admiring the view of the loch. After all, the tree was not private just because they happened to be in it; the ladder, too, belonged to the estate. At the same time Neil felt curiously
10 embarrassed and could not think to start gathering cones again. Calum kept shivering.

They were far from guessing the truth, that Duror had ceased to climb because of fear; that weak and dizzy and full of shame, he was clinging with ignominious tightness; that the dread of the descent was making him sick; and that he had almost forgotten his purpose in ascending to them.

15 At last Neil had to end the suspense.

"Hello, Mr Duror," he called. "It's a grand day, isn't it?"

No reply came.

Neil tried again.

"Do you want to talk to us about something?" he shouted

20 This time, after another long delay, there was a reply. They were surprised by the mildness of his voice. It was so faint too they had to strain to hear it.

"I've got a message for you," he said.

"A message? Is it from Mr. Tulloch?"

There was a pause. "Aye, from him."

25 "Have we to go back home, to Ardmore?" cried Neil hopefully.

"You know these woods belong to Lady Runcie-Campbell?"

"We know that."

"She wants you as beaters in a deer drive this afternoon."

Neil was shocked.

30 "But we're here to gather cones," he yelled. "She can't order us about. She's not our mistress."

"She telephoned Tulloch. He said you've to work for her this afternoon."

"How could he? Didn't he tell us we'd to gather every cone we could? Didn't he ask us to work as much overtime as we liked? What's the good of all that if we're
35 to be taken away for deer drives." Neil's voice grew hoarse with indignation. "My brother's never asked to take part in deer hunts," he shouted. "Mr. Tulloch knows that. I don't believe he knows anything about this. It's just a trick to get us to work for the lady."

Duror was silent. His triumph was become a handful of withered leaves. When he
40 had seen the ladder, he had thought how gratifying it would be to deliver the deadly message to them in the eyrie where they fancied themselves safe. He had not anticipated this lightheadedness, this heaving of the stationary tree, this sickening of his very will to hate. He had never dreamed that he would not be able to do once only what the hunchback did several times a day. It seemed to him that
45 he must therefore be far more ill and decayed than he had thought. He was like a tree still straight, still showing green leaves; but underground death was creeping along the roots.

Questions

23. Summarise what happens in this extract. Make at least four key points.   4

24. Show how the writer creates a tense mood in lines 1–6.   2

25. Look carefully at what Neil says in lines 16–38. Referring closely to the text, show how his attitude to Duror goes through at least two changes.   4

26. Explain what the image in the final sentence tells you about Duror.   2

27. Referring to the extract and to elsewhere in the novel, discuss the conflict between Duror and the cone-gatherers.   8

OR

Text 4 – Prose

If you choose this text you may not attempt a question on Prose in Section 2.

Read the extract below and then attempt the following questions.

The Testament of Gideon Mack by James Robertson

This extract is from Chapter 7.

Another few minutes must have gone by. I forgot where I was and what day it was. The sound was louder than I'd intended. I was only a foot away from the screen, finger hovering near the off switch, and maybe that was why I failed to hear my father's footsteps in the hall. By the time the door opened and his voice filled the room – "Agnes?
5   I thought I heard somebody ..." – there was no point in even bothering to switch the television off. I did, though, and jumped to my feet in a flush of shame and fury.

He closed the door behind him. I stood between him and the television set as if to protect it, as if to say it was not to blame. I could see the wee flames in his cheeks. I bowed my head, fixing my eye on a crack in the skirting board. I heard him say, "Put it back on."

10   "No, no, it doesn't matter, I'm sorry," I mumbled. Entirely the wrong thing. He cut me off, his voice shaking.

"It doesn't *matter*?" he said "Do you dare to disobey me? Put it back on."

I turned and reached for the switch. The television, being warm, came on at once. If my father understood that, he made no allowance for it.

15   "I see you have become very skilled at operating that thing," he said quietly, almost admiringly. "How often have you done this?"

"Never," I said. It was true that I'd not touched the set before on a Sunday. "I promise this is the first time."

"It will be the last," he said. "Come here."

20   He pointed beside him and I went and stood there. His huge right hand descended on my neck and the thumb and fingers gripped it so that I cried out. He increased the pressure. I thought my head would snap off. His breathing was like that of some monstrous creature in its den. The blood in his fingers pulsed furiously against my neck.

Thus we stood in front of the television together, father and son, for the remaining ten
25   minutes of the programme. It felt like an hour. If I squirmed to try and ease the pain, his grip tightened. I hated him then, hated what he was doing to me and hated my own helplessness. *ZAP! BLAM! POW!* I hated the screen with its cartoon punches and I hated the way the parlour echoed with screeching tyres and wisecracks delivered in American accents. I saw it as if through his eyes – cheap, tawdry, meaningless rubbish – and I
30   longed for it to end.

He pushed me from him as the credits rolled and the inane theme music played. "Turn it off," he said. I did as I was told, rubbing my neck and wiping away the tears that he had squeezed out of me.

"What ... is ... that?" he said, dropping the words methodically into the silence.

35   "*Batman*," I said.

"Bat ... man," he said.

"Yes," I said. And then again, "I'm sorry." But I don't think he heard that.

"It is not bat ... man," he said, and I could not stop myself, I was trying to explain, I said, "It *is*."

MARKS

40 "Do not interrupt me," he said. His voice grew louder and louder. "Do not contradict me. It is not bat … man, whatever that means. I'll tell you what it is. It is drivel. It is the most unutterable garbage I have ever witnessed. Garbage from the land of garbage."

Questions

28. Summarise what happens in this extract. Make **three** key points.   3

29. How is the reader made aware, in lines 1–11, of Gideon's nervousness after he hears his father's voice?   2

30. Explain how the writer conveys the aggressiveness of Gideon's father in lines 12–33.   4

31. Show how the father's contempt for American culture is conveyed in lines 34–42.   3

32. Referring to the extract and to elsewhere in the novel, discuss the relationship between Gideon and his father.   8

OR

Text 5 — Prose

If you choose this text you may not attempt a question on Prose in Section 2.

Read the extract below and then attempt the following questions.

Kidnapped by Robert Louis Stevenson

This extract is from Chapter 10 – "The Siege of the Roundhouse".

The sea had gone down, and the wind was steady and kept the sails quiet; so that there was a great stillness in the ship, in which I made sure I heard the sound of muttering voices. A little after, and there came a clash of steel upon the deck, by which I knew they were dealing out the cutlasses and one had been let fall; and after that, silence again.

5 I do not know if I was what you call afraid; but my heart beat like a bird's, both quick and little; and there was a dimness came before my eyes which I continually rubbed away, and which continually returned. As for hope, I had none; but only a darkness of despair and a sort of anger against all the world that made me long to sell my life as dear as I was able. I tried to pray, I remember, but that same hurry of my mind, like a man running, would not

10 suffer me to think upon the words; and my chief wish was to have the thing begin and be done with it.

It came all of a sudden when it did, with a rush of feet and a roar, and then a shout from Alan, and a sound of blows and some one crying out as if hurt. I looked back over my shoulder, and saw Mr. Shuan in the doorway, crossing blades with Alan.

15 "That's him that killed the boy!" I cried.

"Look to your window!" said Alan; and as I turned back to my place, I saw him pass his sword through the mate's body.

It was none too soon for me to look to my own part; for my head was scarce back at the window, before five men, carrying a spare yard for a battering-ram, ran past me and took

20 post to drive the door in. I had never fired with a pistol in my life, and not often with a gun; far less against a fellow-creature. But it was now or never; and just as they swang the yard, I cried out: "Take that!" and shot into their midst.

I must have hit one of them, for he sang out and gave back a step, and the rest stopped as if a little disconcerted. Before they had time to recover, I sent another ball over their heads;

25 and at my third shot (which went as wide as the second) the whole party threw down the yard and ran for it.

Then I looked round again into the deck-house. The whole place was full of the smoke of my own firing, just as my ears seemed to be burst with the noise of the shots. But there was Alan, standing as before; only now his sword was running blood to the hilt, and

30 himself so swelled with triumph and fallen into so fine an attitude, that he looked to be invincible. Right before him on the floor was Mr. Shuan, on his hands and knees; the blood was pouring from his mouth, and he was sinking slowly lower, with a terrible, white face; and just as I looked, some of those from behind caught hold of him by the heels and dragged him bodily out of the round-house. I believe he died as they were doing it.

35 "There's one of your Whigs for ye!" cried Alan; and then turning to me, he asked if I had done much execution.

I told him I had winged one, and thought it was the captain.

"And I've settled two," says he. "No, there's not enough blood let; they'll be back again. To your watch, David. This was but a dram before meat."

MARKS

Questions

33. Show how Stevenson creates a tense atmosphere in lines 1–4.   3

34. What mixed emotions does David feel in lines 5–11?   2

35. Explain briefly **three** ways by which Stevenson makes the events in lines 12–26 dramatic and exciting.   3

36. What impressions is the reader given of Alan Breck in lines 27–39?   2

37. "This was but a dram before meat" (line 39). Explain in your own words what Alan means by this.   2

38. Referring to the extract and to elsewhere in the novel, discuss the relationship between David and Alan Breck.   8

PART C — SCOTTISH TEXT — POETRY

Text 1 — Poetry

If you choose this text you may not write a critical essay on Poetry in Section 2.

Read the extract below and then attempt the following questions.

Anne Hathaway by Carol Ann Duffy

The bed we loved in was a spinning world
of forests, castles, torchlight, clifftops, seas
where he would dive for pearls. My lover's words
were shooting stars which fell to earth as kisses
5 on these lips; my body now a softer rhyme
to his, now echo, assonance; his touch
a verb dancing in the centre of a noun.
Some nights, I dreamed he'd written me, the bed
a page beneath his writer's hands. Romance
10 and drama played by touch, by scent, by taste.
In the other bed, the best, our guests dozed on,
dribbling their prose. My living laughing love –
I hold him in the casket of my widow's head
as he held me upon that next best bed.

Questions

39. Referring to the section "The bed ..." to "... these lips" (lines 1–5), show how the poet conveys a sense of joy and happiness.   **4**

40. In lines 5–10, there are many references to writing poetry and plays.   Choose any two examples of this and explain how each one adds to your understanding of the speaker's feelings.   **4**

41. Look at the last four lines (lines 11–14).

    (a) How does the poet makes clear how different the guests are from the speaker and her lover?   **2**

    (b) What feelings does the speaker show for her lover at the end of the poem?   **2**

42. With close textural reference to this poem and to **at least one** other poem by Carol Ann Duffy, discuss how she explores the theme of love.   **8**

OR

Text 2 — Poetry

If you choose this text you may not attempt a question on Poetry in Section 2.

Read the poem below and then attempt the following questions.

Lucozade by Jackie Kay

My mum is on a high bed next to sad chrysanthemums.
'Don't bring flowers, they only wilt and die.'
I am scared my mum is going to die
on the bed next to the sad chrysanthemums.

5 She nods off and her eyes go back in her head.
Next to her bed is a bottle of Lucozade.
'Orange nostalgia, that's what that is,' she says.
'Don't bring Lucozade either,' then fades.

'The whole day was a blur, a swarm of eyes.
10 Those doctors with their white lies.
Did you think you could cheer me up with a *Woman's Own*?
Don't bring magazines, too much about size.'

My mum wakes up, groggy and low.
'What I want to know,' she says, 'is this:
15 where's the big brandy, the generous gin, the Bloody Mary,
the biscuit tin, the chocolate gingers, the dirty big meringue?'

I am sixteen; I've never tasted a Bloody Mary.
'Tell your father to bring a luxury,' says she.
'Grapes have no imagination, they're just green.
20 Tell him: stop the neighbours coming.'

I clear her cupboard in Ward 10B, Stobhill Hospital.
I leave, bags full, Lucozade, grapes, oranges,
sad chrysanthemums under my arms,
weighted down. I turn round, wave with her flowers.

25 My mother, on her high hospital bed, waves back.
Her face is light and radiant, dandelion hours.
Her sheets billow and whirl. She is beautiful.
Next to her the empty table is divine.

I carry the orange nostalgia home singing an old song.

MARKS

Questions

43. The poet twice refers to Lucozade as "orange nostalgia". What does she mean by this? **2**

44. Briefly describe the mother's mood in lines 1–12. **2**

45. Explain fully how the poet contrasts "grapes" with the "luxury" the mother asks for. **4**

46. Describe the speaker's mood in lines 21–29 and explain how it is conveyed. **4**

47. With close textural reference to this poem and to **at least one** other poem by Jackie Kay, discuss how she explores relationships between generations. **8**

MARKS

OR

Text 3 — Poetry

If you choose this text you may not attempt a question on Poetry in Section 2.

Read the poem below and then attempt the following questions.

Trio by Edwin Morgan

Coming up Buchanan Street, quickly, on a sharp winter evening
a young man and two girls, under the Christmas lights –
The young man carries a new guitar in his arms,
the girl on the inside carries a very young baby,
5   and the girl on the outside carries a chihuahua.
And the three of them are laughing, their breath rises
in a cloud of happiness, and as they pass
the boy says, "Wait till he sees this but!"
The chihuahua has a tiny Royal Stewart tartan coat like a teapot-
10   holder,
the baby in its white shawl is all bright eyes and mouth like favours
       in a fresh sweet cake,
the guitar swells out under its milky plastic cover, tied at the neck
       with silver tinsel tape and a brisk sprig of mistletoe.
15 Orphean sprig! Melting baby! Warm chihuahua!
The vale of tears is powerless before you.
Whether Christ is born, or is not born, you
put paid to fate, it abdicates
         under the Christmas lights.
20 Monsters of the year
go blank, are scattered back,
can't bear this march of three.

– And the three have passed, vanished in the crowd
(yet not vanished, for in their arms they wind
25 the life of men and beasts, and music,
laughter ringing them round like a guard)
at the end of this winter's day.

MARKS

Questions

48. Explain briefly how the poet establishes a happy mood in lines 1–8.　　**2**

49. Look at the descriptions in lines 9–14 of the chihuahua, the baby, and the guitar. Choose any **two** of these and explain how the poet's use of language creates an effective description.　　**4**

50. In lines 15–22 the poet gives his thoughts about what he has just seen. In your own words, explain what he says.　　**4**

51. Describe the poet's mood in the final stanza (lines 23–27).　　**2**

52. With close textual reference to this poem and to **at least one** other poem by Edwin Morgan, discuss how he takes an everyday, ordinary situation and transforms it into something special and thought provoking.　　**8**

OR

Text 4 — Poetry

If you choose this text you may not attempt a question on Poetry in Section 2.

Read the poem below and then attempt the following questions.

Visiting Hour by Norman MacCaig

The hospital smell
combs my nostrils
as they go bobbing along
green and yellow corridors.

5 What seems a corpse
is trundled into a lift and vanishes
heavenward.

I will not feel, I will not
feel, until
10 I have to.

Nurses walk lightly, swiftly,
here and up and down and there,
their slender waists miraculously
carrying their burden
15 of so much pain, so
many deaths, their eyes
still clear after
so many farewells.

Ward 7.
20 She lies
in a white cave of forgetfulness.
A withered hand
trembles on its stalk. Eyes move
behind eyelids too heavy
25 to raise. Into an arm wasted
of colour a glass fang is fixed,
not guzzling but giving.
And between her and me
distance shrinks till there is none left
30 but the distance of pain that neither she nor I
can cross.

MARKS

She smiles a little at this
black figure in her white cave
who clumsily rises
35 in the round swimming waves of a bell
and dizzily goes off, growing fainter,
not smaller, leaving behind only
books that will not be read
and fruitless fruits.

Questions

53. Explain how the speaker's sense of discomfort is conveyed in lines 1–10.   **4**

54. What is the speaker's attitude to the nurses (lines 11–18)? Refer to the text to support your answer.   **2**

55. Choose **two** examples of imagery from lines 19–31 and explain how each one adds to your understanding of the poem.   **4**

56. "...leaving behind only
books that will not be read
and fruitless fruits."

Do you think this is a good way to end the poem? Justify your answer.   **2**

57. With close textual reference to this poem and to **at least one** other poem by Norman MacCaig, discuss how he explores powerful emotions.   **8**

[END OF SECTION 1]

SECTION 2 — CRITICAL ESSAY — 20 marks

Attempt ONE question from this section of the paper from ONE of the Parts A-E.

You may use a Scottish text but <u>not</u> the one used in Section 1.

Your essay should be on a different <u>genre</u> to the one used in Section 1.

Write the number of your chosen question in the margin of your answer.

You should spend about 45 minutes on the essay.

DRAMA

Answers to questions in this part should refer to the text and to such relevant features as characterisation, key scene(s), structure, climax, theme, plot, conflict, setting . . .

1. Choose a play in which there is a character who suffers from a human weakness such as ambition, selfishness, lack of self-knowledge, jealousy, pride, lust . . .

   By referring to appropriate techniques, show how the weakness is revealed, and then explain how this weakness affects both the characters and the events of the play.

2. Choose a play which you feel has a dramatic final scene.

   Describe briefly what happens in the final scene and then, by referring to appropriate techniques, explain how effective the ending is in bringing to a conclusion the central concerns of the text.

PROSE

Answers to questions in this part should refer to the text and to such relevant features as characterisation, setting, language, key incident(s), climax, turning point, plot, structure, narrative technique, theme, ideas, description . . .

3. Choose a novel **or** short story with an ending which you find satisfactory.

   By referring to appropriate techniques, explain why you find the ending satisfactory in bringing to a conclusion the main concerns of the text as a whole.

4. Choose a novel **or** a short story **or** a work of non-fiction which deals with an important human issue (such as the abuse of power, conflict between good and evil, loss of freedom or hatred between individuals or groups).

   By referring to appropriate techniques, show how the author reveals the issue through the portrayal of people and events throughout the text, and show how your understanding of the issue has deepened.

POETRY

Answers to questions in this part should refer to the text and to such relevant features as word choice, tone, imagery, structure, content, rhythm, rhyme, theme, sound, ideas . . .

5. Choose a poem in which the poet creates a particular mood or atmosphere.

By referring to appropriate techniques, show how the poet creates this mood **or** atmosphere.

6. Choose a poem which could be considered as having a powerful message.

By referring to appropriate techniques, show how the poet effectively conveys this message.

FILM AND TV DRAMA

Answers to questions in this part should refer to the text and to such relevant features as use of camera, key sequence, characterisation, mise-en-scène, editing, setting, music/ sound, special effects, plot, dialogue . . .

7. Choose a film **or** TV drama* which creates suspense or tension either in a particular scene **or** throughout the whole film or TV drama.

By referring to appropriate techniques, show how the suspense or tension is created and how it affects your enjoyment of the film or TV drama as a whole.

8. Choose a film **or** TV drama* which both entertains and helps to raise awareness of social issues.

By referring to appropriate techniques, show how the film or TV drama you have chosen succeeds in both these aspects.

* "TV drama" includes a single play, a series or a serial.

LANGUAGE STUDY

Answers to questions in this part should refer to the text and to such relevant features as register, accent, dialect, slang, jargon, vocabulary, tone, abbreviation . . .

9. Consider the specialist language used by any group of people to talk about a particular interest, for example, a sport, a job, a hobby . . .

By referring to specific examples and to appropriate features of language, show how the specialist language used by the group is effective in communicating ideas clearly.

10. Consider how TV programmes aimed at young audiences have an effect on the language young people use.

Identify any recent changes in vocabulary or accent that you are aware of and, by referring to specific examples and to appropriate features of language, explain whether you feel the new words/accents are more effective in communicating than those which they have replaced.

[END OF SECTION 2]

[END OF MODEL PRACTICE PAPER]

Model Paper 3

Whilst this Model Practice Paper has been specially commissioned by Hodder Gibson for use as practice for the National 5 exams, the key reference documents remain the SQA Specimen Paper 2013 and the SQA Past Paper 2014.

For reasons of space, Model Paper 3 does not include Section 1 of the Critical Reading paper.

National
Qualifications
MODEL PAPER 3

English
Reading for Understanding, Analysis and Evaluation

Duration — 1 hour

Total marks — 30

When you are told to do so, open the booklet, read the passage and attempt all the questions, using your own words as far as possible.

Before attempting the questions you must check that your answer booklet is for the same subject and level as this question paper.

On the answer booklet, you must clearly identify the question number you are attempting.

Use **blue** or **black** ink.

Before leaving the examination room you must give your answer booklet to the Invigilator. If you do not, you may lose all the marks for this paper.

HODDER
GIBSON
LEARN MORE

Why Dickens was the hero of Soweto

In this passage, the writer informs us about the effect that books by Charles Dickens, a 19th-century English writer, had on black South African children during the time of racial segregation ("apartheid") in South Africa. "Afrikaans" is the language which was spoken in South Africa by the white rulers before the arrival of democracy in that country.

Hector Pieterson was 12 when he died. Today a museum bearing his name commemorates his death — and hundreds of others — which occurred some 30 years ago at a place whose name has come to symbolise uprising against oppression: Soweto.

Hector was one of thousands of black children who took to the streets on June 16, 1976, in
5 protest about schooling under the apartheid regime in South Africa. When police opened fire on the march it brought the word Soweto to the attention of the world. But less well known is the role that Charles Dickens played in events.

The march was in protest at a government edict making Afrikaans compulsory in schools. From January 1976, half of all subjects were to be taught in it, including ones in which difficulties of
10 translation were often an issue.

To pupils accustomed to being educated in English, the Afrikaans policy was the last of a line insults delivered in the name of "Bantu" or "negative education". They thought being taught in Afrikaans, the language of a regime that had tried to "unpeople" them, would cost them their last remaining freedom — that of thinking for themselves, using their minds.

15 That is where Dickens came in. Many books were banned under apartheid but not the classics of English literature. Pupils arriving hungry at school every day were captivated by the story of a frail but courageous boy named Oliver Twist.

The book was a revelation. Systemised oppression of children happened in England too! They were not alone. Slave labour, thin rations and cruel taunts were part of a child's life in the
20 world outside as well.

One former pupil, now in his forties, says of Dickens: "Four or five of us would be together and discuss the stories. And to think he wasn't banned! The authorities didn't know what was in these books, how they helped us to be strong, to think that we were not forgotten."

Not being forgotten was particularly crucial. The apartheid regime had tried to "vanish" black
25 people. Feeling abandoned and isolated, people turned to Dickens as someone who understood their plight.

But there were not enough books to go round. Few of the crateloads of Shakespeare, Hardy and Dickens shipped from Britain reached the townships. Instead, they came to Soweto in parcels from charities. They were read by candlelight, often out loud, shared in a circle, or passed from
30 hand to hand.

At Morrris Isaacson School, one of the moving forces behind the Soweto protest, which produced two of its leaders, Murphy Morobe, "Shakespeare's best friend in Africa", and Tsietsi Mashinini, there were 1,500 pupils and three copies of *Oliver Twist* in 1976. The former pupils recall waiting months for their turn, with a similar wait for *Nicholas Nickleby*.

35 But it was Oliver that they took to heart: students at one of the country's leading black colleges, Lovedale, formed a committee to ask for more.

Calling it the Board, after Dickens' Board of Guardians, they asked for more lessons, more food — and more and better books. Their reward was to be charged with public violence. All 152 "board" members were expelled from the college and some were jailed.

They felt that Dickens was obviously on their side. Descriptions of Gamfield's "ugly leer" and
40 Bumble's "repulsive countenance" and Oliver being beaten by Mrs Sowerberry and shoved "but nothing daunted" into the dust-cellar were evidence that this English author understood the plight of black South Africans.

Dickens' compassion for the poor linked the people of Soweto to a worldwide literature of tremendous importance.

45 The veteran South African trumpeter Hugh Masekela later chose *Nicholas Nickleby* as his favourite book on a popular radio programme, *Desert Island Discs*, telling the presenter what its author did for people in the townships: "He taught us suffering is the same everywhere."

The love of books that enabled an author dead for more than 100 years to inspire thousands of schoolchildren came mainly from grandmothers who had educated their families orally, then
50 urged them to read widely and learn all that they could.

It also came from people such as the activist Steve Biko, whose own mentor, the Brazilian educator Paulo Freire, spent a lifetime working with forest people who had no formal education, teaching them to "name the world their own way".

That is what the youth of Soweto wanted — a future in their own words. And they got it. By the
55 following year, Afrikaans had been withdrawn from classrooms as unworkable. And so, thanks to the influence of a long-dead British author, the sacrifices of Hector Pieterson and many other Africans have proved to be not entirely in vain — which Dickens himself would surely applaud.

Adapted from an article by Carol Lee in The Times.

MARKS

Questions

1. Explain fully any **two** ways in which the writer makes the opening paragraph dramatic.

    4

2. Referring to lines 1–14, explain **in your own words** why Sowetans were protesting.

    3

3. Why, according to the writer in lines 15–26, was the story of Oliver Twist so popular among young Sowetans?

    4

4. Show how any **two** examples of the writer's word choice in lines 15–20 create sympathy for the character Oliver Twist.

    4

5. Explain the function of the colon in line 35.

    2

6. Referring to lines 27–47, summarise **in your own words** the key evidence the writer uses to show Dickens' popularity among black South Africans.

    4

7. What does the paragraph in lines 37–39 suggest about the Government in South Africa at the time?

    2

8. Look at lines 48–57.

    (a) Explain briefly how each paragraph shows the importance various groups of people attach to education.

    3

    (b) Show how any **two** examples of the writers' use of language in these lines create a very positive and inspiring conclusion to the passage.

    4

[END OF MODEL PRACTICE PAPER]

National Qualifications
MODEL PAPER 3

English
Critical Reading

SECTION 2 — 20 marks

Write ONE critical essay on a previously studied text from Drama, Prose, Poetry, Film and Television Drama or Language.

HODDER GIBSON
LEARN MORE

SECTION 2 — CRITICAL ESSAY — 20 marks

Attempt ONE question from this section of the paper from ONE of the Parts A-E.

You may use a Scottish text but <u>not</u> the one used in Section 1.

Your essay should be on a different <u>genre</u> to the one used in Section 1.

Write the number of your chosen question in the margin of your answer.

You should spend about 45 minutes on the essay.

DRAMA

Answers to questions in this part should refer to the text and to such relevant features as characterisation, key scene(s), structure, climax, theme, plot, conflict, setting . . .

1. Choose a play in which one of the main concerns is love **or** jealousy **or** betrayal **or** reconciliation.

   Explain what the concern is, and by referring to appropriate techniques show how it is explored throughout the play.

2. Choose a scene from a play in which suspense or tension is built up.

   By referring to appropriate techniques, show how this suspense or tension is built up and what effect this scene has on the play as a whole.

PROSE

Answers to questions in this part should refer to the text and to such relevant features as characterisation, setting, language, key incident(s), climax, turning point, plot, structure, narrative technique, theme, ideas, description . . .

3. Choose a novel **or** a short story in which a character is in conflict with his or her friends or relatives or society.

   By referring to appropriate techniques, show how the conflict arises and what effect it has on the character's fate in the novel or short story as a whole.

4. Choose a novel **or** a short story **or** a work of non-fiction in which setting is an important feature.

   By referring to appropriate techniques, explain how the writer creates the setting, and then go on to show how this feature contributes to your understanding of the text as a whole.

POETRY

Answers to questions in this part should refer to the text and to such relevant features as word choice, tone, imagery, structure, content, rhythm, rhyme, theme, sound, ideas . . .

5. Choose a poem which reflects on an aspect of human behaviour in such a way as to deepen your understanding of human nature.

   Describe the aspect of human behaviour which you have identified and, by referring to appropriate techniques, show how the poem brought you to a deeper understanding of human nature.

6. Choose a poem which portrays an interesting character.

   By referring to appropriate techniques, show how the poet makes the character interesting.

FILM AND TV DRAMA

Answers to questions in this part should refer to the text and to such relevant features as use of camera, key sequence, characterisation, mise-en-scène, editing, setting, music/ sound, special effects, plot, dialogue . . .

7. Choose a film **or** TV drama* in which the main character is an individual for whom we feel sympathy.

   By referring to appropriate techniques, show how the character is portrayed in such a way that we feel sympathy.

8. Choose an opening sequence from a film which effectively holds your interest and makes you want to watch the rest of the film.

   By referring to appropriate techniques, show what elements of the opening sequence have this effect, and how they relate to the film as a whole.

* "TV drama" includes a single play, a series or a serial.

LANGUAGE STUDY

Answers to questions in this part should refer to the text and to such relevant features as register, accent, dialect, slang, jargon, vocabulary, tone, abbreviation . . .

9. Consider the ways that young people use the internet to communicate and socialise, for example: social networking sites, instant messaging, chat rooms, blogs . . .

   By referring to specific examples and to appropriate features of language, explain how such communication differs from formal English, and what its attractions are for young people.

10. Consider a text which you find to be persuasive, for example: an advertisement, a speech, a newspaper article . . .

    By referring to specific examples and to appropriate features of language, show how persuasive techniques have been used to convince you.

[END OF SECTION 2]

[END OF MODEL PRACTICE PAPER]

NATIONAL 5

2014

National Qualifications 2014

X724/75/01

English
Reading for Understanding, Analysis and Evaluation

WEDNESDAY, 30 APRIL

1:00 PM – 2:00 PM

Total marks — 30

Attempt ALL questions.

Write your answers clearly in the answer booklet provided. In the answer booklet you must clearly identify the question number you are attempting.

Use **blue** or **black** ink.

Before leaving the examination room you must give your answer booklet to the Invigilator; if you do not you may lose all the marks for this paper.

Hey, parents, leave those kids alone.

In many ways, nothing changes. We love our children. We want our children to grow up to be competent, decent human beings fit for adult purpose. These are the main things, and in these we have, I think we are all agreed, not done too badly. Our children, and I'll generalise here, are not serial axe murderers or kitten drowners. Our children do make
5 an effort — at least on special occasions anyway — to repay the enormous investment of time, energy, money and emotion we have poured into them. Children are programmed to please, to be loved, and to love us back.

So we are not here to examine our children. What we should do is try to find out where we have gone so terribly wrong. Before we come to the wretchedly indulgent state of
10 modern parenting, though, I suppose I'd better set out my stall. Inevitably, when one becomes a parent, one can't help revisiting one's own childhood to make comparisons.

When I was little, we were given no choices — about what we ate, what we wore, what we did, where we went to school, when we went to bed etc. I could only choose what to read.

15 There was not so much stuff (many of my son's 15-year-old friends have iPods, iPads, MacBooks, unlimited access to their parents' credit cards, Pay Pal, eBay and iTunes accounts — and not just iPhones, but BlackBerrys too), so we made our own fun.

Our parents provided us with the essentials, then got on with their own lives. Which makes me realise that my parents were brilliant, not for what they did, but more for
20 what they didn't do.

So we were fed, we were clothed, we were loved, and we had all the books we could read. But there was not the expectation of having every wish granted, as there is now, and that is the best thing that my parents could ever have given us.

I remember only once going to a restaurant in the UK. It was a motorway café on the
25 A303. My father told us, wincing as he looked at the laminated text, with its stomach-churning pictograms, that we could have the spag bol. From the children's menu.

We had a TV, but as we lived in Belgium there was nothing to watch apart from two American sitcoms, which came on only once a week.

My parents were so hard up that when we went to England for holidays on the family farm
30 on Exmoor — mainly spent "wooding" for winter fuel on rainswept hillsides — my father would invariably book cheap overnight ferry crossings from the Continent. He would never shell out for a cabin, despite the 1am or 3am departure slots. Instead, he would tell us to go to sleep in the back of the car, parked in the lower deck, where we would eventually pass out from suffocation or diesel fumes.

35 We never had friends round for "playdates". Keeping children busy and happy was not a parental priority. If we were bored, that was our own fault. In fact, there was nothing to do for weeks on end except rake leaves (my father once made us spend a whole half-term raking leaves) and read on our beds. Occasionally my mother would shout up the stairs: "Stop reading!" Imagine that now, when children are on their laptops in their rooms,
40 looking at . . . I don't even want to imagine.

As for school, well, reports were read, not dwelt upon, as they were not parents' business, but ours. As for parental involvement, all I can tell you is that my father's proudest boast as a parent is that he never, once, attended a parent-teacher meeting at any one of our schools.

45 It never did me any harm, but still, I can't repeat this sensible, caring regime of character-building, toughening, benign neglect for my own children . . . and nor, it appears, can anyone else. Now examples of "wet parenting" abound.

Page two

We also live in a world where a manic mum calls herself a Tiger Mother and writes a bestselling book by the same name about how to produce straight-A violin-playing
50 tennis-champ superkids, and where pushy, anxious helicopter parents hover over every school. A friend reports that when her son was due to visit the Brecon Beacons on a school camping trip this summer, three mothers pulled out their sons because the weather forecast was "rainy".

University dons are also complaining of a traumatic level of parental over-involvement
55 just at the exact moment that mummies and daddies are supposed to be letting go.

It was the complete opposite in my day. When I was on my gap year, I called my father from Israel in September and told him I'd decided not to take up my place at university. I announced that I wanted to stay in Galilee with a handsome local shepherd. For ever.

My father didn't miss a beat. "Great scheme!" he cried, astutely divining that if he
60 approved the plan, I would never carry it out.

In my lifetime, parenthood has undergone a terrifying transition. Becoming a mother or father is no longer something you just are. It is something you do, like becoming a vet — complete with training courses, parenting vouchers, government targets and guidelines, and a host of academics and caring professionals (as well as their websites,
65 and telephone helplines) on hand 24/7 to guide you through what to expect when your twentysomethings return home.

Parenting has become subsidised and professionalised, even though anyone can (and, frankly, does) have a baby, after which they become parents.

I love being a parent, most of the time anyway, but we should immediately
70 de-professionalise it, on the grounds that: one, it's unpaid; and two, thanks to the economy, lack of housing and jobs etc, you never get to retire.

Rachel Johnson, in The Times

MARKS

1. Look at line 9, where the writer gives the view that, nowadays, parents "have gone . . . terribly wrong".

   Explain **in your own words** what the writer goes on to say has gone wrong.   2

2. Explain any way in which the sentences in lines 12 – 14 help to provide a link between ideas at this point in the passage.   2

3. Look at lines 24 – 40, where the writer develops the idea of her family being "hard up".

   Show fully how examples of the writer's use of such features of language as **word choice** or **sentence structure** helps to convey her ideas effectively.   4

4. Look at lines 45 – 47.

   Explain what is meant by the expression "benign neglect", and explain what is surprising about this expression.   3

5. Look at lines 48 – 55.

   With reference to **three** examples of the writer's **word choice** from these lines, show fully how she makes clear her disapproval of what she calls "wet parenting".   6

6. In the expression "straight-A violin-playing tennis-champ superkids" the writer tries to achieve a humorous, mocking tone.

   Explain with reference to her use of language how successful you think she has been in achieving this tone.   2

7. Look at lines 59 – 60.

   Show fully how the writer conveys her father's **apparent** attitude, and his **actual attitude**, to her plan.   4

8. Look at lines 61 – 66, and then explain **as far as possible in your own words** what similarities the writer sees between "Becoming a mother or father" and "becoming a vet".   2

9. In this article, the writer points out several differences between parenting and childhood when she was little and parenting and childhood now (she refers to "a terrifying transition", line 61).

   As far as possible in your own words, summarise what some main differences are.   5

[END OF QUESTION PAPER]

Acknowledgement of Copyright

Extract is adapted from an article in The Times, 15 October 2012

National Qualifications 2014

X724/75/02

English Critical Reading

WEDNESDAY, 30 APRIL

2:20 PM – 3:50 PM

Total marks — 40

SECTION 1 — Scottish Text — 20 marks

Read an extract from a Scottish text you have previously studied.

Choose ONE text from either

Part A — Drama   Pages 2–7

or

Part B — Prose   Pages 8–17

or

Part C — Poetry   Pages 18–25

Attempt ALL the questions for your chosen text.

SECTION 2 — Critical Essay — 20 marks

Attempt ONE question from the following genres — Drama, Prose, Poetry, Film and Television Drama, or Language.

Your answer must be on a different genre from that chosen in Section 1.

You should spend approximately 45 minutes on each Section.

Write your answers clearly in the answer booklet provided. In the answer booklet you must clearly identify the question number you are attempting.

Use **blue** or **black** ink.

Before leaving the examination room you must give your answer booklet to the Invigilator; if you do not you may lose all the marks for this paper.

SECTION 1 — SCOTTISH TEXT — 20 marks

PART A — SCOTTISH TEXT — DRAMA

Text 1 — Drama

If you choose this text you may not attempt a question on Drama in Section 2.

Read the extract below and then attempt the following questions.

***Bold Girls* by Rona Munro**

Marie's house. Belfast. Late afternoon. Present day

It is irons and ironing boards and piles of clothes waiting to be smoothed, socks and pegs and damp sheets waiting for a break in the Belfast drizzle for the line; it's toys in pieces and toys that are just cardboard boxes and toys that are new and gleaming and flashing
5 *with lights and have swallowed up the year's savings. It's pots and pans and steam and the kettle always hot for tea; it's furniture that's bald with age and a hearth in front of the coal fire that's gleaming clean.*

At the moment it's empty, an unnatural, expectant emptiness that suggests this room is never deserted; it's too stuffed with human bits and pieces, all the clutter of housework
10 *and life.*

There is a small picture of the virgin on one wall, a large grainy blow-up photo of a smiling young man on the other. He has a seventies haircut and moustache.

Deirdre is not in this room, she is crouching on all fours on her own talking out of darkness in which only her face is visible. She is wary, young.

15 DEIRDRE: (*moving from all fours*) The sun is going down behind the hills, the sky is grey. There's hills at the back there, green. I can't hardly see them because the stones between here and there are grey, the street is grey. Somewhere a bird is singing and falling in the sky. I hear the ice cream van and the traffic and the helicopter overhead.

Black-out; after a few minutes Lights come up on Marie's house.

20 *Marie bursts into the room with her arms laden with four packets of crisps, two of Silk Cut and a packet of chocolate biscuits. She is cheerful, efficient, young. She drops one of the crisps, tuts in exasperation, and looks at it*

MARIE: (shouting back out the door) Mickey! Mickey were you wanting smoky bacon?... Well this is salt and vinegar . . . Well, why did you not say? Away you and swap this . . .
25 Catch now. (She hurls the bag) No you cannot . . . No . . . because you'll not eat your tea if you do! (At the doorway) Mickey, pick up those crisps and don't be so bold.

Marie comes back into the room and starts two jobs simultaneously. First she puts the crisps etc away, then she fills a pan with water and throws it on the stove. She starts sorting her dry washing into what needs ironing and what doesn't; she sorts a few items
30 *then starts peeling potatoes; all her movements have a frenetic efficiency.*

MARKS

Questions

1. Look at the description of Marie's house. By referring to word choice and/or sentence structure, explain what impression this creates of Marie's daily life.   **4**

2. With close reference to the text, explain what Deirdre's **actions** and **speech** tell us about her relationship to her surroundings. You could consider: word choice, tone, the use of imagery etc . . .   **4**

3. The playwright introduces Marie. What do we find out about:

    (*a*) her attitude towards Mickey;   **2**

    (*b*) her attitude towards her daily routine?   **2**

4. The play goes on to develop our understanding of how challenging life is in many respects for the "bold girls". By referring to this extract and at least one other example from the play, discuss what these challenges are.   **8**

[Turn over

OR

Text 2 — Drama

If you choose this text you may not attempt a question on Drama in Section 2.

Read the extract below and then attempt the following questions.

Sailmaker by Alan Spence

Extract from Act Two

ALEC:	Look at the state ae us. We're livin like bloody Steptoe and Son! Nae light. Place is like a midden. When did we last gie it a good clean? Needs gutted.
	Look at it!
DAVIE:	It's hard son. It's no easy on yer own.
5 ALEC:	So ye go an get bevvied. Forget it all.
DAVIE:	Ye'd think ah came in steamin every night!
	Christ ah need a wee break once in a while. Like the night. Nae harm in it. Good company. Wee sing song. Right gents, a wee bit order there. One singer one song. That lassie's a rare singer. Sang Honky Tonk Angels.
10	She's the one ah told ye about.
ALEC:	(*Sarcastic*) The really nice person.
DAVIE:	She wis.
ALEC:	Who was that lady I saw you with last night?
DAVIE:	That was no lady, that was a really nice person.
15	Nae harm in it.
ALEC:	It's always the same. Every time ye meet a wumman she's a really really really nice person.
	Why don't ye just admit that ye fancy her?
	(DAVIE *slaps him, exits*)
20	Ach aye, yirra good boy son. Wallop!
	Bad. Bad. Bad.
	(*Pause*)
	Wallop.
	(*Darkness. Spotlight on* ALEC)
25	I keep goin back.
	What is it I'm tryin to remember?
	What is it I'm tryin to say?
	There's somethin I've lost. Something I've forgotten.
	Sometimes in the middle of the night . . .
30	What is it I'm looking for?
	God knows.

MARKS

Questions

5. **In your own words**, summarise what happens in this part of the play. Make **two** key points.

2

6. Think about how Alec and Davie are feeling during their dialogue with one another (lines 1—19).

   (a) Show how Alec's language reflects his feelings.

2

   (b) Although he does not say very much, Davie experiences a range of emotions during his dialogue with his son. With close reference to the text, explain what **at least two** of these are.

4

7. Alec is left alone at the end of this extract.

   With reference to word-choice and sentence structure, explain clearly his state of mind at this stage in the play.

4

8. By referring to this extract, and to elsewhere in the play, explain how the character of Alec develops and changes as he grows older.

8

[Turn over

OR

Text 3 — Drama

If you choose this text you may not attempt a question on Drama in Section 2.

Read the extract below and then attempt the following questions.

Tally's Blood **by Ann Marie di Mambro**

This scene takes place in the back of the Pedreschi's shop.

ROSINELLA: You see the way Italians are getting on now, eh? Beginning to make a wee bit money? Because they're prepared to WORK that's why. I don't know anybody who works so hard as the Italian men.

Hughie in: with pail and mop.

5 HUGHIE: That's the tables cleared and the front shop mopped, Mrs Pedreschi, and the chip pan cleaned out. Is the milk boiled?

ROSINELLA: Should be.

She turns attention back to Lucia, Hughie lifts pot from stove and pours contents into two pails: he covers them and sets them aside, working like a trojan.

10 ROSINELLA: And the way they love their families. Nobody loves their families like the Italians. You want to stay for a wee bit pasta, Hughie? It's your favourite. Rigatoni.

HUGHIE: No thanks, Mrs Pedreschi. I better get up the road. Bridget's going out and I don't like my mammy left on her own.

15 ROSINELLA: Bridget's going out is she? Don't tell me she's winching?

HUGHIE: No. Her and Davie are going up to Charmaine's the night — to go over all the arrangements. My mammy's no up to it.

ROSINELLA: That's right. When's the wedding now?

Hughie and Lucia exchange glances: he makes gesture of "go ahead" to her. Lucia shakes
20 *head.*

Hughie: Saturday.

ROSINELLA: And where are they going to stay?

HUGHIE: At Charmaine's.

ROSINELLA: It's funny that, isn't it, but that's the way they do it here. In Italy a girl
25   must go to her husband's house. That's why you must have land if you've got sons.

Massimo in.

ROSINELLA: So that'll be your mammy left with her eldest and her youngest, eh? I don't see your Bridget ever marrying, do you? You see, Lucia, there's a lot
30   of women Bridget's age no married. The war killed that many young men. I'm right there, amn't I Massimo?

MASSIMO: You got those pails ready, son?

HUGHIE: I'll bring them through.

MARKS

MASSIMO: And give's a hand to put these shutters up before you go.

35 *Hughie and Massimo out: Rosinella watches him go.*

ROSINELLA: I'm right about that Davie, amn't I Lucia? Give it five or six months, Hughie'll be telling us he's an uncle again. Mind you, I suppose his mother must feel it, right enough. Can you find me a wee envelope hen, a wee poke or something? What was I saying . . . ah yes . . . See what I mean
40   about Italian men. Just take that brother of Hughie's. Getting married on Saturday, give him two or three days and he'll be out DRINKING with his pals.

Rosinella shooshes up when Hughie comes in, followed by Massimo: all locked up. Massimo takes off his apron, reaches for a bottle of wine.

45 MASSIMO: Thanks, Hughie son. You want a wee glass of wine?

HUGHIE: I better not, Mr Pedreschi. I better get up the road.

ROSINELLA: Hang on a minute, son. (She has slipped a couple of notes into the poke, gives it to Hughie) Here, give this to your brother from me. Instead of a present. Help them out a wee bit, eh? (Hughie hangs back, embarrassed)
50   . . . Take it.

Questions

9. (a) Rosinella makes stereotypical statements about Italians and/or Scots which are shown to be false in this extract. Identify **two** statements and explain how the playwright shows they are false.   **4**

   (b) Explain how you think the audience would react to this falseness.   **2**

10. Think about the character Rosinella.

   (a) How is Rosinella shown to be kind or caring in this extract?   **2**

   (b) How is Rosinella shown to be unkind or unpleasant in this extract?   **2**

11. Identify **two** examples of colloquial or conversational language from the extract.   **2**

12. This extract deals with racial stereotypes. With close reference to this extract and elsewhere in the play explain how the issue of racism is explored.   **8**

[Turn over

PART B — SCOTTISH TEXT — PROSE

Text 1 — Prose

If you choose this text you may not attempt a question on Prose in Section 2.

Read the extract below and then attempt the following questions.

The Cone-Gatherers by **Robin Jenkins.**

In this extract, a deer hunt, at which Neil and Calum have been told to help out, is coming to its violent end.

The drive was nearly over. Only a hundred or so yards away were the waiting guns. Frightened by the noises approaching them from the rear, and apprehensive of the human silence ahead, the five roe deer were halted, their heads high in nervous alertness. When Calum saw them, his cry was of delight and friendship, and then of terrified warning as
5 the dogs too, and Duror, caught sight of them and rushed in pursuit. Silently, with marvellous grace and agility over such rough ground, the deer flew for the doom ahead. Their white behinds were like moving glints of sunlight; without them their tawny hides might not have been seen in the autumnal wood.

Calum no longer was one of the beaters; he too was a deer hunted by remorseless men.
10 Moaning and gasping, he fled after them, with no hope of saving them from slaughter but with the impulse to share it with them. He could not, however, be so swift or sure of foot. He fell and rose again; he avoided one tree only to collide with another close to it; and all the time he felt, as the deer must have, the indifference of all nature; of the trees, of tall withered stalks of willow herb, of the patches of blue sky, of bushes, of piles
15 of cut scrubwood, of birds lurking in branches, and of the sunlight: presences which might have been expected to help or at least sympathise.

The dogs barked fiercely. Duror fired his gun in warning to those waiting in the ride. Neil, seeing his brother rush into danger, roared to him to come back. All the beaters, except Charlie far in the rear, joined in the commotion; the wood resounded with their exultant
20 shouts. Realising this must be the finish or kill, Graham, recuperating on the road, hopped back over the fence into the wood and bellowed loudest of all.

As Duror bawled to his dogs to stop lest they interfered with the shooting, and as the deer hesitated before making the dash across the ride, Calum was quite close to them as silent, desperate, and heroic, they sprang forward to die or escape. When the guns
25 banged he did not, as Neil had vehemently warned him to do, fall flat on the ground and put his fingers in his ears. Instead, with wails of lament, he dashed on at demented speed and shot out onto the broad green ride to hear a deer screaming and see it, wounded in the breast and forelegs, scrabbling about on its hindquarters. Captain Forgan was feverishly reloading his guns to fire again. Calum saw no one else, not even the lady
30 or Mr Tulloch, who was standing by himself about twenty yards away.

Screaming in sympathy, heedless of the danger of being shot, Calum flung himself upon the deer, clasped it around the neck and tried to comfort it. Terrified more than ever, it dragged him about with it in its mortal agony. Its blood came off onto his face and hands.

While Captain Forgan, Young Roderick, and Lady Runcie-Campbell stood petrified by this
35 sight, Duror followed by his dogs came leaping out of the wood. He seemed to be laughing in some kind of berserk joy.

MARKS

Questions

13. Look at the first paragraph and describe the changing emotions Calum experiences when he sees the deer.

2

14. In lines 5—8 how does the writer emphasise the sadness of what is about to happen to the deer?

2

15. Identify two examples of how the writer's language in lines 9—16 convey Calum's clumsy panic as he tries to help the hunted animals.

2

16. Look again at lines 24—33. Show how the writer conveys the chaos of the moment when Calum reaches and tries to help the wounded deer.

4

17. How unusual do you find Duror's reaction in lines 34—36 to Calum ruining the deer drive?

2

18. Discuss how Duror is portrayed in this extract and elsewhere in the novel.

8

[Turn over

OR

Text 2 — Prose

If you choose this text you may not attempt a question on Prose in Section 2.

Read the extract below and then attempt the following questions.

The Testament of Gideon Mack by James Robertson

I went running every second or third day. I ran not as a member of a club, not in training for competitions (although I have run marathons for charity), not even to keep fit (although it had that effect), but because I enjoyed it. Yes, running filled me with joy, contentment, as nothing else did. It took me out of myself. Also, it was how I released
5 the energy inside me: as if the fire blazing away in there was my fuel. If I went four days without a run, I grew hot and tense and felt as if my chest was about to explode. I *needed* to run. It was how I got the heat out of my system.

Running made me aware both of the countryside in which I lived and of my physical self. When I set off through the streets of Monimaskit, I could feel the disapproval of some of
10 my parishioners boring into the back of my neck — there was something just *no richt* about a minister in shorts, and sweating. But once out of the town I left all that behind me. I avoided traffic-heavy main roads and ran on narrow, deserted unclassifieds, farm tracks, paths that led me through woods and alongside fields and over burns. I ran along the shore, I ran up into the low hills, I ran beside the crashing of the sea on sand and
15 shingle and I ran above the roaring of the Keldo Water as it fought through the Black Jaws on its way to that sea. I loved the idea of myself — was this vanity? — running among the shadows of trees, against the backdrop of hills, in the echo of birdsong and bellowing cows. I could run for a couple of hours at a time if I chose, barely pausing at gates or stiles, sensitive to the different noises my trainers made when I went up or down a hill, or
20 when I moved from hard road to soft path or grass. Usually I ran in the late afternoon, the dead time between daytime appointments and evening visits and meetings, and I seldom met anybody else. A woman walking her dog, perhaps, or a couple of lads on their bikes. Sometimes the woman would recognise me and say hello. Sometimes she'd recognise me but pretend not to, embarrassed by the ministerial knees. If the boys had a
25 clue who I was, they never let on.

I loved that time of day in all seasons and all weathers, the bright hot stillness of summer and the dark moody dampness of winter. I loved it for itself, but running made it more special still. Running emptied my head of work, the Kirk, the world. Difficult issues and awkward individuals were repelled by the force of my energy, and their ghosts faded into
30 the trees. In Israel young fanatics with explosives strapped to their bodies were wiping themselves and busloads of hated strangers off the planet; insect species were being extinguished every five minutes in the Amazon forest; military coups were being bloodily launched in Africa; dams were being built in China, making tens of thousands homeless; but in Keldo Woods, alone and immune and having slipped his clerical collar, Gideon Mack
35 was running. Sometimes a line from a song or a hymn got trapped in my head and I ran to its rhythm, half-enjoying it and half-annoyed by it. Phrases from the Scriptures that became strange and mantra-like in the repetition: *Nec tamen consumebatur*; "The Lord is with thee, thou mighty man of valour"; MENE, MENE, TEKEL UPHARSIN. Sometimes I heard my own voice in there, bits of poems I'd read, things I wished I'd said at the right
40 moment, heroic and true things I might say in the future — nothing, as it's turned out, remotely connected with what I would actually say.

Sometimes I saw myself as I do now — as if in a film, splashing through puddles to a soundtrack by Vangelis: *when I run I feel God's pleasure*. But that was somebody else: Eric Liddell, the Flying Scotsman, a missionary, a kind of saint. *The loneliness of the*
45 *long-distance runner*: phrases like that would enter my head and bounce around in there as I ran; but that was someone else again, a Borstal boy, a figure of fiction. I was somewhere in between — an escapee from my professional hypocrisy, a minister off the leash, a creature neither wholly real nor wholly imagined, hurrying through an ancient landscape. Yes, even then I suspected what I now know to be true: that life itself is not
50 wholly real. Existence is one thing, life quite another: it is the ghost that haunts existence, the spirit that animates it. Running, whether in the rain or sun, felt like life.

Questions

19. Using examples from this extract to support your points, explain the different reasons why Gideon Mack enjoys running.   **4**

20. What does this extract reveal about Mack's attitude to his job? Give evidence from the extract to support your answer.   **2**

21. Look closely at the **language** used in this extract.

    (a) Show how **sentence structure** helps the reader understand how much Gideon Mack enjoys running.   **3**

    (b) Choose one example of **imagery** used to help the reader understand the importance of running to Gideon Mack and explain how it does so.   **3**

22. Discuss one aspect of Gideon Mack's character which features in this extract and is developed elsewhere in the novel.   **8**

[Turn over

OR

Text 3 — Prose

If you choose this text you may not attempt a question on Prose in Section 2.

Read the extract below and then attempt the following questions.

Kidnapped by Robert Louis Stevenson

In this extract, which is from Chapter 9 of the novel, David Balfour sees Alan Breck Stewart for the first time as he arrives on the Covenant.

We had run down a boat in the fog, and she had parted in the midst and gone to the bottom with all her crew, but one. This man (as I heard afterwards) had been sitting in the stern as a passenger, while the rest were on the benches rowing. At the moment of the blow, the stern had been thrown into the air, and the man (having his hands free, and
5 for all he was encumbered with a frieze overcoat that came below his knees) had leaped up and caught hold of the brig's bowsprit. It showed he had luck and much agility and unusual strength, that he should have thus saved himself from such a pass. And yet, when the captain brought him into the round-house, and I set eyes on him for the first time, he looked as cool as I did.

10 He was smallish in stature, but well set and as nimble as a goat; his face was of a good open expression, but sunburnt very dark, and heavily freckled and pitted with the small-pox; his eyes were unusually light and had a kind of dancing madness in them, that was both engaging and alarming; and when he took off his great-coat, he laid a pair of fine silver-mounted pistols on the table, and I saw that he was belted with a great sword.
15 His manners, besides, were elegant, and he pledged the captain handsomely. Altogether I thought of him, at the first sight, that here was a man I would rather call my friend than my enemy.

The captain, too, was taking his observations, but rather of the man's clothes than his person. And to be sure, as soon as he had taken off the great-coat, he showed forth
20 mighty fine for the round-house of a merchant brig: having a hat with feathers, a red waistcoat, breeches of black plush, and a blue coat with silver buttons and handsome silver lace; costly clothes, though somewhat spoiled with the fog and being slept in.

"I'm vexed, sir, about the boat," says the captain.

"There are some pretty men gone to the bottom," said the stranger, " that I would
25 rather see on the dry land again than half a score of boats."

"Friends of yours?" said Hoseason.

"You have none such friends in your country," was the reply. "They would have died for me like dogs."

"Well, sir," said the captain, still watching him, "there are more men in the world than
30 boats to put them in."

"And that's true, too," cried the other, "and ye seem to be a gentleman of great penetration."

"I have been in France, sir," says the captain, so that it was plain he meant more by the words than showed upon the face of them.

35 "Well, sir," says the other, "and so has many a pretty man, for the matter of that."

MARKS

"No doubt, sir," says the captain, "and fine coats."

"Oho!" says the stranger, "is that how the wind sets?" And he laid his hand quickly on his pistols.

"Don't be hasty," said the captain. "Don't do a mischief before ye see the need of it.
40 Ye've a French soldier's coat upon your back and a Scotch tongue in your head, to be sure; but so has many an honest fellow in these days, and I dare say none the worse of it."

Questions

23. Look at paragraph 1 (lines 1—9) and summarise the circumstances of how Alan Breck Stewart came to arrive on the Covenant. You should make at least four key points.   4

24. Look at paragraph 2 (lines 10—17).

     In your own words, explain what David Balfour's first impressions were of Alan Breck Stewart's physical appearance and character.   4

25. Look at the conversation between Alan Breck Stewart and Captain Hoseason (lines 23—42).

     Show how any **two** examples of the writer's use of language contributes to the creation of tension in the dialogue.   4

26. With reference to this extract and to elsewhere in the novel, discuss the development of David and Alan's relationship.   8

[Turn over

OR

Text 4 — Prose

If you choose this text you may not attempt a question on Prose in Section 2.

Read the extract below and then attempt the following questions.

The Telegram by Iain Crichton Smith

The elder had passed the Murrays. The next house was her own. She sat perfectly still. Oh, pray God it wasn't hers. And yet it must be hers. Surely it must be hers. She had dreamt of this happening, her son drowning in the Atlantic ocean, her own child whom she had reared, whom she had seen going to play football in his green jersey and white
5   shorts, whom she had seen running home from school. She could see him drowning but she couldn't make out the name of the ship. She had never seen a really big ship and what she imagined was more like the mailboat than a cruiser. Her son couldn't drown out there for no reason that she could understand. God couldn't do that to people. It was impossible. God was kinder than that. God helped you in your sore trouble. She began
10 to mutter a prayer over and over. She said it quickly like the Catholics. O God save my son O God save my son O God save my son. She was ashamed of prattling in that way as if she was counting beads but she couldn't stop herself, and on top of that she would soon cry. She knew it and she didn't want to cry in front of that woman, that foreigner. It would be weakness. She felt the arm of the thin woman around her shoulders, the thin
15 arm and it was like first love, it was like the time Murdo had taken her hand in his when they were coming home from the dance, such an innocent gesture, such a spontaneous gesture. So unexpected, so strange, so much a gift. She was crying and she couldn't look . . .

"He has passed your house," said the thin woman, in a distant firm voice, and she looked
20 up. He was walking along and he had indeed passed her house. She wanted to stand up and dance all around the kitchen, all fifteen stone of her, and shout and cry and sing a song but then she stopped. She couldn't do that. How could she do that when it must be the thin woman's son? There was no other house. The thin woman was looking out at the elder, her lips pressed closely together, white and bloodless. Where had she learnt that
25 self control? She wasn't crying or shaking. She was looking out at something she had always dreaded but she wasn't going to cry or surrender or give herself away to anyone.

And at that moment the fat woman saw. She saw the years of discipline, she remembered how thin and unfed and pale the thin woman had always looked, how sometimes she had had to borrow money, even a shilling to buy food. She saw what it
30 must have been like to be a widow bringing up a son in a village not her own. She saw it so clearly that she was astounded. It was as if she had an extra vision, as if the air itself brought the past with all its details nearer. The number of times the thin woman had been ill and people had said that she was weak and useless. She looked down at the thin woman's arm. It was so shrivelled, and dry.

35 And the elder walked on.

MARKS

Questions

27. Look closely at lines 1—18.

    How does the writer use language effectively to create tension?   4

28. Look closely at the description of the thin woman in lines 19—26.

    Show how the writer uses word choice to demonstrate:

    (*a*) her fear;   2

    (*b*) her self-control.   2

29. In your own words, summarise the main difficulties the thin woman has had to overcome in her life. You should make at least four points.   4

30. By referring to this story, and to at least one other story by Iain Crichton Smith, show how he is successful in creating a character or characters we can feel sympathy for.   8

[Turn over

OR

Text 5 — Prose

If you choose this text you may not attempt a question on Prose in Section 2.

Read the extract below and then attempt the following questions.

Away in a Manger by Anne Donovan

This year the nativity was bigger than life-sized. The figures were bronze statues, staunin on a carpet of straw and surrounded by what looked like a hoose made of glass. It was placed tae wan side of the square, inside a fence. Sandra thought it was quite dull lookin. Weans liked bright colours and these huge people were kind of scary. She minded
5 the wee plastic figures of Mary and Joseph she used tae set carefully in place every Christmas, leavin the baby Jesus tae last. They'd fitted intae the palm of her haund. She'd need tae get a crib for Amy. Sandra wisnae very religious, no religious at all, really, but still, it was nice for the wee ones tae have a crib.

"Is that a manger, Mammy?" Amy pointed.

10 "That's right. D'you know who all the people are?"

Amy sucked at her mitt and looked carefully at the figures. "That's Mary and that's Joseph — and that's the baby Jesus. And that's a shepherd wi his sheep. But who's that, Mammy?"

"They're the three wise kings. Look — they've got presents for the baby Jesus."

15 "But who's that, Mammy? Behind the cow."

Huddled in the straw, hidden in a corner behind the figure of a large beast, lay a man. He was slightly built, dressed in auld jeans and a thin jaicket. One of his feet stuck oot round the end of the statue and on it was a worn trainin shoe, the cheapest kind they sold in the store. Sandra moved round tae get a better look at him. He was quite young, wi a
20 pointed face and longish dark hair. A stubbly growth covered his chin. He seemed sound asleep.

"Is he an angel, Mammy?"

Sandra didnae answer. She was lookin at the glass structure wonderin how on earth he'd got in. One of the panels at the back looked a bit loose, but you'd think they'd have an
25 alarm on it. Lucky for him they never — at least he'd be warm in there. She was that intent on the glass panels that she'd nearly forgotten he wisnae a statue. Suddenly he opened his eyes. They were grey.

Amy grabbed her mother's arm and started jumpin up and down.

"Mammy, look, he's alive! Look Mammy. He's an angel!"

MARKS

Questions

31. Using your own words as far as possible, summarise the main events in this extract. You should make at least two key points.

2

32. Look at lines 1—3. The writer uses a number of techniques to show how Amy tries to makes sense of the scene. Identify two techniques and explain their effects.

4

33. Look at lines 7—8 from "Sandra wisnae...". The writer creates the impression of Sandra thinking. Choose any one aspect of the writer's use of language and explain its effect.

2

34. Look at lines 16—20. The writer uses word choice to create a detailed picture of the man. Identify **two** separate examples of the writer's word choice from these lines and comment on their effects.

4

35. With reference to this story and at least one other story by Donovan, discuss how any one theme is explored.

8

[Turn over

PART C — SCOTTISH TEXT — POETRY

Text 1 — Poetry

If you choose this text you may not attempt a question on Poetry in Section 2.

Read the poem below and then attempt the following questions.

War Photographer **by Carol Ann Duffy**

In his darkroom he is finally alone
with spools of suffering set out in ordered rows.
The only light is red and softly glows,
as though this were a church and he
5　a priest preparing to intone a Mass.
Belfast. Beirut. Phnom Penh. All flesh is grass.

He has a job to do. Solutions slop in trays
beneath his hands, which did not tremble then
though seem to now. Rural England. Home again
10　to ordinary pain which simple weather can dispel,
to fields which don't explode beneath the feet
of running children in a nightmare heat.

Something is happening. A stranger's features
faintly start to twist before his eyes,
15　a half-formed ghost. He remembers the cries
of this man's wife, how he sought approval
without words to do what someone must
and how the blood stained into foreign dust.

A hundred agonies in black and white
20　from which his editor will pick out five or six
for Sunday's supplement. The reader's eyeballs prick
with tears between the bath and pre-lunch beers.
From the aeroplane he stares impassively at where
he earns his living and they do not care.

MARKS

Questions

36. As the photographer prepares to develop the film we learn important things about him.

    Identify two important things we learn about him from stanza one.   2

37. Show how two examples of the poet's use of language in stanza two highlight the effect the photographer's work has had on the photographer.   4

38. Show how one example of the poet's use of language contributes to the dramatic effect of stanza three.   2

39. How effective do you find any two aspects of the final stanza as a conclusion to the poem?

    Your answer might deal with ideas and/or language.   4

40. Using close textual reference, show how the presentation of the main character in this poem is similar or different to the presentation of the main character in another poem or poems by Duffy which you have read.   8

[Turn over

OR

Text 2 — Poetry

If you choose this text you may not attempt a question on Poetry in Section 2.

Read the poem below and then attempt the following questions.

In the Snack-bar by Edwin Morgan

A cup capsizes along the formica,
slithering with a dull clatter.
A few heads turn in the crowded evening snack-bar.
An old man is trying to get to his feet
5 from the low round stool fixed to the floor.
Slowly he levers himself up, his hands have no power.
He is up as far as he can get. The dismal hump
looming over him forces his head down.
He stands in his stained beltless gabardine
10 like a monstrous animal caught in a tent
in some story. He sways slightly,
the face not seen, bent down
in shadow under his cap.
Even on his feet he is staring at the floor
15 or would be, if he could see.
I notice now his stick, once painted white
but scuffed and muddy, hanging from his right arm.
Long blind, hunchback born, half paralysed
he stands
20 fumbling with the stick
and speaks:
'I want – to go to the – toilet.'

It is down two flights of stairs but we go.
I take his arm. 'Give me – your arm – it's better,' he says.
25 Inch by inch we drift towards the stairs.
A few yards of floor are like a landscape
to be negotiated, in the slow setting out
time has almost stopped. I concentrate
my life to his: crunch of spilt sugar,
30 slidy puddle from the night's umbrellas,

MARKS

table edges, people's feet,

hiss of the coffee-machine, voices and laughter,

smell of a cigar, hamburgers, wet coats steaming,

and the slow dangerous inches to the stairs.

Questions

41. (*a*) Identify two of the poem's main ideas or central concerns that are introduced in this extract.

2

   (*b*) Show how any two examples of the poet's use of language in stanza 1 help to make these concerns clear to readers.

4

42. Explain how the poet's own role in what is happening in the snack-bar changes from stanza 1 to stanza 2.

2

43. Look at lines 23—34. Show how the poet uses language to emphasise the difficulty of the start of the journey to the toilet.

4

44. By closely referring to the text of this and at least one other Morgan poem, show how Morgan uses language effectively to create interesting characters.

8

[Turn over

OR

Text 3 — Poetry

If you choose this text you may not attempt a question on Poetry in Section 2.

Read the poem below and then attempt the following questions.

Basking Shark **by Norman MacCaig**

To stub an oar on a rock where none should be,
To have it rise with a slounge out of the sea
Is a thing that happened once (too often) to me.

But not too often—though enough I count as gain
5 That once I met, on a sea tin-tacked with rain,
That roomsized monster with a matchbox brain.

He displaced more than water He shoggled me
Centuries back—this decadent townee
Shook on a wrong branch of his family tree.

10 Swish up the dirt and, when it settles, a spring
Is all the clearer. I saw me, in one fling,
Emerging from the slime of everything.

So who's the monster? The thought made me grow pale
For twenty seconds while as, sail after sail,
15 The tall fin slid away, and then the tail.

MARKS

Questions

45. Look at stanza 1. What event is described in this stanza and how does MacCaig react? Refer to the poet's language in your answer.

3

46. Referring closely to stanza 2, show how MacCaig uses word choice to convey how he feels about the encounter.

4

47. "He displaced more than water". Explain what this line means and show how the poet in the rest of the stanza develops this idea further.

3

48. Choose an example of word choice in stanza 4 and explain how effective you find this example.

2

49. MacCaig often describes his personal experiences in his poetry, using these to explore wider themes. Referring closely to this poem and to at least one other poem by MacCaig, show how he uses personal experience to explore wider themes.

8

[Turn over

OR

Text 4 — Poetry

If you choose this text you may not attempt a question on Poetry in Section 2.

Read the poem below and then attempt the following questions.

Lucozade **by Jackie Kay**

My mum is on a high bed next to sad chrysanthemums.
"Don't bring flowers, they only wilt and die."
I am scared my mum is going to die
on the bed next to the sad chrysanthemums.

5 She nods off and her eyes go back in her head.
Next to her bed is a bottle of Lucozade.
"Orange nostalgia, that's what it is," she says.
"Don't bring Lucozade, either," then fades.

"The whole day was a blur, a swarm of eyes.
10 Those doctors with their white lies.
Did you think you could cheer me up with a Woman's Own?
Don't bring magazines, too much about size."

My mum wakes up, groggy and low.
"What I want to know," she says, "is this:
15 where's the big brandy, the generous gin, the Bloody Mary,
the biscuit tin, the chocolate gingers, the dirty big meringue?"

I am sixteen; I've never tasted a Bloody Mary.
"Tell your father to bring a luxury," says she.
"Grapes have no imagination, they're just green.
20 Tell him: stop the neighbours coming."

I clear her cupboard in Ward 10B, Stobhill Hospital.
I leave, bags full, Lucozade, grapes, oranges,
sad chrysanthemums under my arms,
weighted down. I turn round, wave with her flowers.

25 My mother, on her high hospital bed, waves back.
Her face is light and radiant, dandelion hours.
Her sheets billow and whirl. She is beautiful.
Next to her the empty table is divine.

I carry the orange nostalgia home singing an old song.

Questions   MARKS

50. Look at stanzas 1 and 2 (lines 1—8).

Why does the poet's mother not want her to bring flowers or Lucozade?   **2**

51. Referring to lines 9—20, show how the poet gives the reader a clear impression of the mother's character or personality.   **4**

52. Explain how the poet uses language in lines 21—29 to indicate a clear change in the girl's feelings.   **6**

53. Identify at least one theme from this poem. Using close textual reference, show how the theme (or themes) is explored in this poem, and in at least one other poem by Jackie Kay.   **8**

[END OF SECTION 1]

[Turn over

SECTION 2 — CRITICAL ESSAY — 20 marks

Attempt ONE question from the following genres — Drama, Prose, Poetry, Film and Television Drama, or Language.

Your answer must be on a different genre from that chosen in Section 1.

You should spend approximately 45 minutes on this Section.

DRAMA

Answers to questions on Drama should refer to the text and to such relevant features as characterisation, key scene(s), structure, climax, theme, plot, conflict, setting . . .

1. Choose a play in which there is a character who is important in relation to the theme of the play.

   Referring to appropriate techniques, explain how this character affects our understanding of this theme.

2. Choose a play in which there is a key scene.

   Briefly describe what happens in this scene then, by referring to dramatic techniques, go on to explain why the scene is important to the play as a whole.

PROSE

Answers to questions on Prose should refer to the text and to such relevant features as characterisation, setting, language, key incident(s), climax, turning point, plot, structure, narrative technique, theme, ideas, description . . .

3. Choose a novel **or** short story **or** work of non-fiction which has a key incident.

   Give a brief account of the incident, and by referring to appropriate techniques, show how this incident is important to the text as a whole.

4. Choose a novel **or** short story in which there is a character involved in some form of conflict.

   By referring to appropriate techniques, show how the character comes to be involved in this conflict and how the conflict develops throughout the text.

POETRY

Answers to questions on Poetry should refer to the text and to such relevant features as word choice, tone, imagery, structure, content, rhythm, rhyme, theme, sound, ideas . . .

5. Choose a poem which you find particularly thought-provoking.

   By referring to poetic techniques, explain how the poet makes this poem so thought-provoking.

6. Choose a poem which deals with human experience.

   By referring to poetic techniques, show how the poet makes this experience come alive and helps you appreciate the poem as a whole.

FILM AND TELEVISION DRAMA

Answers to questions on Film and Television Drama should refer to the text and to such relevant features as use of camera, key sequence, characterisation, mise-en-scène, editing, setting, music/sound, special effects, plot, dialogue . . .

7. Choose the opening or closing scene or sequence from a film **or** television drama*.

   By referring to appropriate techniques, explain why you find it an effective opening or closing scene or sequence.

8. Choose a film or television drama* which has a character who either supports or threatens the main character.

   By referring to appropriate techniques, explain how this character plays an important role in the film/television drama as a whole.

* "television drama" includes a single play, a series or a serial.

[Turn over

LANGUAGE

Answers to questions on Language should refer to the text and to such relevant features as register, accent, dialect, slang, jargon, vocabulary, tone, abbreviation . . .

9. Choose two advertisements, and consider the language used.

   By referring to the language techniques used, explain how effective they are at persuading you.

10. Consider the differences in language between two groups of people – for example people who live in different areas, or who have different jobs.

   By referring to appropriate language techniques, explain the main differences in language use between the two groups.

[END OF SECTION 2]

[END OF QUESTION PAPER]

Acknowledgement of Copyright

Part A Text 1   Extract is taken from *"Bold Girls"* by Rona Munro, ISBN 9780340655276. Published by Hodder Education.

Part A Text 2   Extract is taken from *"Sailmaker Plus"* by Alan Spence, ISBN 9780340973035. Published by Hodder Education.

Part A Text 3   Extract is taken from *"Tally's Blood"* by Ann Marie di Mambro, ISBN 9781471808401. Published by Hodder Education.

Part B Text 1   Extract is taken from *"The Cone Gatherers"* by Robin Jenkins, ISBN 9781841959894. Published by Canongate Books Ltd.

Part B Text 2   Extract is taken from *"The Testament of Gideon Mack"* by James Robertson, ISBN 9780141049663. Published by Penguin Books Ltd.

Part B Text 3   Extract is taken from *"Kidnapped"* by Robert Louis Stevenson. Public Domain.

Part B Text 4   Extract is taken from *"Telegram"* by Iain Crichton Smith from The Red Door, The Complete English Stories 1949-1976, ISBN 1841581607. Published by Birlinn.

Part B Text 5   Extract is taken from *"Away in a Manger"* by Anne Donovan from Hieroglyphics and Other Stories, ISBN 9781841955193. Published by Canongate Books Ltd.

Part C Text 1   Poem, *"War Photographer"* by Carol Ann Duffy, is taken from New Selected Poems 1984-2004, ISBN 9780330433945. Published by Picador.

Part C Text 2   Poem, *"In the Snack-bar"* by Edwin Morgan, is taken from Edwin Morgan New Selected Poems, ISBN 1857544595. Published by Carcanet Press Ltd.

Part C Text 3   Poem, *"Basking Shark"* by Norman MacCaig, is taken from The Poems of Norman MacCaig (edited by Ewan McCaig), ISBN 9781846971365. Published by Polygon.

Part C Text 4   Poem, *"Lucozade"* by Jackie Kay, is taken from Darling: New & Selected Poems, ISBN 9781852247775. Published by Bloodaxe Books, 2007.

NATIONAL 5 | ANSWER SECTION

SQA AND HODDER GIBSON NATIONAL 5 ENGLISH 2014

READING FOR UNDERSTANDING, ANALYSIS AND EVALUATION

1. Candidates should show they understand the meaning of the phrase by referring to examples which illustrate the idea.

   Any three from:

   - she gives examples/mentions specific famous people whom we think we know well
   - she uses "assume" to continue the idea of "illusion"
   - she uses "familiar" to continue the idea of "intimacy"
   - she uses "know everything there is to know" to continue the idea of "intimacy"
   - we think we know all about what David Beckham wears
   - we feel we know personal details about Prince William
   - we know all about how and when JK Rowling wrote her books/we know as much about JK Rowling's method of writing as we do about her.

2. Candidates should demonstrate their understanding of the similarities between JK Rowling's life/experiences and Cinderella's life/experiences.

   Any four ideas from:

   - both "endured" cold living conditions
   - both were on their own/single
   - both were poor
   - both had their lives altered for the better
   - both found husbands.

3. Candidates should explain how the word choice shows the negative effects of fame.

   Any two from:

   - "begging letters" implies unpleasant/unwanted attention
   - journalists "rifling" through her bins suggests invasion of privacy/indiscriminate searching and/or unpleasant/unwanted attention
   - photographers "lurking" on the beach implies covert/hidden/suspicion/being observed from a distance and/or unpleasant/unwanted attention
   - "strangers" implies people she does not know giving her unwanted attention
   - "accosted" implies unwanted attention/a sense of danger
   - "in the supermarket" implies she cannot perform everyday tasks.

4. Candidates should identify the advantages and disadvantages of fame as expressed by JK Rowling.

   Each advantage or disadvantage supported by detailed comment can be awarded a maximum of two marks.

Advantages:
- a sense of validation: "I don't feel like quite such a waste of space anymore."
- Implied relationship with her fans.

Disadvantages:
- she feels guilty about her wealth
- fears life after Harry – she is worried about being taken seriously as an adult writer/that she will not be able to move on
- she feels she will only be known for writing about Harry Potter.

5. Candidates should identify a rhetorical question and discuss its effect.

   Any one question identified plus one explanation from:

   - "William, of course, has nothing to sell – or has he?" Plus effect of the question which is to question the marketability of Prince William's qualities
   - "Is he willing to surrender the chance of a relatively normal life to be the modern face of monarchy?" Plus effect of the question which is to emphasise the dilemma Prince William faces.

6. Candidates should demonstrate understanding of the ways in which JK Rowling feels she is "fortunate" by giving evidence from the text.

   Any four ideas from:

   - her fame is not based on who she is
   - her fame is not based on what she looks like
   - her fame is not based on her family connections
   - she is famous for her imagination/writing/characters
   - people discuss her work and not her
   - paraphrased version of "we know Harry, and his magic is likely to last."

7. Candidates should infer the writer's attitude to JK Rowling and support this with evidence from the text.

   One mark for identifying the attitude and one mark for relevant quotation.

   Writer's attitude – positive, admiring. Plus at least one piece of evidence from the following list:

   - "reassure"
   - "success"
   - "her own invention"
   - "millions"
   - "his magic is likely to last".

8. Candidates should choose one of the images and analyse its effect.

   For three marks, candidates should state the comparison and show how it is linked to the example used in the passage. This would be considered a full analysis.

   Freeze-frame = a still from a moving image/photograph

   Logo = brand name

   Crashing edifice = a falling structure.

For example:

Fame is compared to a photograph which cannot be changed. This shows how difficult it would be for JK Rowling to change her career path.

9. Candidates should summarise the nature of fame, according to the writer.

Any four points from:

Key points:

- we think we know famous people well

- we are surprised to hear famous people in reality

- advantages of fame (could be several)

- disadvantages of fame (could be several)

- reasons for fame, eg personality, skill, family.

NATIONAL 5 ENGLISH SPECIMEN QUESTION PAPER

CRITICAL READING

SECTION 1 – Scottish Text

SCOTTISH TEXT — DRAMA

Text 1 – Drama — *Tally's Blood* **by Ann Marie di Mambro**

1. Answers may focus on the contrast between Rosinella and Massimo or may focus entirely on Massimo:

   - Rosinella is seen to be "*head in hands*" and "*looks up wearily*" showing she is looking for kindness;

   - however Massimo is described to be acting "*coldly*" and/or with "*no sympathy at all*" which suggests that he is angry with her.

2. *Possible answers include:*

   - The dash after Hughie indicates that Rosinella has cut him off/isn't willing to listen to his point of view.

   - Massimo is asking lots of questions to try and get some explanation as to what Rosinella is thinking.

   - Rosinella is giving short answers which are blunt but reveal her pain is not allowing her to think properly.

   - The dash before "all of a sudden" shows Massimo is shocked/taken aback/pausing for thought/trying to understand.

   - Rosinella's repetition of "I don't care" shows she has lost all interest in Scotland and the shop.

   - The short sentences in "Shut it. Sell it." show a complete disregard for the shop/life in Scotland/Massimo's hard work.

3. Candidates should make four separate points about why Massimo is upset/angry for 1 mark each.

   Possible answers include:

   - Rosinella has never wanted to go to Italy before/always made excuses in the past

   - but now she wants to go to Italy because Lucia is there

   - she has been (constantly) open/vocal about things that have caused her pain

   - Massimo has always been sympathetic to her pain

   - but Rosinella has not really considered how other people have suffered also

   - he realises that she is selfish but wishes he didn't know that

   - he wishes that he had children of his own (particularly a son)

   - He regrets the way he may have treated his father.

4. Candidates should identify two separate points for 1 mark each. It is possible to gain 2 marks for a fully developed answer.

   Possible answers include:

   she is too possessive over Lucia

   she doesn't want Lucia to have anyone else

   she doesn't realise that other people love Lucia too

in doing things for Lucia she has been meeting her own needs not Lucia's

she still loves herself more than Lucia

she hasn't always done the right thing for Lucia.

5. Candidates should discuss the portrayal of the relationship between Massimo and Rosinella in this extract and elsewhere in the play.

Possible answers include:

Massimo and Rosinella arguing about how to discipline Lucia, eg when she refuses to take the dress off, when Lucia swears, when Lucia wants to go to the wedding with Hughie, etc. They both accuse each other of being too soft. Ultimately Rosinella is a bit tougher, but not much.

Rosinella and Massimo argue about his treatment during the war as he wants to forget it but she says she can't.

They are both distraught when Lucia has to go back to Italy and there are arguments about being ready to give her back, going to the airport, Rosinella's refusal to "cheer up", Rosinella's treatment of Hughie, etc.

When Rosinella goes to Italy she tells Lucia that she and Massimo are not getting on.

Playful arguments
They often pretend to be annoyed with each other, eg calls her a "daft wee besom" with affection, Rosinella cuffs Massimo,
"Good natured banter between Massimo and Rosinella"
There are also comments such as "The best thing that ever happened to you was the day you met me" (Massimo).

Lack of romance
Rosinella asking about the shop before Massimo's welfare.

Love
Physical affection, eg *"Massimo smiles with great affection, squeezes her cheek"*.

Rosinella's concern when Massimo is taken away, eg crying, prayers, candles, waiting outside the cells, etc.

When Rosinella and Massimo are reunited after the war.

The story of how they met and got married: love at first sight, forbidden love, romantic elopement, Rosinella fainted when she first saw Massimo, etc.

Their reunion at the end of the play when Massimo comes to Italy to get Rosinella and they pretend to re-enact the night they ran away together.

The final lines of the play are Massimo declaring his love for Rosinella followed by them embracing.

Candidates may choose to answer in **bullet points** in this final question, or write a number of linked statements. There is **no requirement** to write a "mini essay".

Up to 2 marks can be achieved for identifying elements of **commonality** as identified in the question.

A further 2 marks can be achieved for **reference to the extract given.**

4 additional marks can be awarded for similar references to at **least one other text/part of the text** by the writer.

In practice this means:

Identification of commonality (eg: theme, central relationship, importance of setting, use of imagery, development in characterisation, use of personal experience, use of narrative style, or any other key element...)

from the extract:

1 × relevant reference to technique

1 × appropriate comment

or

1 × relevant reference to idea

1 × appropriate comment

or

1 × relevant reference to feature

1 × appropriate comment

or

1 × relevant reference to text

1 × appropriate comment

(maximum of 2 marks only for discussion of extract)

from at **least one other text/part of the text:**

as above (× 2) for **up to 4 marks**

Text 2 — Drama — *Bold Girls* by Rona Munro

6. Candidates should make three separate points for 1 mark each.

   Quotation is likely but not necessary. Candidates can illustrate their understanding by referring to the content of the extract.

   Possible answers include:

   • Cassie hints to Marie that Martin has made a girl pregnant

   • Marie realises that Cassie and Nora have been arguing

   • Cassie is worried because Joe will be freed from prison in less than a year

   • Cassie tells Marie she is repulsed by Joe

   • Marie assures Cassie she will be there to support her in the future

   • there is a police raid on the social club

   • Deirdre says the whole town is a prison.

7. Candidates should demonstrate that Cassie is repulsed by the idea of Joe being anywhere near her. She is worried that she will not cope with him being back home.

   Candidates should quote one example of word choice and show how it shows her repulsion/concern.

   Examples of word choice showing her repulsion include:

   • "I can't stand the smell of him." suggests lack of tolerance/senses repulsed

   • "the greasy, grinning beer bellied smell of him" suggests lack of attraction/ugliness

   • some candidates may comment on the alliteration in this quote

   • "winking away" suggests lack of sincerity

   • "dreaming of" suggests lack of realism

   • "wriggling his fat fingers over me" suggests exploitative behaviour

   • "like I'm a poke of chips" suggests lack of permanence behind his feelings, some candidates may comment on the simile

   • "I don't want him in the house in my *bed*" suggests she does not want anything sexual.

   Examples of word choice showing she is worried:

   • "Oh I'm just bad. I am." suggests she has a darker side

   • "I'll go crazy." suggests she is worried about her mental/emotional health.

8. (a) Candidates should consider both stage directions and dialogue in their response.

   Both characters should be considered and at least one comment should be made about each character.

   Candidates should quote and explain to show the **different character traits**

   Example of stage direction about Cassie:

   "Slowly Cassie smiles at her" suggests she is more guarded in showing her feelings.

   Example of stage direction about Marie:

   "(Putting a hand on Cassie's arm)" suggests Marie is more reassuring.

Examples of dialogue given to Cassie:

   • "They can just look and think what they like." suggests Cassie is more self-confident

   • "I'm just bad Marie" suggests Cassie puts herself down more

   • "...she's bad now. Ask my mummy." suggests a more child-like quality

Examples of dialogue given to Marie:

   • "Cassie, what's wrong?" suggests Marie is more caring

   • "No. I never knew that." suggests Marie is less likely to gossip

   • "Have you had words?" suggests Marie is more likely to sense disharmony

   • "I know. It'll be all right Cassie." and "You'll cope." suggests Marie is more reassuring

   • "I won't let you..." (etc) suggests Marie is more protective.

   (b) Candidates should demonstrate an understanding of Deirdre's personality as being harsh and unattractive (at this point in the play).

   Whilst no further stage directions are given to her, the fact that Deirdre speaks only in a different light to the rest of the scene should be commented upon for full marks.

   Examples of stage directions about Deirdre:

   Up to 3 marks could be gained for answers which explore the fact that her whole dialogue in this extract takes place in the "hard light". This changes the mood of the scene to a more harsh/hostile mood and establishes Deirdre as a cold/hostile character. When she finishes speaking, the lights revert to "normal".

   Examples of dialogue given to Deirdre:

   Up to 3 marks could be gained for answers which explore the fact that there are several references to injury/causing injury/violence which suggest ruthlessness about Deirdre.

   Some possible references include:

   • "brick in your hand"/"hit skin and it'll burst open"/"hit bones and they'll break"/"hear them snap"/ "smell the petrol"/"you'll be breathing fire"/"throw fire in a bottle and it runs everywhere"
   Relevant comment on any of the above (up to 2)

   • "get a car, fast car"/"drive it till its wheels burn"/ leave it smoking, burning, exploding" suggest thrill seeking
   Relevant comment on any of the above (up to 2)

   • "The whole town's a prison"/"we're all in a prison" suggest she feels trapped/hopelessness/ despair

   • relevant comment on any of the above (up to 2).

9. Candidates must demonstrate understanding of at least two different dramatic techniques from this extract and in at least another part of the play. Answers should refer to specific techniques.

   Full answers will deal with two features as: characterisation, setting, monologue, lighting changes, cross-conversations, colloquialisms, symbolism...

Candidates may choose to answer in **bullet points** in this final question, or write a number of linked statements. There is no requirement to write a "mini essay".

Up to 2 marks can be achieved for identifying elements of **commonality** as identified in the question.

A further 2 marks can be achieved for **reference to the extract given**.

4 additional marks can be awarded for similar references to **at least one other text/part of the text** by the writer.

<u>In practice this means:</u>

Identification of **commonality** (eg: theme, central relationship, importance of setting, use of imagery, development in characterisation, use of personal experience, use of narrative style, or any other key element…)

from the extract:

1 × relevant reference to technique

1 × appropriate comment

or

1 × relevant reference to idea

1 × appropriate comment

or

1 × relevant reference to feature

1 × appropriate comment

or

1 × relevant reference to text

1 × appropriate comment

(maximum of 2 marks only for discussion of extract)

from at **least one other text/part of the text:**

as above (× 2) for **up to 4 marks**

Text 3 — Drama — *Sailmaker* by Alan Spence

10. Candidates should identify four points from this scene.

    Candidates should use their own words as far as possible.

    Possible answers include:

    - Alec is asked a difficult/challenging question about his faith
    - Alec cannot answer it as the answer is not in a book/ he hasn't learned it …
    - Alec runs away from the Mission rather than facing the challenge
    - Alec returns to the life he knows – symbolised by his kicking over the midden bin
    - Alec is no longer interested in religion.

11. Candidates should show how the word choice used illustrates Alec's discomfort.

    And

    Candidates should show how the sentence structure used illustrates Alec's discomfort.

Possible answers include:

Word choice

- "Feel the big black woman lookin at me" – suggests that he is the focus of attention/nowhere to hide/ eyes boring into him/intimidated by her …
- "Terrified" – reflects feeling of intense fear as he cannot answer the question
- "She looks right at me" – feels threatened/ intimidated
- "looked down at the floor" – tries to avoid eye-contact as he is embarrassed that he cannot answer
- "could feel myself blush" – suggests his embarrassment as he cannot answer
- "hot" – probably not that hot in the building – this reflects his feelings as he sweats in fear
- "feeling a wee bit sick" – reflects his fear
- "get some fresh air" – looking for a way of escaping/ avoiding the question

Sentence structure

- lots of questions reflect his insecurity/inability to answer/embarrassment
- list in lines 21–22 reflects the series of actions as he runs away
- ellipsis in line 22 reflects his lack of answer
- repetition – "I didn't know" (line 26) – emphasises his lack of response
- final sentence sums up his only decisive action.

12. (a) Candidates should identify an aspect of Alec's character which is exemplified by his use of English.

    Much of the extract features what Alec has learned (eg from the Catechism) and reflects his changing status.

    Candidates should then justify their choice.

    Possible answers include:

    Alec is growing up becoming more educated middle class distanced from his roots.

    (b) Candidates should identify an aspect of Alec's character which is exemplified by his use of the occasional Scots word.

    Candidates should then justify their choice.

    Possible answers include:

    To show/remind/illustrate (to the audience) that

    - occasionally Alec forgets his new-found education/ status
    - he is growing up – he is not completely educated yet
    - Alec still belongs in his working-class background
    - when challenged, Alec returns to what he knows best – his Scots background and roots.

13. Candidates should show how the theme of social class is developed in this extract and elsewhere in the play.

    Candidates may choose to answer in **bullet points** in this final question, or write a number of linked statements.

    There is **no requirement** to write a "mini essay".

    Up to 2 marks can be achieved for identifying elements of **commonality** as identified in the question.

A further 2 marks can be achieved for **reference to the extract given**.

4 additional marks can be awarded for similar references to **at least one other text/part of the text** by the writer.

<u>In practice this means:</u>

Identification of commonality (eg: theme, central relationship, importance of setting, use of imagery, development in characterisation, use of personal experience, use of narrative style, or any other key element…)

from the extract:

1 × relevant reference to technique

1 × appropriate comment

or

1 × relevant reference to idea

1 × appropriate comment

or

1 × relevant reference to feature

1 × appropriate comment

or

1 × relevant reference to text

1 × appropriate comment

(maximum of 2 marks only for discussion of extract)

from at **least one other text/part of the text:**

as above (× 2) for **up to 4 marks**

SCOTTISH TEXT – PROSE

Text 1 – Prose – *The Telegram* by Iain Crichton Smith

14. Suggested answers may include any two of the following plus explanation of the effect:

- **Contrast:** the village "appeared quiet" but "much had gone on" – emphasises the turmoil that the war has brought
- **Tone:** irony of "their ships had sunk in seas which they had never seen" – emphasises that they are involved in a war which they understand little about
- **Repetition** of "drowned" – emphasises the tragic loss of lives
- **Sentence inversion:** "What the war…did not know" – emphasis on the war at the start of the sentence to highlight its impact
- **Metaphor:** "strange plague" – emphasises destructive nature; kills large numbers indiscriminately
- **Word choice:** "meaninglessly" – emphasises the pointless loss of life; "randomly" – everybody is at risk

15. *Suggested answers:*

- "Strange missile" – the telegram is like a deadly weapon/they are unfamiliar with/brings devastation to a family
- "a weapon"/"desolation" – emphasises the destructive force of the telegram/brings news of death and destroys the family

16. Answers must highlight the differences between the women. Candidates must use their own words as indicated.

Suggested answers:

Thin woman

- "ambitious" for her son/wants him to have opportunities/sent him to university/was an officer in the navy
- she is poor – "only had a widow's pension…"
- seen as an outsider – "an incomer"
- not well liked in the village –"not popular"

Fat woman

- doesn't have the same ambitions for her son "left school at fourteen"/"ordinary seaman"/"had to salute the thin woman's son"
- had a sense of belonging in the village – "had lived in the village all her days"/"was a native".

17. *Suggested answers:*

- "watched"/"watching": suggests they are unable to take their eyes off it
- "feverishly": suggests state of panic/terror
- "plague" – sees it as something dreadful/deadly like a disease which will wipe out many people.

18. Candidates should discuss how Iain Crichton Smith builds tension in this story and in at least one other story.

Candidates may choose to answer in **bullet points** in this final question, or write a number of linked statements. There is **no requirement** to write a "mini essay".

Up to 2 marks can be achieved for identifying elements of **commonality** as identified in the question.

A further 2 marks can be achieved for r**eference to the extract given**.

4 additional marks can be awarded for similar references to **at least one other text/part of the text** by the writer.

<u>In practice this means:</u>

Identification of commonality (eg: theme, central relationship, importance of setting, use of imagery, development in characterisation, use of personal experience, use of narrative style, or any other key element…)

from the extract:

1 × relevant reference to technique

1 × appropriate comment

or

1 × relevant reference to idea

1 × appropriate comment

or

1 × relevant reference to feature

1 × appropriate comment

or

1 × relevant reference to text

1 × appropriate comment

(maximum of 2 marks only for discussion of extract)

from at **least one other text/part of the text:**

as above (× 2) for **up to 4 marks**

Text 2 — Prose — *A Chitterin' Bite* by Anne Donovan

19. *Possible answers include:*

Agnes
"Ah said we'd meet…" shows Agnes' assertiveness/bossy nature (etc)

Mary
"What?…/ah'll gie it a try."
Shows Mary's hesitation/uncertainty (etc)

20. • omission of sentence openings hurries the action
- use of commas creates faster pace
- use of a series of verbs suggests rushed activity
- use of verbs (such as "swimming"/"scrambling"… etc) suggests hurried activity
- not using complete sentences suggests hurry.

21. *Any two examples for 1 mark each:*
- single line sentence
- single line paragraph
- tone suggested by use of question mark
- brevity of her retort "what?"
- unlinks her arm from Agnes
- use of verbs with emotional charge "marched" suggesting anger/huff/desire to leave Agnes and "starin" suggesting her separation from Agnes
- tone of irritation/annoyance/ associated with, "Well, you don't need me tae come too" or idea of her being in a huff.

22. **Jimmy**
- "broad nose" unattractive
- further attention to unattractive qualities of the nose, "a bit bent tae the side"
- reference to the hair is unappealing "straight dirty-fair"/"side shed"

Shuggie
- "the pal" suggesting that Mary does not want to know him any better
- "stauning hauf behind him" as he too is nervous but this is viewed as unattractive by Mary
- He is small "wee" and slight "skinny" both of which suggest she is not attracted to him or even repelled by him.
- "laddie" suggesting he is too young
- "baby cheeks" which are ill-defined and puffed out like an infant's
- Simile, "red lips like a lassie" making him seem effeminate and unattractive.

23. Candidates should discuss an aspect of the narrative style in this story and in at least one other story by Donovan.

Candidates may choose to answer in **bullet points** in this final question, or write a number of linked statements. There is **no requirement** to write a "mini essay".

Up to 2 marks can be achieved for identifying elements of **commonality** as identified in the question.

A further 2 marks can be achieved for **reference to the extract given**.

4 additional marks can be awarded for similar references to **at least one other text/part of the text** by the writer.

In practice this means:

Identification of commonality (eg: theme, central relationship, importance of setting, use of imagery, development in characterisation, use of personal experience, use of narrative style, or any other key element…)

from the extract:

1 × relevant reference to technique

1 × appropriate comment

or

1 × relevant reference to idea

1 × appropriate comment

or

1 × relevant reference to feature

1 × appropriate comment

or

1 × relevant reference to text

1 × appropriate comment

(maximum of 2 marks only for discussion of extract)

from at **least one other text/part of the text:**

as above (x 2) for **up to 4 marks**

Text 3 — Prose — *The Cone-Gatherers* by Robin Jenkins

24. Identification of feature/expression (1 mark), explanation (1 mark)
- Use of semi colon - what follows this punctuation is a detailed account of what she felt during that run.
- Complex/lengthy sentence; suggesting the interminable run to the place.

- "Furthest limits of her being" – she is at the very end of her ability to face what she thinks she will find.
- "ten minutes"/reference to time emphasises how far away it was
- "without which she could never return" suggesting the high stakes of her mission.

25. 1 mark for each point:
- concerned that Manson, who has gone ahead to help Calum, should receive due reward
- as Manson's boss, he expects that he will also receive some kind of reward.

26. *Possible answers include:*
- "(Potently) beautiful" – she recognises power/attractiveness of landscape
- "Vast" – idea of scale/scope
- "Bright" – suggestion of positive connotations
- "Detailed as a dream" - suggesting a heightened perception
- "Dream" – suggesting unreality
- "Wonderful interpretation", if it could only be known – a sense that there is hidden meaning in what is happening
- reference to the "warship" – intrusion of something sinister into something beautiful
- "Pines" - the pine trees representing something in the landscape with which she identifies/which moves her.

27. *1 mark for each point:*
- Tearing her clothes on the whins
- Splintering the bracken

28. Duror has been destroyed/feels anguished/has no satisfaction by what he has done.

In spite of the fact he has hated him/wanted him dead.

29. Candidates should discuss how the theme of death is explored in this extract and elsewhere in the novel.

Candidates may choose to answer in **bullet points** in this final question, or write a number of linked statements. There is **no requirement** to write a "mini essay".

Up to 2 marks can be achieved for identifying elements of **commonality** as identified in the question.

A further 2 marks can be achieved for **reference to the extract given**.

4 additional marks can be awarded for similar references to **at least one other text/part of the text** by the writer.

In practice this means:

Identification of **commonality** (eg: theme, central relationship, importance of setting, use of imagery, development in characterisation, use of personal experience, use of narrative style, or any other key element…)

from the extract:

1 × relevant reference to technique

1 × appropriate comment

or

1 × relevant reference to idea

1 × appropriate comment

or

1 × relevant reference to feature

1 × appropriate comment

or

1 × relevant reference to text

1 × appropriate comment

(maximum of 2 marks only for discussion of extract)

from at **least one other text/part of the text**:

as above (× 2) for **up to 4 marks**

Text 4 – Prose – *The Testament of Gideon Mack* by James Robertson

30. Straightforward summary of the passage, award 1 mark for each key point made.

31. *Possible answers include:*

Cave:
- "gloomy" suggesting dark, unpleasant, etc
- "black as tar" to describe the water again has negative connotations of the colour black and the idea of tar is distasteful; "twa great slaverin' hounds" suggests aggression, fear.

Gentleman:
- "black-avised" (given in glossary as "dark-featured") suggests menace through the connotations of black.

32. *Possible answers include:*
- Feisty/brave – it is said she had guessed who the stranger was but didn't care/she physically fought with him
- Selfish – married for money/ bargains her maid's life so she can go free
- Crafty – sees a way to be with her real love (without her husband knowing)
- Reckless – knowingly bargains with the devil

33. Candidates should discuss the use of narrative style in this extract and elsewhere in the novel.

Candidates may choose to answer in **bullet points** in this final question, or write a number of linked statements. There is **no requirement** to write a "mini essay".

Up to 2 marks can be achieved for identifying elements of **commonality** as identified in the question.

A further 2 marks can be achieved for **reference to the extract given**.

4 additional marks can be awarded for similar references to **at least one other text/part of the text** by the writer.

In practice this means:

Identification of **commonality** (eg: theme, central relationship, importance of setting, use of imagery, development in characterisation, use of personal experience, use of narrative style, or any other key element…)

from the extract:

1 × relevant reference to technique

1 × appropriate comment

or

1 × relevant reference to idea

1 × appropriate comment

or

1 × relevant reference to feature

1 × appropriate comment

or

1 × relevant reference to text

1 × appropriate comment

(maximum of 2 marks only for discussion of extract)

from at **least one other text/part of the text**:

as above (× 2) for **up to 4 marks**

Text 5 — Prose — *Kidnapped* by Robert Louis Stevenson

34. Candidates should comment on the two sides to his character which David discerns through his initial impressions.

    1 mark to be awarded for amusing/informative; 1 mark awarded for ruined/inebriated/looked down upon/ pitiful, etc.

    Possible answers include:

    Gloss of:

    - "entertained" - amused
    - "very words of speakers" – amused and/or informed
    - "show us where they stood" – amused and/or informed
    - "drunk"/"wreck" - ruined/inebriated/looked down upon/pitiful

35. Marks awarded for:
    - David's response
    - example of writer's use of language
    - comment on language used

    Possible answers include:

    Response: disapproval, condemnation, etc

    Word choice:
    - "eschew" – avoidance
    - "like disgrace" – scandalous.

    Sentence structure:
    "neither ...Christian ... nor gentleman" – neither/nor structure – implies that those who play cards are neither Christian nor gentleman thus negative implications.

    Extended metaphor:
    "testimony"/"judge" – implications of wrongdoing and application of justice.

36. (a) Cluny's tone (1 mark);
    Appropriate reference to sentence structure (1 mark);
    Comment on reference (1 mark)

    Possible answers include:

    Cluny's **tone**: anger, annoyance, frustration, shock, etc

Sentence structure:

- Repeated questions – emphasising his shock at David's comments
- Short opening sentence of line 19 "Cluny stopped mingling the cards." – dramatic impact of the sudden arrest of the action indicating his shock.

(b) Name technique (1 mark);
    Explanation of what is meant by technique (1 mark)
    The phrase emphasises the lengths to which Alan will go to defend David.

    Possible answers include:

    Hyperbole
    Alan emphasises the extremes he would go to in defence of David.

    or

    Metaphor
    Emphasising that he is willing to go through pain and danger in support of David.

37. Two reasons required for 1 mark each.

    Gloss of:
    - "I am very wearied" – he is tired;
    - "it was a promise to his father" – an important compact/assurance made not to play cards.

38. Candidates should discuss the complex relationship between David and Alan, with reference to this extract and elsewhere in the novel.

    Candidates can comment on the "complexity" of their relationship in several ways. The following would be the expected routes to answering this question but they are not the only ones:

    - Complexity can be seen through their opposition to each other in terms of their attitudes and politics;
    - Complexity can be seen in their relationship being one built upon deep friendship but also built upon disagreement

    Candidates may choose to answer in **bullet points** in this final question, or write a number of linked statements. There is **no requirement** to write a "mini essay".

    Up to 2 marks can be achieved for identifying elements of **commonality** as identified in the question.

    A further 2 marks can be achieved for **reference to the extract given**.

    4 additional marks can be awarded for similar references to **at least one other text/part of the text** by the writer.

    <u>In practice this means:</u>

    Identification of commonality (eg: theme, central relationship, importance of setting, use of imagery, development in characterisation, use of personal experience, use of narrative style, or any other key element...)

    from the extract:

    1 × relevant reference to technique

    1 × appropriate comment

    or

    1 × relevant reference to idea

    1 × appropriate comment

    or

1 × relevant reference to feature

1 × appropriate comment

or

1 × relevant reference to text

1 × appropriate comment

(maximum of 2 marks only for discussion of extract)

from at **least one other text/part of the text**:

as above (x 2) for **up to 4 marks**

SCOTTISH TEXT — POETRY

Text 1 — Poetry — *Havisham* by Carol Ann Duffy

39. (a) 2 marks can be awarded for two main ideas or concerns shown in stanza one.

Only 1 mark should be awarded for one main idea or concern.

- the contradictory nature of love/possibility of loving and hating one person at the same time
- the psychological damage caused by hate
- the pain of rejection
- the power/enduring nature of hate
- the violence/aggression/desire for revenge which accompanies obsessive love.

(b) 2 marks can be awarded for example of language helping to clarify or illustrate meaning.

Other examples from stanza one are acceptable.

- the contradiction of "beloved"/"sweetheart" and "bastard" suggests inner conflict.
- the positioning of "Not" at the start of the sentence suggests strong, negative feelings.
- the word choice of "dark" suggests evil/mystery.
- the word choice of "green" suggests jealousy.
- the imagery of "pebbles for eyes" suggests a hardening of the emotions/a coldness of spirit.
- the comparison of tendons to "ropes" suggests threat/constraint.
- the word choice of "strangle" suggests a destructive/threatening action.

40. 2 marks can be awarded for example of language helping to clarify or illustrate meaning.

Other examples from stanza one are acceptable.

- the positioning/isolating of "Spinster" suggests self-disgust at her unmarried status.
- the word choice of "stink" suggests decay/loss of personal hygiene.
- the word choice of "whole" suggests excessive period spent in bed.
- the word choice of "yellowing" suggests fading/decaying over time of the dress.
- the word choice of "trembling" suggests the fear of her reflection showing what she has become.
- the reductive or onomatopoeic use of "caw" suggests less than human behaviour.
- the distortion/onomatopoeia of "Nooooo" suggests her grief has made her incoherent.

- the juxtaposition of "her, myself" suggests confusion of identity.
- the use of enjambment between stanzas two and three/the positioning of "to me?" re-focuses attention on the cause of her distress.
- the word choice of "curses" suggests the depth of hatred for her ex-lover.
- the qualification of the curses as "sounds not words" suggest her hate/anger has made her incoherent.

41. 2 marks can be awarded for example of language helping to clarify or illustrate meaning.

Other examples from stanza one are acceptable.

- The word choice of "better" suggests an improvement brought about by her dreams.
- The word choice of "lost body over me" suggests the return of physical intimacy in her dreams.
- The word choice of "fluent" suggests the ability to give expression to her desires in her dreams (compared to her incoherence when awake).
- The ambiguity of "fluent tongue" suggests the sexual content of her dreams.
- Various examples of word choice in "body over me … down" are open to a variety of sexual interpretations indicating the content of her dreams.

42. Candidates should show understanding of the term "conclusion" and show how the content of the last lines continues the ideas and/or language from the rest of the poem.

Example plus comment – any two will gain 4 marks.

Only one use of language will gain a maximum of 2 marks.

Other examples from the last lines are acceptable.

- The word choice of "suddenly bite awake" suggests the suddenness/pain of her return to consciousness.
- The enjambment/juxtaposition of "Love's/hate" suggests a return of the conflicting emotions experienced when conscious.
- The juxtaposition of "Love's hate … white veil" suggests her feelings of hatred hiding behind appearance of love.
- The image of "red balloon bursting" suggests sudden destruction of her dreams.
- The onomatopoeia/isolation of "Bang" suggests the sudden/frightening return to reality.
- The word choice of "stabbed" portrays her violent reaction/antipathy to anything suggestive of marriage.
- The word choice of "male corpse" suggests a conclusion to the violence directed at her ex-lover/a desire to constrain and control.
- The assonance of "long slow honeymoon" suggests a savouring of the sexual aspect of marriage.
- The juxtaposition of "corpse" and "honeymoon" suggests the need to sexually control her errant lover.

- The idea contained in "Don't think .... b-b-b-breaks" highlights the psychological damage caused by her rejection/her inability to resolve her inner conflict/ her incoherence.
- The typography of "b-b-b-breaks" suggests the unremitting nature of her grief.

43. Candidates should show awareness of the ideas and/or language of this poem and at least one other by Duffy.

Candidates may choose to answer in **bullet points** in this final question, or write a number of linked statements. There is **no requirement** to write a "mini essay".

Up to 2 marks can be achieved for identifying elements of **commonality** as identified in the question.

A further 2 marks can be achieved for **reference to the extract given**.

4 additional marks can be awarded for similar references to **at least one other text/part of the text** by the writer.

In practice this means:

Identification of commonality (eg: theme, central relationship, importance of setting, use of imagery, development in characterisation, use of personal experience, use of narrative style, or any other key element...)

from the extract:

1 × relevant reference to technique

1 × appropriate comment

or

1 × relevant reference to idea

1 × appropriate comment

or

1 × relevant reference to feature

1 × appropriate comment

or

1 × relevant reference to text

1 × appropriate comment

(maximum of 2 marks only for discussion of extract)

from **at least one other text/part of the text:**

as above (x 2) for **up to 4 marks**

Text 2 — Poetry — *Bed* **by Jackie Kay**

44. Any four main ideas explored in the poem for 1 mark each.

Quotation is not necessary but is likely.

Four separate points should be made for the 4 marks.

Possible answers include:

- the speaker is treated well by her daughter
- the speaker feels she is a burden
- the speaker is bed bound
- the speaker is reliant on her daughter to carry out even the most basic of tasks
- there has been some role reversal between the daughter and the mother in terms of who does the caring
- their relationship has suffered

- the speaker describes her loss of looks
- the speaker has lived in the same community for generations
- her house is not as well maintained as it used to be
- the speaker cannot eat solids
- the speaker can suffer from mood swings/can be grumpy
- the speaker feels trapped in her bedroom
- the speaker wonders how her daughter will feel when she dies.

45. Candidates should select evidence which shows/ describes the speaker's helplessness/reliance on others.

Candidates must identify and comment upon one feature of **word choice** AND one feature of **sentence structure** for full marks.

Relevant quotation in relation to word choice (1 mark).

Appropriate comment (1 mark).

Relevant quotation in relation to sentence structure (1 mark).

Appropriate comment (1 mark).

NB: answers should be from lines 1–20 only.

Possible answers in relation to word choice include:

- "Am a burden" suggests she has to be carried/ supported
- "Stuck here" suggests lack of freedom/movement
- "big blastit bed" (alliteration of plosive sound) suggests her frustration at being bed bound
- "year in, year oot," repetition suggests she cannot improve
- "she has tae dae fir me" suggests reliance on daughter
- "Am her wean noo" suggests regressive nature of independence
- "some skinny chicken" suggests physical deterioration
- "Aw A' dae is" suggests restrictive nature of activities
- "sit an look oot this windae" suggests lack of variety of past times

Possible answers in relation to sentence structure include:

- Use of enjamb(e)ment in the first few stanzas suggests the speaker's outpouring of guilt at her situation. (eg at the end of line 1: "she is/an Am a burden...").
- Repeated balanced nature of sentences in opening three stanzas suggest the consequences of the speaker's helplessness.

  (eg at the start of stanza two: "There's things she has tae dae fir me/A wish she didnae huv tae dae." Suggests regret at helplessness).
- Parenthesis in lines 15—16

"(an yet as a young wuman A' took pride in ma guid smooth skin" sums up how attractive/proud the speaker was when she was younger).

- Use of short sentences (mono syllabic in places) sum up her helpless situation. Eg, line 17:

"Aw A' dae is sit an look oot this windae.".

- Use of dash at the end of line 18 introduces example of inability to maintain the window.

46. (a) Candidates should refer to lines 16—40 in their answers to this question.

    2 marks could be awarded for selection of one quotation followed by a detailed comment or two quotations with more straightforward comments.

    Possible answers include:

    - "A've seen hale generations graw up" suggests the neighbours stay constant

    - "an simmer doon" suggests the neighbours can be rowdy/boisterous

    - "the Kerrs have disappeared" suggests a long-standing family has left the area

    - "Campbells ur still here" suggests they remain a constant presence

    - "A've no seen ony Campbell in a long time" suggests lack of movement/transparency/daughter is lying about constancy of neighbours to reassure speaker.

    (b) Candidates should show an understanding of the idea that the speaker feels "trapped" in her surroundings/hopeless about her life.

    2 marks could be awarded for selection of one quotation followed by a detailed comment or two quotations with more straightforward comments.

    Possible answers include:

    - "A' dinny believe her" suggests some conflict between the speaker and her daughter

    - "Aye fine" suggests reluctant acceptance of the food she is given

    - "great heaving sigh" suggests boredom

    - "crabbit tut" suggests annoyance

    - "ma froon" suggests unhappiness

    - "Am jist biding time" suggests she is waiting on the inevitable

    - "drab wee prison" suggests feelings of entrapment

    - "how wull she feel?" suggests reflection about her daughter's feelings.

47. Candidates should show understanding of the central relationship in this poem and at least one other by Jackie Kay. The mother has become reliant on her daughter. There has been some role reversal. The mother feels guilty at having to rely on her daughter. The daughter may resent the monotony of caring for her mother but does it out of loyalty.

    Candidates are expected to refer to the central relationship in at least one other poem by Jackie Kay. They should provide quotations and/or close references to the text in support of their answer.

    They should refer specifically to poetic devices used in the texts and the impact of these devices (in helping the reader to understand the nature of the central relationship) should be evaluated.

    Candidates may choose to answer in **bullet points** in this final question, or write a number of linked statements. There is **no requirement** to write a "mini essay".

    Up to 2 marks can be achieved for identifying elements of **commonality** as identified in the question.

    A further 2 marks can be achieved for reference to the extract given.

4 additional marks can be awarded for similar references to **at least one other text/part of the text** by the writer.

<u>In practice this means:</u>

Identification of commonality (eg: theme, central relationship, importance of setting, use of imagery, development in characterisation, use of personal experience, use of narrative style, or any other key element…)

from the extract:

1 × relevant reference to technique

1 × appropriate comment

or

1 × relevant reference to idea

1 × appropriate comment

or

1 × relevant reference to feature

1 × appropriate comment

or

1 × relevant reference to text

1 × appropriate comment

(maximum of 2 marks only for discussion of extract)

from at **least one other text/part of the text:**

as above (× 2) for **up to 4 marks**

Text 3 — Poetry — *Aunt Julia* by Norman MacCaig

48. *Possible answers include:*

    - Repetition of "very" establishes strong/extrovert/eccentric personality.

    - Repetition of "I could not" establishes extent to which MacCaig did not know her/could not get to know her/lack of closeness between them.

    - Direct statement of fact about Aunt Julia establishes at outset she is central to poem/her strong personality.

    - Aunt Julia placed as first phrase establishes her as central concern.

49. *Possible answers include:*

    - "She wore men's boots" – strong, doing "male" tasks, worked outdoors, hardworking

    - "when she wore any" – used to working outdoors, "at one" with nature/earth

    - "her strong foot stained with peat" – working outdoors, over many years

    - "while her right hand drew yarn marvellously out of the air" -idea of magical, delicate, skilful, gentle work.

50. *Possible answers include:*

    "She was buckets and water flouncing into them" suggests her tasks were part of her/her life, energetic, at one with nature, tough/hardworking/energetic

    or

    "She was winds pouring wetly round house-ends" – suggests her tasks were part of her/her life, at one with nature/climate, tough/hardworking/energetic

    or

"She was brown eggs, black skirts and a keeper of threepenny bits in a teapot" suggests her tasks were part of her/her life, "dull"/earthy colours, thrifty/self-sufficient, focus on setting/the home

51. *Possible answers include:*

- "By the time I had learned a little"/now that he is older/more mature/later in life he reflects that he cannot now communicate with her/that he has missed opportunity

- "silenced"/"absolute black"/finality of death means he cannot now develop his relationship with her/that he has missed opportunity

- "But I hear her still"/he imagines her in the present/her voice haunts him suggests he is nostalgic about the past/is still influenced by her

- "with so many questions unanswered" suggests a sense of futility/lack of resolution.

52. Candidates should show understanding of how MacCaig uses observation of people or places in this poem and at least one other.

Candidates may choose to answer in **bullet points** in this final question, or write a number of linked statements. There is **no requirement** to write a "mini essay".

Up to 2 marks can be achieved for identifying elements of **commonality** as identified in the question.

A further 2 marks can be achieved for **reference to the extract given**.

4 additional marks can be awarded for similar references to **at least one other text/part of the text** by the writer.

<u>In practice this means:</u>

Identification of commonality (eg: theme, central relationship, importance of setting, use of imagery, development in characterisation, use of personal experience, use of narrative style, or any other key element…)

from the extract:

1 × relevant reference to technique

1 × appropriate comment

or

1 × relevant reference to idea

1 × appropriate comment

or

1 × relevant reference to feature

1 × appropriate comment

or

1 × relevant reference to text

1 × appropriate comment

(maximum of 2 marks only for discussion of extract)

from at **least one other text/part of the text:**

as above (× 2) for **up to 4 marks**

Text 4 — Poetry — *Trio* **by Edwin Morgan**

53. *Possible answers include:*

- he uses present tense to give a sense of immediacy

- he uses "quickly" to indicate speed

- he uses "sharp" to indicate coldness, icy weather

- he mentions Christmas lights to give a festive feel

- use of short phrases/punctuation indicates business, speed of movement, urgency

54. For 6 marks, candidates should refer to three examples of how language is used to create a positive atmosphere.

Possible answers:

- "three of them are laughing" – the three are all happy/united in their laughter"

- "their breath rises in a cloud of happiness" – suggests again they are united as one and enveloped by their happiness

- "Wait till he sees this but!" – direct speech/colloquial language expresses the boy's happy anticipation of the pleasure his gift will bring.

or

- Reference to aspect of the positive description of the gifts, eg "tiny Royal Stewart tartan coat like a teapot-holder" – description of dog's coat reveals it is made of a very brightly coloured tartan.

or

- Simile compares the dog's coat to a teapot holder. Both are small, soft objects designed to keep something cosy suggesting the dog is loved.

- "baby in its white shawl all bright eyes and mouth like favours in a fresh sweet cake" – description of baby's shawl reveals it is protected against the cold/white, suggests the innocence of the baby.

or

- Simile compares baby's eyes and mouth to the decorations on a wedding cake. Both are small, pretty things. Wedding is a celebration of love, suggesting how much love there is for the baby.

- "guitar swells out under its milky plastic cover tied at the neck with silver tinsel tape and a brisk sprig of mistletoe" – description of cover suggests guitar is also protected from the elements

or

- word choice of "swells"/"milky" suggest pregnancy/birth and suggest the guitar is full of life

or

- "silver tinsel tape" makes it obvious guitar has been decorated as it is a gift

or

- "sprig of mistletoe" suggests it is being given with love.

55. (a) Candidates should identify two central concerns for 1 mark each

    Possible answers:

    - friendship/love defeat problems
    - camaraderie brings strength to cope with life's problems
    - that formal religion isn't as important as people loving and caring for one another
    - the importance of music as a means to express emotion.

    (b) Candidates should select any aspect of lines 15—27 and offer an evaluative comment on how it enforces one of the central concerns identified in 4(a).

    Candidates may refer to ideas and/or language.

    Candidates need not name specific literary techniques that they quote.

    Possible answers:

    - "The vale of tears is powerless before you" – effective use of the Biblical metaphor for the world's problems to emphasise the strength of the trio.
    - "Monsters of the year go blank" – effective to present life and its problems as monsters that are also beaten by the trio. Their friendship defeats all such problems.
    - Parenthesis/brackets in lines 24—26 – allow the poet to reflect on the trio's deeper significance emphasising their strength.
    - "Whether Christ is born, or is not born" – it doesn't matter if Christ really lived or not, effectively enforces idea of love being more important that religion.
    - "Abdicates" – effective word choice to indicate formal religion surrenders when faced with the power of their friendship.
    - "Laughter ringing round them like a guard" – effective simile to highlight that the laughter they share protects them like a guard would from all life can throw at them.
    - "Orphean sprig!" – reference to Orpheus who is a famous musician in Greek legend, and to the mistletoe, emphasises the importance of music as a way of expressing emotion.
    - List of the three objects the members of the trio are carrying/"Orphean sprig! Melting baby! Warm Chihuahua!"

    or

    - Conjunction "and" used to link "men and beasts, and music" highlights how the poet sees music as being just as important as the other two.

56. Candidates should show awareness of relevant ideas and/or language features in this poem and at least one other Morgan poem.

    Candidates may choose to answer in **bullet points** in this final question, or write a number of linked statements. There is **no requirement** to write a "mini essay".

    Up to 2 marks can be achieved for identifying elements of **commonality** as identified in the question.

    A further 2 marks can be achieved for **reference to the extract given**.

4 additional marks can be awarded for similar references to at **least one other text/part of the text** by the writer.

In practice this means:

Identification of commonality (eg: theme, central relationship, importance of setting, use of imagery, development in characterisation, use of personal experience, use of narrative style, or any other key element…)

from the extract:

1 × relevant reference to technique

1 × appropriate comment

or

1 × relevant reference to idea

1 × appropriate comment

or

1 × relevant reference to feature

1 × appropriate comment

or

1 × relevant reference to text

1 × appropriate comment

(maximum of 2 marks only for discussion of extract)

from **at least one other text/part of the text:**

as above (× 2) for **up to 4 marks**

SECTION 2 — Critical Essay

Bands are not grades. The five bands are designed primarily to assist with placing each candidate response at an appropriate point on a continuum of achievement. Assumptions about final grades or association of final grades with particular bands should not be allowed to influence objective assessment.

	20–18	17–14	13–10	9–5	4–0
The candidate demonstrates:	• **a high degree of familiarity** with the text as a whole • **very good understanding** of the central concerns of the text • a line of thought that is **consistently** relevant to the task	• **familiarity** with the text as a whole • **good understanding** of the central concerns of the text • a line of thought that is **relevant** to the task	• **some familiarity** with the text as a whole • **some understanding** of the central concerns of the text • a line of thought that is **mostly relevant** to the task	• **familiarity with some aspects** of the text • **attempts** a line of thought **but this may lack relevance to the task**	Although such essays should be rare, in this category, the candidate's essay will demonstrate one or more of the following • it contains numerous errors in spelling/grammar/ punctuation/ sentence construction/ paragraphing • knowledge and understanding of the text(s) are not used to answer the question • any analysis and evaluation attempted are unconvincing • the answer is simply too thin
Analysis of the text demonstrates:	• **thorough awareness** of the writer's techniques, through analysis, making **confident** use of critical terminology • **very detailed/thoughtful** explanation of stylistic devices supported by a **range of well-chosen** references and/or quotations	• **sound awareness** of the writer's techniques through analysis, making **good** use of critical terminology • **detailed explanation** of stylistic devices supported by **appropriate** references and/ or quotation	• **an awareness** of the writer's techniques through analysis, making **some** use of critical terminology • explanation of stylistic devices supported by **some appropriate** references and/ or quotation	• **some awareness** of **the more obvious** techniques used by the writer • **description of some** stylistic devices followed by limited reference and/or quotation	
Evaluation of the text is shown through:	• **a well developed** commentary of what has been enjoyed/ gained from the text(s), supported by a **range** of well-chosen references to its relevant features	• **a reasonably developed** commentary of what has been enjoyed/ gained from the text (s), supported by **appropriate** references to its relevant features	• **some** commentary of what has been enjoyed/gained from the **text(s)**, supported by **some appropriate** references to its relevant features	• **brief** commentary of what has been enjoyed/gained from the **text(s), followed by brief** reference to its features	
The candidate:	• uses language to communicate a line of thought **very clearly** • uses **spelling, grammar, sentence construction and punctuation which are consistently** accurate • structures the essay **effectively to enhance** meaning/ purpose • uses paragraphing which is **accurate and effective**	• uses language to communicate a line of thought **clearly** • uses spelling, grammar, sentence construction and punctuation which are **mainly** accurate • structures the essay **well** • uses paragraphing which is **accurate**	• uses language to communicate a line of thought **at first reading** • uses spelling, grammar, sentence construction and punctuation which are **sufficiently** accurate • attempts to structure the essay **in an appropriate way** • uses paragraphing which is sufficiently accurate	• uses language to communicate a line of thought which may be disorganised and/or difficult to follow • makes significant errors in spelling/grammar/ sentence construction/ punctuation • has not structured the essay well • has made significant errors in paragraphing	
In summary, the candidates essay is:	thorough and precise	very detailed and shows some insight	fairly detailed and relevant	lacks detail and relevance	superficial and/or technically weak

NATIONAL 5 ENGLISH MODEL PAPER 1

READING FOR UNDERSTANDING, ANALYSIS AND EVALUATION

1. *Any four of the following for 1 mark each:*
   - tennis players are very superstitious
   - they believe that certain behaviour can affect results
   - research was carried out on pigeons
   - it was discovered that they could be made to believe that certain actions …
   - … caused certain outcomes …
   - … even though there was no connection.

2. (a) *Any two of the following for 1 mark each:*
   - he believes in the power of superstition
   - he is irrational
   - he is unshakeable/dogmatic
   - he is unaware of his irrational stance.

   (b) *Reference to/explanation of any 2 of the following for one mark each:*
   - use of "even"
   - as a cricketer, he is thought to be more intelligent than other sportspeople
   - use of "even though"
   - "threadbare and smelly" – not what we would expect of a professional sportsman
   - prepared to inconvenience team-mates.

3. *Any four of the following for 1 mark each:*
   - a superstition can be based on a false belief …
   - … and therefore can lead to unnecessary behaviour
   - but mostly this causes no damage …
   - … provided observing it does not cause huge inconvenience
   - a superstition can be based on a genuine danger/fear …
   - … in which case observing it is beneficial.

4. Key features (*any two from*):
   - repeated/parallel structure, consisting of
   - "some believe/like …"
   - followed by comma
   - followed by "but"
   - semicolons create list.

   Conveys point by (*any two from*):
   - illustrating just how many different ways people don't let superstition influence them too much
   - showing how similar all these beliefs are
   - showing how easy it is to find examples.

5. (a) It can be seen as either effective or not effective:

effective because	just as a spectrum contains a whole range/variety/scale (of colours)	so there is a (wide) range of superstitions/(illogical) behaviours/perceptions/beliefs
not effective because	the (bright) colour imagery implied	is not apt or fitting or helpful to describe/illustrate the (melancholy) subject

   (b) *Any of the following:*
   - it illustrates his point about the range of "irrationality" by providing an extreme example of superstition
   - it illustrates his point that superstition taken to excess/dogmatically insisted upon has an unhelpful/deleterious effect/outcome
   - he is using reference to a team game to show the influence of superstition on others.

   (c) *Any of the following:*
   - the reference to the elements of help and hindrance recaps the idea of ambivalence explored elsewhere in the passage
   - (metaphor) "kick (the ritual into touch)" reprises references to football/sport used earlier
   - "With a rabbit's foot, obviously" reprises the cynical/sceptical/humorous tone seen elsewhere.

6. *Any two of the following for 2 marks each:*
   - "funny bunch" – slang, off-hand way to describe sportspeople
   - "bring the world collapsing" – exaggeration
   - "poor dears" – mock concern
   - "Yes, really" – suddenly as if speaking directly to reader
   - "feathered fellows" – as if they're human
   - "I know, I know" – pretending to be hearing readers' derision
   - "(pigeons) unavailable for interview" – as if they're human, mocking the standard official response to a difficult question
   - "got up the noses" – slang (plus playful mixing of literal and metaphorical)
   - "abode" – deliberately exaggerated way to describe a cave
   - "scarpers"— (old fashioned) slang sounds out of place for such a threat
   - "his five-a-day" – anachronistic reference to modern nutritional theory.

7. *Any four of the following for 1 mark each (may be in bullet point form or in prose):*
   - superstitions can been observed in eminent sportspeople
   - pigeons can be trained to act as if superstitious
   - superstition arises when there is a belief that one action can lead directly to another …

- ... even when no connection exists
- some/most superstitions are harmless ...
- ... and observing them can bring comfort/hope/peace of mind
- some superstitions lead to damaging behaviour.

NATIONAL 5 ENGLISH MODEL PAPER 1

CRITICAL READING

SECTION 1 – Scottish Text

Generic instructions for the 8 marks questions on all texts.

Candidates may choose to answer in **bullet points** in this final question, or write a number of linked statements. There is **no requirement** to write a "mini essay".

Up to 2 marks can be achieved for identifying elements of **commonality** as identified in the question.

A further 2 marks can be gained for **reference to the extract given.**

4 additional marks can be awarded for similar references to **at least one other text/part of the text** by the writer.

<u>In practice this means:</u>

Identification of commonality (e.g.: theme, central relationship, importance of setting, use of imagery, development in characterisation, use of personal experience, sue of narrative style, or any other key element ...)

from the extract:

1 × relevant reference to technique	1 × appropriate comment

OR

1 × relevant reference to idea	1 × appropriate comment

OR

1 × relevant reference to feature	1 × appropriate comment

OR

1 × relevant reference to text	1 × appropriate comment

(maximum of 2 marks only for discussion of extract)

from at least one other/text part of the text:

as above (× 2) for up to 4 marks

SCOTTISH TEXT — DRAMA

Text 1 — Drama — *Bold Girls* by Rona Munro

1. Candidates should make general and/or specific points about the way Deirdre's words and/or actions will make the audience see her as strange.
   Possible answers include:
   - the very fact of her intrusion into Marie's home
   - she is generally uncommunicative
   - she is generally ungrateful for shelter/food
   - her blunt opening question/absence of any apology for intrusion
   - her ignoring of Nora's remark
   - when asked again, merely gestures
   - her eventual response is surly, discourteous ("sullen")
   - the blunt, monosyllabic "Back of the school there."
   - the loud, aggressive repetition of "Back of the school there."
   - "nods" and "shrugs" – basic gestures only
   - no acknowledgement of/thanks for tea/biscuits
   - method of eating ("furtively and ravenously").

2. Candidates should make for each of the three women a general comment about her treatment of Deirdre and support it with appropriate reference to the extract. *Possible answers include:*

Marie:

- helpful, welcoming, kind
- invites her in/offers tea/doesn't ask questions

Nora:

- inquisitive/a little suspicious/hostile
- asks (and repeats) questions about where she is from, what has happened to her

Cassie:

- suspicious, fearful
- looks away when Deirdre catches her eye.

3. Candidates should show an understanding of what is happening at this moment in the play. *Possible answers include:*

- As a distraction from the tension/nervousness created by Deirdre's behaviour.

4. Candidates should an awareness of Deirdre's role in this extract and elsewhere in the play as "a catalyst", whose intrusion into the lives of Marie and Cassie has dramatic consequences.

General instructions for marking this question are given on page 171.

Text 2 — Drama — *Sailmaker* by Alan Spence

5. Candidates should make four separate points for 1 mark each. Quotation is likely but not necessary. *Possible answers include:*

- Davie tells Billy he has lost his job
- Billy says it's not Davie's fault/not fair/criticises employers
- Davie is very defeatist/thinks he's got nothing going for him
- Billy says he might be able to get him a job
- Davie displays little enthusiasm
- Billy tries to keep Davie's spirits up.

6 Candidates should show how the sentence structure used illustrates Davie's feelings.

Possible answers include:

- exclamation shows his feeling of hopelessness, defeat
- use of italics shows how resentful he feels about "them"
- series of short sentences suggests disengaged, depressed, given up
- series of questions suggests at a loss, feels hopeless.

7. Candidates should refer to both characters and quote from or refer to the text. *Possible answers include:*

- Davie has very little to say/is monosyllabic/sounds defeated
- Bill talks at greater length/offers hope/ encouragement.

8. Candidates should demonstrate an understanding of Davie's personality as it is revealed in these lines.

Possible answers include:

- unambitious/never one to get excited – "wouldnae be much"
- feels sort of powerless to affect anything – *"shrugs"*
- takes life as it comes – "better than nothing"
- keen to rationalise/make best of situation – "that was a lousy job anyway"
- mild surprise at something trivial – "Amazin how it gets on top of ye"
- resigned acceptance of everything – "Och aye. No to worry."
- clichéd optimism (or possible ironic repetition of Billy earlier) – "Never died a winter yet"

9. Candidates should show an awareness of how Davie's words and actions here and elsewhere in the play are used to present his character.

General instructions for marking this question are given on page 171.

Text 3 — Drama — *Tally's Blood* by Ann Marie di Mambro

10. Candidates should make three separate points about Rosinella's character. Quotation is likely but not necessary. *Possible answers include:*

- Rosinella and Massimo argue (over Rosinella's spoiling of Lucia)
- Massimo admires Lucia's schoolbag
- Lucia refuses to take off her dress
- Massimo suggests a compromise
- the compromise works.

11. Candidates should make two separate points for 1 mark each. Quotation/reference is likely but not necessary. *Possible answers include:*

- she loves Lucia
- she is generous towards Lucia/is prepared to spoil her
- she is selfless/altruistic
- she is unashamed of her generosity.

12. Candidates should refer to and/or explain the various ways by which Lucia's behaviour is intended to portray her as a five-year-old. *Possible answers include:*

- the stubbornness implied by repetition (of "No" and/ or "I want to keep it on")
- the quick change(s) of mood from playful to petulant
- starting to shout
- yielding to adult compromise
- perhaps she is aware all along that one of them will weaken …

13. Candidates should quote examples of obviously "Scottish" turns of phrase.
    Possible answers include:
    - "see when I …"
    - "wee"
    - "lassie"
    - "wean"
    - "no" (for "not")
    - "tatties"
    - "hen"
    - "I says".

14. Candidates should discuss the portrayal of the relationship between Lucia and her adoptive parents in this extract and elsewhere in the play.

    General instructions for marking this question are given on page 171.

SCOTTISH TEXT — PROSE

Text 1 — Prose — *The Cone-Gatherers* by Robin Jenkins

15. Candidates should select two appropriate words or phrases or language features and relate each one to "the violence of the storm".

    Appropriate reference (1 mark). Explanation (1 mark).

    Possible answers:
    - "flashed" suggests sudden movement, frightening
    - "crashed" suggests something loud, destructive
    - "shattered" suggests completely broken by a single blow
    - "hurled" suggests that in the brothers' mind the storm has potential to throw them viciously from the tree
    - "fragments" bits of the tree have been reduced to tiny pieces
    - "terrified" the storm has the power to frighten an inanimate object
    - repetition of "every" emphasises dominance, power of the storm
    - "torn its roots" tree seems to have been pulled apart.

16. Candidates should show how two words clarify Neil's impatience.
    Possible answers:
    - "flung" suggests as quick, careless movement
    - "snatched up" suggests a quick, unthinking movement
    - "shouted" suggests he is urging Calum to move
    - "gasped" suggests rapid breathing, losing patience
    - "clutched" suggests frantic holding on.

17. Candidates should identify four key points Neil makes, using their own words as far as possible.
    Possible answers:
    - for the sake of his (Neil's) health
    - for the sake of Calum's health
    - to avoid danger of lightning
    - the beach hut can be reached quickly
    - not to be afraid of LRC's possible anger

    - they won't cause any damage to the hut
    - no one will know they been there.

18. Candidates should identify and explain at least one feature of these lines which shows Calum's childlike innocence/naivety.
    Possible answers:
    - "They'll get all wet, Neil." – rather pathetic statement of the obvious
    - "Aye, that's right" – doesn't realise that Neil's repeating of these words is sarcastic
    - he takes Neil's question about the sun literally
    - murmurs his response as if frightened to disagree with Neil

19. Candidates should discuss the relationship between Calum and Neil in this extract and elsewhere in the novel.

    General instructions for marking this question are given on page 171.

Text 2 — Prose — *The Testament of Gideon Mack* by James Robertson

20. Candidates should show how Miss Craigie is presented as an intimidating character.
    Possible answers include:
    - "Just come in, for heaven's sake" brusque, irritable, impatient
    - "*If locked go away*" the notice is unwelcoming, abrupt
    - "Can't you read?" almost aggressive, demeaning
    - undermines Gideon's attempt to be apologetic with sarcastic response
    - "Oh, it's you" in a clearly unwelcoming tone
    - "distaste" shows her disapproval of Gideon/of the Kirk
    - her reputation as believing Kirk to be "a scabrous outbreak …" sees Kirk/religion as a disease, something that blights society.

21. Candidates should show how the dialogue conveys the friction between the two characters.
    Possible answers include:
    - general point: every one of Gideon attempts at politeness is turned against him by her curt responses
    - her immediate contradiction of what he says about the clerical collar
    - her (logical but) rude response when he says he's been reading her book and wants to ask some questions
    - her (understandable but) unnecessary comment about knowing what the word "supplementary" means.

22. Candidates should show how the writer's sentence structure and imagery help to describe the layout of Miss Craigie's hallway.

    Possible answers include:

    Sentence structure:
    - the colon (after "location") introduces explanation of what he realises the reason for the layout

- the colon (after "placed") introduces explanation of both the "pre-existing" and the "strategically placed"
- the list beginning "plant-stand" illustrates the large number of objects involved **and/or** creates an imitation of the step-by-step nature of the arrangement

Imagery:

- "a kind of domestic rock-face" just as a rock face can be climbed with the help of pre-planned places to grip hold or to pause so she is able to make a dangerous route less hazardous
- "horizontal climbing-wall" just as a climbing wall is ascended vertically with artificial aids, so she can move along her hallway aided by these objects.

23. Candidates should discuss the relationship between Gideon and Miss Craigie.

General instructions for marking this question are given on page 171.

Text 3 — Prose — *Kidnapped* by Robert Louis Stevenson

24. Candidates should show an understanding of the relationship between Alan's remark and the details in paragraph 1.
Possible answers:

- James must have gone mad
- showing so much light
- will attract the Redcoats.

25. Candidates should make a sensible inference from Alan's introduction.
Possible answers:

- that David is a man of status "gentleman", "laird"
- that David is important, notorious, mysterious "give his name the go-by".

26. Candidates should give at least one point for each character for full marks, and should use their own words as far as possible.
Possible answers:

Alan:

- not bothered
- attitude of win-some-lose-some
- pleased that the Red Fox is dead

James:

- thinks it's bad news
- with dire consequences
- wishes Red Fox still alive
- Appin will be blamed, will suffer
- fears for his family.

27. Candidates should relate specific details and/or language features in these lines to the creation of a sense of panic.
Possible answers:

- list-like structure of sentence beginning "Some were" suggests extensive, frantic, disorderly activity
- list of weapons ("guns, swords …") suggests they are all lumped together
- "no kind of order" – indicates lack of a controlling hand

- "struggled together for the same gun" – shows unruly, disorganised behaviour
- "ran into each other" – almost cartoon-like disorder
- "continually turning about from his talk" – shows his lack of concentration, desperate to get some order into the men's activity
- "orders … never understood" – impression of futile activity, almost anarchic
- "anxious and angry" – clear signs of confusion and panic.

28. Candidates should discuss the characterisation of Alan Breck in this extract and elsewhere in the novel.

General instructions for marking this question are given on page 171.

Text 4 — Prose — *Mother and Son* by Iain Crichton Smith

29. Candidates should show how an unpleasant impression of the mother is created.

Possible answers include:

- "mouth tightly shut" suggests cruel, harsh, unbending
- "prim" suggests straitlaced, prissy, moralising
- "anaemic" suggests cold, pale, lifeless
- "bitter smile" suggests hostile, nasty
- comparisons with insurance man suggests smile is insincere, for show only
- comparison with "witch" suggests evil, wicked, power to harm.

30. Candidates should show how the man's/son's reaction is made clear.

Possible answers include:

- "cursed vindictively" suggests aggressive, spiteful response
- "helplessly" suggests the hopelessness he feels
- "some state of innocence … to which he could not return" suggests resentment at loss of previous, better existence
- "still and dangerous" suggests something violent, destructive bubbling beneath the surface.

31. Candidates should explain in own words the tone/delivery of the son's comment.

Possible answers include:

- flat, unemotional
- automatic, unthinking
- detached.

32. Candidates should show how the hostility between the two characters is made clear.

Possible answers include:

- exclamation mark shows it's not a question but a criticism
- "snapped" suggests sharp, aggressive tone
- "pettishly" suggests petulant, irritable, almost childish
- "sitting there moping while …" direct criticism for neglecting his duties
- "don't know why we christened you" insulting his very birthname

- "My father was never ..." openly demeaning son with comparison
- repetition of "All right, all right" suggests irritable, bad-tempered
- "get a new record for your gramophone" insulting comment, comparing her to a machine
- the added "hundreds of times" emphasises how much it annoys him
- "she wasn't to be stopped" shows her as relentless, persistent
- "mooning about the house" she sees his behaviour as pointless, childish
- "pacing up and down" she sees him as distracted, acting strangely
- "taken to the asylum" open allegation that he is not sane
- "something wrong with their heads" insulting his father's family, shifting blame away from hers
- "in your family but not in ours" insulting one side of the family, defending her own.

33. Candidates should discuss how Crichton Smith explores conflict between characters.

    General instructions for marking this question are given on page 171.

Text 5 — Prose — *Zimmerobics* by Anne Donovan

34. Candidates should show how the narrator's physical discomfort is conveyed by two examples of the writer's use of language.

    Possible answers include:

    - "jaggy pains" shows she experiences sharp bursts of pain
    - "vertebrae grinding" suggests her bones are crunching, grating against each other
    - onomatopoeic "clicking and clunking" suggests rattling, noisy, malfunctioning
    - simile "like the central heating boiler starting up" suggests (light-heartedly) she is a cumbersome machine.

35. Candidates should identify two aspects of Catherin's personality and support each with reference to the text.

    Possible answers include:

    - not interested in aunt – minimal response of "Uh-huh"
    - obsessively tidy – "busy rearranging ornaments on the mantelpiece"
    - unsympathetic – "gave me one of her looks"
    - great believer in virtue of activity – "I should take more interest"
    - persistent – "always trying to get me"
    - brisk, bossy – has organised TV for aunt unasked or her habit of speaking in short, curt sentences.

36. Candidates should show how the contrast between the two women.

    Possible answers include:

    - aunt is content to do nothing, while niece has no time for inactivity
      - "daydream"/"lost inside my own head" and
      - "not in her nature to daydream ..."

- aunt has forgotten about film when Catherine next visits, while it's the first thing niece asks about
- "I was caught off my guard" and
  - "Did you enjoy the film?"
- aunt has no interest in being sociable, while niece thinks meeting people is important
  - "I'd rather just sit here" and
  - "go and meet people"
- aunt is content "inside my own head", while niece criticises her for having no interest in "anything outside yourself"
- aunt is not bothered about order or routine, while niece is like a "stapler", suggesting she is functional, mechanical, controlling
- a good response could be made by comparing the imagery of the stapler with the connotations of the Zimmer.

37. Candidates should discuss the writer's exploration of conflict in "Zimmerobics" and at least one other story.

    General instructions for marking this question are given on page 171.

SCOTTISH TEXT — POETRY

Text 1 — Poetry — *Originally* by Carol Ann Duffy

38. Candidates should identify key events in the poem.
    Possible answers include:

    - the speaker (and her family) move to a new home/country
    - at first she feels out of place
    - eventually she assimilates
    - by the end she is uncertain of her origins/where she came from.

39. (a) Candidates should provide a simple explanation of what the statement means.
    Possible answers include:

    - childhood involves moving from one stage to another
    - nothing remains the same for any child
    - change is normal for any child.

39. (b) Candidates should refer to language/techniques in order to show the distinction the poet makes between "slow" and "sudden" change.
    Possible answers include:
    Slow:
    - structure of "leaving you standing, resigned, up an avenue" creates a unhurried pace
    - word choice of "resigned" suggests submissive, inactive
    - "no one you know" suggests loneliness, isolation
    Sudden:
    - structure of "Others are sudden. / Your accent wrong." sounds jerky, rushed
    - structure of "Your accent wrong" very compressed/minor sentence like a sudden accusation
    - series of plosive consonants ("Corners ... pebble-dashed estates, big boys") creates harsh, rushed, slightly aggressive tone.

40. Candidates should show how the speaker's feelings of uncertainty are conveyed.

    Possible answers include:

    - repetition of "or" shows she has no clear memory of when things changed

    - series of questions shows she is unsure/seeking answers

    - "only think" suggests she knows it may not be the case

    - list of things possibly lost ("a river …") suggests there is a wide range of possibilities/she is unsure exactly what might have been lost

    - her need to clarify strangers' question by asking "Originally?" suggests she is not sure what the question actually means to her

    - word choice of "hesitate" conveys need to pause and think

    - "hesitate" placed crucially as the last word emphasises her inability to answer a straight question.

41. Candidates should discuss similarities and/or differences – in language and/or ideas – between *Originally* and at least one other poem by Duffy.

    General instructions for marking this question are given on page 171.

Text 2 — Poetry — *Hyena* by Edwin Morgan

42. Candidates should identify specific poetic techniques and link each to the threatening nature of the hyena in these lines

    Possible answers include:

    - repetition of "I am" creates dogmatic, arrogant figure

    - direct address to "you" creates sense of reader/listener being directly targeted

    - alliteration of "fierce without food" focuses attention on the hyena's aggressive nature

    - sibilance in "eyes/screwed/slits/sun" creates hissing, snake-like sound

    - word choice of "You must believe" sounds dogmatic, overbearing.

43. (a) Candidates should suggest why the poet repeats Africa in the similes.
    Possible answers include:

    - since the hyena is an African animal

    - shows hyena comparing himself to an entire continent which suggests self-importance

    - the repetition suggests hyena is rigid, inflexible

    - lack of variation suggests hyena is unimaginative.

43. (b) Candidates should identify a specific feature of sentence structure and link it to an element of the poet's description.
    Possible answers include:

    - list of verbs suggests range of movements

    - the simplicity of the sentences/statements suggests the single-mindedness of the hyena

    - repetition of "I" + verb suggests self-confidence

    - brutal shortness/simple monosyllabic nature of final sentence highlights the stark conclusion of the hyena's activities.

44. Candidates should explore a number of ways by which the poet conveys the harshness of the hyena's world.
    Possible answers include:

    - the slightly menacing tone of "Do you like my song?"

    - description of moon as "hard and cold" makes it seems unwelcoming, hostile

    - reversal of more common romantic, pleasant associations of "moon"

    - "slave of darkness" has connotations of evil, vampire-like

    - "stone walls and the mud walls" suggest (primitive) prison-like conditions

    - "ruined places" suggests desolation, destruction

    - "sniff a broken drum" – imagery of destruction, something with a purpose now ruined

    - "I bristle" – as if prepared for action

    - use of "howl" conveys the reality of the "song" as wild, aggressive

    - "howl my song to the moon" suggests madness, lunacy

    - final question is almost taunting.

45. Candidates should discuss the view of the natural world Morgan presents in "Hyena" and in at least one other poem.

    General instructions for marking this question are given on page 171.

Text 3 — Poetry — *Assisi* by Norman MacCaig

46. Candidates should choose an appropriate example of the poet's use of language and explain how it adds to the description.

    Possible answers include:

    (a) the dwarf:

    - detail of "hands on backwards" suggests deformity, distortion, unable to function properly

    - alliteration/sibilance in "sat, slumped" suggests lifeless, deflated

    - word choice of "slumped" suggests drooping, wilting

    - imagery/simile "like a half-filled sack" suggests incomplete, lacking substance, inhuman, inferior material

    - alliteration "tiny twisted" focuses attention, slightly harsh

    - detail of "tiny twisted legs" emphasises the distortion, out of proportion

    - imagery of "(from which) sawdust (might run)" suggests less than human, left-over material

    - comparison with "ruined temple" elevates him to something holy, magnificent, worthy of worship

    - structure of "eyes wept pus" stark, monosyllabic description emphasises the horror

    - word choice of "pus" associated with ill-health, infection, highly distasteful

    - sound "wept pus" – clash of sounds ("-pt p-") is very harsh, bitter

    - enjambment in "back … higher/than his head" highlights the dislocation

- word choice of "lopsided" emphasises the distortion, visual difference.

(b) the church:

- "three tiers" – suggests (over)elaborate, like a decorated wedding cake
- plural "churches" – suggests excess, overkill
- "honour of St Francis" – perhaps hints at lack of "honour" to the living.

(c) the tourists:

- word choice of "rush of tourists" – suggests they were not bothering to take much in, over-hasty
- word choice/sound of "clucking" – compares them to hens, lacking individuality, not very bright
- alliteration in "clucking contentedly" – creates an imitative, slightly mocking effect
- word choice of "contentedly" – suggests smugness
- word choice of "fluttered" – suggests light, insubstantial.

47. Candidates should identify an attitude shown by the poet to the priest and support this with at least one appropriate reference.

Possible answers include:

Attitude:

- dismissive, scornful, contemptuous, mocking, angry

Support:

- ignores the dwarf
- more interested in the tourists/showing off to them
- patronising tone of "how clever it was"
- unconscious irony in "reveal to the illiterate the goodness/of God", as if only the illiterate need this explained
- rather unctuous "the goodness/of God and the suffering/of His Son", especially since he ignores the suffering of the dwarf before his eyes
- "he scattered/the grain of the Word" – tongue-in-cheek continuation of the "hens" metaphor, suggesting he is like a pompous preacher.

48. Candidates may find these lines effective or not, but for full marks must refer to the lines and to the poem as a whole.

Possible answers include:

- despite his physical deformities, the dwarf has an inner beauty (equivalent to that of St Francis)
- his voice is described as "sweet", implying delicate, pleasant he is compared with a "child," implying innocence he is compared with a "bird", implying natural beauty, freedom of movement
- the whole poem is about seeing/failing to see the real person the blindness/hypocrisy of the Church.

49. Candidates should discuss how MacCaig creates sympathy (not necessarily for a person/people) in *Assisi* and in at least one other poem.

General instructions for marking this question are given on page 171.

Text 4 – Poetry – *My Grandmother's Houses* **by Jackie Kay**

50. Candidates should identify aspects of personality (not physical attributes). Quotation/reference is not required. *Possible answers:*

- she is a hard/conscientious worker
- she dominates her granddaughter/is frequently giving orders
- she is subservient to/in awe of/afraid of her "betters"
- she is not well educated/lacks sophistication
- she wants her granddaughter to be seen in a good light
- she is a strict/violent disciplinarian.

51. Candidates should show some ability to deconstruct the chosen image.

Possible answers:

- "like an octopus's arms" (to describe the way the rooms lead off the hall) suggests a large number/going in all directions/a bit scary
- "a one-winged creature" (to describe the grand piano) makes to piano seem alive, a little mysterious.

52. Candidates should identify aspects of the woman's personality and support each with an appropriate quotation/reference.

Possible answers:

- she is/thinks she is superior/of a higher class "posh"
- she is insincere/putting on a show "all smiles"
- she is (superficially at least) kindly "Would you like ..."
- she is (superficially at least) encouraging/friendly "Lovely", "beautiful"
- she is patronising "Lovely", "beautiful"
- she is insensitive, verging on racist "skin the colour of café au lait"
- she is not very p.c. "skin the colour of café au lait"
- she is high-handed, officious, haughty "You just get back to your work".

53. Candidates should show understanding of the presentation of people in the chosen text(s).

General instructions for marking this question are given on page 175.

SECTION 2 – Critical Essay

Please see the assessment criteria for the Critical Essay on page 169.

NATIONAL 5 ENGLISH MODEL PAPER 2

READING FOR UNDERSTANDING, ANALYSIS AND EVALUATION

1. 1 mark for selection and one mark for comment.
   Any two from:
   - "wrecking" – suggests destruction, violence, etc
   - "vandals" – suggests mindless destruction, etc
   - "Genghis Khan" – associated with uncivilised behaviour, etc
   - "destroying" – suggests demolishing, tearing down, etc
   - "pillaging" – suggests looting, stealing, etc
   - alliteration ("pillaging out punctuation") – adds some weight to the criticism
   - "savaging" – suggests viciously tearing apart, etc
   - alliteration ("savaging our sentences") – adds some weight to the criticism
   - "textese" – suffix "-ese" is pejorative
   - "slanguage" – combines 'language' with 'slang', which is looked down on
   - "virus" – suggests disease, something harmful, etc
   - "bleak" – suggests poverty of language
   - "bald" – suggests plainness of language
   - "shorthand" – suggests superficial, etc
   - "drab" – suggests dreariness, monotony, etc
   - "masks" – suggests concealment, deceit, etc.

2. (a) • reaction to texting has been both positive and negative
       • reaction to others was negative.
   (b) 1 mark for selection of feature and one mark for comment.
       - use of "ever" ("has there ever been") – suggests he thinks it could be unique
       - list of reactions – shows just how wide-ranging they are
       - use of (rhetorical) question – to make reader think it must be something remarkable.

3. Any three of the following for 1 mark each:
   - people think it's something entirely new, but it's not
   - people think it's only young people who use it, but it's not
   - people think it impedes reading and writing, but (possibly) it actually improves it
   - people think it will cause lasting harm, but its effect will be slight/short-lived.

4. 1 mark for selection of word and one mark for comment.
   Any two from:
   - "hysteria" – suggests critics are in panic, raising irrational objections, etc
   - "swallowed whole" – suggests critics' gullibility, etc
   - "stories"/"reports" – suggests critics are prepared to believe unverified accounts

   - "incessantly" – suggests critics are obsessive, won't stop to consider other arguments
   - "hoax" – suggests critics are prepared to believe something made up.

5. *Reference to and/or explanation of the significance of any three of the following for 1 mark each:*
   - historical pedigree (for use of initials)
   - "English literary tradition" – sounds dignified, academic, established, accepted as being of value, etc
   - reference to OED – the most respected dictionary, hallmark of quality, etc
   - reference to four highly respected writers.

6. 1 mark for each of the following explanations:
   - line 55: precedes/introduces an expansion/explanation of the "extraordinary number of ways ..."
   - line 57: precedes/introduces an expansion/explanation of what "Professional writers" do
   - line 60: creates pause before adding the most the contentious aspect, the one about which critics blame texting most.

7. 1 mark for selection of word or feature and one for comment.
   Any two from:
   - two similar sentences at start – suggests a balance, calmness, nothing to get worked up about
   - "merely" – minimises any negative effect
   - "creative" – suggests something imaginative, positive, worthy, etc
   - "suit the demands" – suggests something helpful, co-operative, etc
   - "no ... not ... not" – repetition assures us all the bad things will not happen
   - "evolution" – suggests growth, improvement, etc.

8. Any five of the following for 1 mark each (may be in bullet point form or in prose):
   - features criticised in texting have a long historical pedigree
   - text language is an understandable response to the design of the keypad
   - text language is an understandable way to save time
   - abbreviations are common elsewhere
   - people, especially children, enjoy playing with language
   - playing with language helps develop linguistic skills
   - texters are already skilled in the use of language
   - there is no correct form of English (from which texters are deviating).

NATIONAL 5 ENGLISH MODEL PAPER 2

CRITICAL READING

SECTION 1 – Scottish Text

SCOTTISH TEXT – DRAMA

Text 1 – Drama – *Tally's Blood* **by Ann Marie di Mambro**

1. (a) 1 mark for acceptable aspect of character and 1 mark for valid textual reference.
    Possible answers include:

    - self-centred – ignores Lucia's attempts to speak
    - snobbish/class-conscious – looks up/wants to impress to Palombos; looks down on others (the type who boast "Ma lassie cleaned four chickens.")
    - traditional – determined to marry Lucia to an Italian
    - ambitious for Lucia – wants to marry her into a "good" family
    - fantasist/delusional – convinced Lucia is "daft for" Silvio Palombo.

    (b) *Either of the following:*

    - her repeated "He's okay" – polite but very committal/no enthusiasm at all
    - the repeated "Auntie Rosinella …?" – interrogative tone, trying to change the subject (to her wish to attend the wedding).

2. *Any three of the following for 2 marks each:*

    - she maintains that Italian men work harder than others – but the audience can actually see Hughie working hard ("like a Trojan")
    - she maintains that "Nobody loves their families like the Italians" – but immediately after that Hughie declines to stay for some food, because of a duty he feels to his mother
    - she displays obvious distaste for extra-marital sex (seen as a typical fault of Scottish people), when the audience is in no doubt about what happened between Franco and Bridget
    - she is contemptuous of Scottish men's propensity for alcohol ("Give him two or three days …") – but within seconds we see Hughie declining the offer of a drink from Massimo.

3. Candidates should discuss the role of Hughie in the extract and in the play as a whole.

    General instructions for marking this question are given on page 171.

Text 2 – Drama – *Bold Girls* **by Rona Munro**

4. A contrast clearly defined and suitable textual reference for 2 marks.

    Any of the following:

    - Cassie's extroversion versus Marie's shyness
    - Cassie's confidence versus Marie's timidity
    - Cassie's self-centredness versus Marie's obliging nature
    - Cassie's exuberance versus Marie's diffidence.

Reference could be made to any of the following to support any of the contrasts:

Words:

- Marie: "Well, maybe …"
- Marie: the rather feeble meat pie joke – attempted humour
- Cassie "great diet"
- Cassie: "really feel the benefit"
- Cassie: "Let them".

Actions:

- Marie: *"shuffling cautiously"*
- Marie: *"glances round nervously"*
- Cassie: *"dancing … extravagant"*
- Cassie: *"beams, applauding"*.

5. A valid aspect of the relationship and appropriate textual support for 2 marks.

    Possible answers include:

    - Marie cares for/is concerned about Cassie ("Cassie, what's wrong?", "Have you had words?")
    - Marie is supportive of Cassie ("It'll be all right Cassie.", "I'll just be across the road, I won't let you go crazy.")
    - Cassie feels she can confide in Marie ("I tell you Marie I can't stand the *smell* of him.")
    - Cassie knows Marie is unshockable, knows she can exaggerate with her ("I'm just bad, Marie, didn't you know?")
    - there is a kind of unspoken understanding between them (*"Slowly Cassie smiles at her."*).

6. *Possible answers include:*

    - the use of italics to emphasise her disgust/contempt
    - "greasy" – suggests unhealthy, slimy, etc
    - "grinning" – suggests leering, unpleasant, etc
    - "beer bellied" – suggests self-indulgence, unpleasant, sloppy appearance
    - "winking away" – suggest lecherous, unsavoury, etc
    - "wriggling" – makes him sound worm-like
    - "fat fingers" – suggests clumsy, distasteful, etc
    - "like I'm a poke of chips" – he treats her as a commodity, something for his own gratification
    - alliteration ("greasy, grinning", "beer bellied", "fat fingers") – harsh sounds emphasise her revulsion
    - climactic structure of the last sentence – builds to the horror of "my *bed*".

7. Answers should focus on the relationship between Marie and Cassie and should take account of the revelations in Scene Four.

    General instructions for marking this question are given on page 171.

Text 3 — Drama — *Sailmaker* by Alan Spence

8. Any four valid points.

   Possible answers include:

   - he is not earning a lot from his job
   - he is gambling heavily
   - he has suffered a significant loss (backing a favourite)
   - he is in debt to the bookie
   - he is paying high interest/not paying off original sum.

9. Any one valid character point and textual support.

   Possible answers include:

   - generous – extends loan
   - caring – wants to know what the problem is
   - knows his brother well – suspects drink/knows it's not just the job
   - persistent – doesn't let Davie fob him off
   - nosey/intrusive – keeps asking questions about brother's private life.

10. *Possible answers include:*

    - he knows his brother is (sort of) joking
    - he realises brother is trying to relieve some tension
    - he is amused at the fact brother can bring his sectarianism into anything
    - he realises that the bookie's religion is not going to change anything.

11. The key point is the contrast between Davie's steadfast optimism and Billy's realistic/cynical view of life; identifying this and making reference to at least two different parts of the exchange should gain 4 marks.

    Reference could be made to several occasions when a hopeful comment by Davie is countered by a pessimistic/realistic putdown from his brother, e.g.:

    - the scathing "Whatever that is" showing that Billy lacks Davie's faith
    - the blunt assertions "It's a mug's game. The punter canny win" in response to Davie's rather feeble "Things've got tae get better"
    - the frustrated "Flingin it away!" in response to Davie's dogged "Got tae keep trying"
    - a further contrast can be identified in lines 42–49 where Billy's desire for positive action is met with Davie's passivity ("Ah knew his terms") , culminating in his shoulder-shrugging "Whit a carry on, eh?".

12. Answers should deal with a number of relevant aspects of how money problems and escape are explored, e.g.:

    - Davie's gambling
    - Davie's drinking
    - Billy's move to Aberdeen for work
    - exchanges between Alec and Ian about work prospects
    - the idea of education as a way to betterment
    - football (and sectarianism) as a diversion from poverty
    - religion as an "escape"
    - specific details of Davie's and Alec's situation.

    General instructions for marking this question are given on page 171.

SCOTTISH TEXT — PROSE

Text 1 — Prose — *In Church* by Iain Crichton Smith

13. **Before** (any three of):

    - British officer (Colin Macleod) leaves the trenches
    - comes across a ruined church
    - meets a deserter who lives in the crypt
    - the deserter had been studying for the ministry
    - insists on delivering a sermon.

    After:

    - he shoots Colin.

14. *Possible answers include:*

    - "forced" – under compulsion, against his will
    - "what they call" – implies he doesn't agree
    - his outlook ("gaze") was different from the army's
    - "despised" – looked down on with contempt
    - "feared" – caused him alarm
    - list of the men's shortcomings – emphasises how many there were
    - "fornicated" – immoral behaviour
    - "spat" – disgusting, unhealthy
    - "filthily" – lack of hygiene, lack of self-respect.

15. *Possible answers include:*

    - contrasts the horrors of war with a friendly/sociable game of football
    - contrasts the horrors of war with the sociable activity of sharing photographs
    - contrasts civilised behaviour of German officer with the bombardment to follow
    - contrasts the banality of looking at watch with horrors to come.

16. *Possible answers include:*

    - used to think God was on the side of the innocent, but no longer
    - believes God is "absent"
    - God has left him alone to suffer
    - God has left the world to suffer
    - God doesn't care
    - God has allowed mankind to engage in the destruction of war.

17. Answers should focus on Crichton Smith's characterisation.

    General instructions for marking this question are given on page 171.

Text 2 — Prose — *Away in a Manger* by Anne Donovan

18. *Possible answers include:*

    - "shimmerin wi light" – alluring, attractive, etc
    - "brightness sharp against the gloomy street" – contrast to emphasise the appeal of the square
    - "like the plastic jewellery sets wee lassies love" – connotations of precious jewels, bright and shiny, children's enjoyment of play
    - "in a mad rhythm" – uncontrolled, zany, exhilarating, etc

- "ae their ain" – idea of freedom, lack of constraint, etc
- "bells ringin and snow fallin" – association with Christmas fun (plus rhythmical pattern to heighten the sense of involvement)
- "Reindeer and Santas, holly, ivy, robins ..." – list to emphasise to the sheer number of attractions
- "bleezin wi light" – as if on fire, extraordinarily bright, etc
- "fillin the air" – the sound is pervasive, dominates the senses
- "like a cracklin heavenly choir" – as if angels are present; suggestions of warmth, comfort, etc.

19. A well-made point for 2 marks and a less assured response for 1 mark.

    Possible answers include:

    - to convey the excitement of others around them
    - to give the impression of a babble of disembodied voices everywhere
    - to give a rapid glimpse of some of the attractions (reindeer, star, tree).

20. *Possible answers include:*

    - in the past people on the benches were easily identified as down-and-outs
    - today they looked no different from ordinary shoppers.

21. *Possible answers include:*

    - Amy tugging at mother's arm to attract attention
    - Sandra's "Whit song?" as if she's not been paying attention
    - Sandra's "Do you?" as if struggling to show some interest
    - Amy's gushing detail about school and Mrs Anderson
    - Sandra's very uninterested "Oh."
    - Sandra's "What's no your favourite?" – she hasn't been paying attention at all
    - Amy initiates guessing game
    - Sandra won't play along ("Don't know.")
    - Amy's wheedling "Guess, Mammy, you have tae guess."
    - Sandra joins in to keep the peace (because she knows that's how to get it over with)
    - Amy quickly resorts to "Gie in?"
    - Sandra accepts with alacrity
    - Amy's triumphant "Ah've won!" ...
    - ... followed almost without a break by a question demanding an explanation.

22. Answers should focus on the development of the parent/child relationship in the extract and in another story. Of the stories on the set list, the most profitable will be: *All That Glisters* or *Dear Santa* or, to a lesser degree, *Virtual Pals*.

    General instructions for marking this question are given on page 171.

Text 3 – Prose – *The Cone Gatherers* by Robin Jenkins

23. *Possible answers include:*

    - Duror is unable to climb tree
    - Neil is initially polite

- Duror delivers message to Calum and Neil about the deer drive
- Neil protests strongly
- the effect on Duror of being unable to climb the tree is evident.

24. *Possible answers include:*

    - the use of a series of rather threatening sounds – "scrapes", "thumps", "cracked", "barked"
    - the frequency of short sentences – creates a breathless, staccato effect
    - the alternation between sound and silence – creates suspense
    - the references to waiting, once for "three or four minutes" – an agonisingly long time.

25. There should be reference to at least three of the following in order to establish two changes, with each attitude supported by some valid reference to the text:

    - friendly/polite (line 16)
    - helpful (line 19)
    - hopeful/anticipating good news (lines 23 and 25)
    - non-committal/defensive (line 27)
    - angry/slightly aggressive (lines 30–31)
    - disbelieving/indignant (lines 33–35)
    - very assertive (lines 35–37).

26. Clear explanation for 2 marks and 1 mark for a less confident explanation. *A possible answer is:*

    - on the outside he appears normal/healthy, but a malignant force is destroying him from within.

27. Answers should focus on the conflict between Duror and the Cone-Gatherers.

    General instructions for marking this question are given on page 171.

Text 4 – Prose – *The Testament of Gideon Mack* by James Robertson

28. *Possible answers include:*

    - Gideon is watching TV (on a Sunday)
    - his father returns unexpectedly
    - his father is furious
    - his father forces him to watch rest of programme
    - his father delivers a condemnation of American culture.

29. *Possible answers include:*

    - switches off the TV even though he knows there is no point
    - "jumped to my feet" – sudden action implying nervousness
    - "a flush of shame and fury" – embarrassment and resentment
    - futile action of trying to protect the TV set
    - "bowed my head" – can't look his father in the face
    - fixes eye on crack – trying to shut out the presence of his father
    - "mumbled" suggests he is confused, in a panic.

30. *Possible answers include:*
    - use of italics to convey tone of voice
    - rhetorical question to express fury at disobedience
    - hint of cutting sarcasm in "you have become very skilled at operating that thing"
    - "huge right hand descended on my neck" – sense of monstrous threat
    - "thumb and fingers gripped" – conveys the tightness, painfulness of the action
    - "increased the pressure" – making it even worse
    - "thought my head would snap off" – no thought for Gideon's pain
    - "breathing was like that of some monstrous creature in its den" – the comparison dehumanises his father, makes him sound like a mythical destroyer
    - "If I squirmed ... his grip tightened" – no mercy, prepared to inflict even greater pain
    - "he pushed me" – forceful, aggressive action.

31. *Possible answers include:*
    - the way he says "What ... is ... that?" as if spitting out the words in disgust
    - his refusal to call the programme by it correct name, preferring "Bat ... man" as if the words are disgusting
    - "whatever that means" – implying it might mean anything
    - "drivel" – he thinks it's worthless, idiotic
    - "unutterable garbage" – he considers it to be like rubbish, indescribably useless
    - "Garbage from the land of garbage." – repetition/ alliteration – harsh consonant conveys anger, disgust
    - "land of garbage" – implying whole country is contaminated.

32. Answers should focus on the relationship between Gideon and his father.

    General instructions for marking this question are given on page 171.

Text 5 — Prose — *Kidnapped* by Robert Louis Stevenson

33. Three brief references and comment for 1 mark each.

    Possible answers include:
    - "steady"/"quiet"/"great stillness" – idea of unnerving peacefulness, calm before the storm, etc
    - "muttering voices" – can't be made out, so slightly threatening, etc
    - "clash of steel" – sudden sharp noise to break the silence, use of onomatopoeia
    - "dealing out the cutlasses" – disturbing idea of dangerous weapons being handed out, an idea of what David and Alan will have to face
    - return to "silence" – again nerve-racking, uneasy, etc.

34. *Any two of the following for 1 mark each:*
    - uncertainty
    - fear
    - hopelessness
    - anger
    - desire for it to be over.

35. Any three valid points with some textual support for 1 mark each.

    Possible answers include:
    - "all of a sudden" – surprise, frightening
    - "a rush of feet" – speed, threat, etc
    - "a roar" – aggressive sound
    - "and ... and ... and" – structure (list form) gives impression of one action following quickly after another
    - "someone crying out as if hurt" – uncertainty
    - "I cried" – the exclamation shows his state of alarm
    - "Look to your window!" – Alan's response draws attention to more danger
    - "pass his sword through the mate's body" – gruesome killing
    - "drive the door in" – idea of force, threat
    - "But it was now or never" – idea of last chance, resolved to fate
    - "shot into their midst" – reckless, desperate action
    - "the whole party threw down the yard and ran for it" – sense of victory (albeit short-lived).

36. *Possible answers include:*
    - bloodthirsty ("his sword was running blood to the hilt")
    - proud ("himself so swelled with triumph")
    - impressive appearance ("looked to be invincible")
    - believer in cause ("There's one of your Whigs for ye!").

    A possible answer is:
    - callous ("asked if I had done much execution").

37. What they've experienced so far is nothing much ("but a dram"); much worse, a more substantial battle is yet to come ("meat").

38. Answers should focus on the relationship between David and Alan.

    General instructions for marking this question are given on page 171.

SCOTTISH TEXT — POETRY

Text 1 — Poetry — *Anne Hathaway* by Carol Ann Duffy

39. *Possible answers include:*
    - "a spinning world" – suggests speed, exhilaration, etc
    - "castles" – suggests fairy-tale romance, luxury, security, etc
    - "torchlight" – suggests carnival atmosphere, brightness, etc
    - "clifftops" – suggests dizzy height, dominance, distant horizons, etc
    - "forests, castles, torchlight, clifftops, seas" – list suggests profusion of exciting features
    - "dive for pearls" – suggests romantic, exotic, etc
    - "shooting stars" – suggests brightness, speed, exhilaration, etc
    - "kisses/on these lips" – tactile, sensual, etc.

40. *Possible answers include:*

    NB: The comments given below are suggestions only; there will be other, perfectly acceptable, interpretations.

    - "rhyme" – suggesting the lovers' connectedness, sense of belonging together, fulfilling each other
    - "assonance" – suggesting they are similar, connected, but retaining some individuality
    - "verb dancing in the centre of a noun" – suggesting her lover's ability to bring life, movement, action … this is a complex image which allows many analyses
    - "he'd written me" – as if she is his creation, she owes everything to him
    - "a page beneath his writer's hands" – presents her as a passive recipient of his creativity
    - "drama (played)" – as if the senses referred to are actors in some greater performance.

41. (a) *Possible answers include:*
    - "dozed" – sleeping (with a suggestion of indolence), while the others are more energetically and pleasurably engaged
    - "dribbling" – connotations of old age and messiness compared with the others' apparent vitality and clarity of purpose
    - "prose" – suggests their lives are dull, ordinary, uninspired, unlike the imaginative "poetry" of the others' love-making.

    (b) *Possible answers include:*
    - fondness
    - respect
    - sadness at his death
    - devotion.

42. Answers should focus on the development of the theme of love in this poem and another by Duffy. Of the poems on the set list, the most profitable will be: *Valentine* or *Havisham* or, to a lesser degree *Mrs Midas*.

    General instructions for marking this question are given on page 171.

Text 2 — Poetry — *Lucozade* by Jackie Kay

43. *Possible answers include:*
    - refers to the colour of the drink
    - it is something associated with childhood/happier times.

44. *Possible answers include:*
    - negative: "they only wilt and die", "Don't bring …"
    - passive: "nods off", "fades"
    - dismissive: "Orange nostalgia, that's what that is"
    - tired of hospital experience: "whole day was a blur, a swarm of eyes"
    - distrusting: "Those doctors with their white lies."
    - scornful/cutting: "Did you think you could cheer me up with a *Woman's Own*?"

45. *Possible answers include:*
    - "grapes have no imagination, they're just green" – shows she has no interest in them, because they are featureless, dull, have nothing to appeal to her …

    Whereas

    - "the big brandy, the generous gin, the Bloody Mary, the biscuit tin, the chocolate gingers, the dirty big meringue?' – seem livelier, more appealing because of their association with sharp taste, colour, excess, … (appropriate comment could be made also on the alliteration, the list structure and the self-indulgent glee of "dirty big meringue").

46. *Possible answers include:*

    Mood:
    - happy, upbeat, optimistic, positive, reassured, …

    References:
    - "clear her cupboard" – hint of a new start, getting rid of the unwanted
    - "bags full" – sense of a job well done
    - "wave with her flowers" – cheerful gesture
    - "My mother … waves back" – gesture is reciprocated, sense of connection
    - "face is light and radiant" – she can see brightness, almost angelic light
    - "sheets billow and whirl" – sense of freshness, unrestrained movement
    - "She is beautiful" – a straightforward statement of affection
    - "the empty table is divine" – by clearing away all the unwanted things, she has made a simple table seem somehow holy
    - "singing an old song" – implying contentedness and connection with her mother.

47. Answers should focus on the way a relationship between generations is presented and explored in *Lucozade* and another poem by Jackie Kay. Any of the poems on the set list would be suitable.

    General instructions for marking this question are given on page 171.

Text 3 — Poetry — *Trio* by Edwin Morgan

48. *Possible answers include:*
    - "Christmas lights" – bright and cheerful, association with festivity, etc
    - "the three of them are laughing" – everyone is in a good mood
    - "a cloud of happiness" – even their breath is associated with joy
    - "Wait till he sees this but!" – sense of anticipation, pleasure in giving.

49. *Possible answers include:*

    The chihuahua:
    - cute, appealing, vulnerable ("tiny")
    - colourful, perhaps a little dignified ("Royal Stewart tartan")
    - a little ridiculous, incongruous ("coat like a teapot-holder")

The baby:

- clean, pure ("white shawl")
- radiant, alert ("all bright eyes")
- like a good luck charm ("mouth like favours")
- sweet, appealing, nourishing ("in a fresh sweet cake")

The guitar:

- like something alive, organic ("swells out")
- bright, associated with decoration and with giving ("silver tinsel tape")
- associated with celebration, mystical powers ("brisk sprig of mistletoe").

50. Four basic points for 1 mark each, but some answers will provide a convincing response by dealing with fewer than four points.

    Possible answers include:

    - they are objects of wonder/admiration
    - they are a celebration of life
    - they render Christ's birth in a sense irrelevant
    - they have the power to defy death
    - they are united like a conquering army
    - they can overcome any threat.

51. *Possible answers include:*

    - positive ("vanished … yet not vanished")
    - uplifted, inspired ("…they wind/the life of men…")
    - confident, safe ("laughter ringing them round like a guard")
    - saddened, depressed ("vanished … end … winter").

52. Answers should focus on how the poet "transforms the ordinary". Of the poems on the set list, the most profitable will be: "In the Snack-bar" or "Winter" or "Good Friday". It is acceptable in this question to write about a poem by Morgan which is not on the set list.

    General instructions for marking this question are given on page 171.

Text 4 — Poetry — *Visiting Hour* by Norman MacCaig

53. *Possible answers include:*

    - "combs my nostrils" – sense of irritation
    - "bobbing along" – uneven movement
    - "green and yellow corridors" – association with sickness, nausea
    - "seems a corpse" – uncertain. disorientated
    - "vanishes" – sense of mystery
    - "I will not feel, I will not/feel, until/I have to" – jerky rhythm conveys tension, disorientation.

54. *Possible answers include:*

    - admiration of their calmness
    - respect for their ability to cope with death/suffering
    - appreciation of their bright, uncomplaining approach/attitude.

55. *Possible answers include:*

    - "white cave of forgetfulness" – comparison of room to a "cave" conveys idea of seclusion, isolation from rest of world
    - "trembles on its stalk" – comparison of arm to "stalk" conveys its thinness, fragility
    - "a glass fang is fixed,/not guzzling but giving" – comparison of drip to a "fang" creates ghoulish/ slightly amusing idea of vampire in reverse
    - "the distance of pain" – suggests that pain can in some way be measured and that he is aware of how much she is suffering.

56. There are many possible responses and each has to be judged on its merits. Better answers will explore the oxymoron of "fruitless fruits" and/or the futility of "books that will not be read" and/or the impact of "only". Some sense of the speaker's mood/feelings should be included.

57. Answers should focus on the way strong emotion is presented and explored in *Visiting Hour* and another poem by MacCaig. Of the poems on the set list, the most profitable will be: *Aunt Julia* or *Memorial* or *Sounds of the Day* or, to a lesser degree, *Assisi*.

    General instructions for marking this question are given on page 171.

SECTION 2 – Critical Essay

Please see the assessment criteria for the Critical Essay on page 169.

NATIONAL 5 ENGLISH
MODEL PAPER 3

READING FOR UNDERSTANDING, ANALYSIS AND EVALUATION

1. *Any two of the following:*
   - the bluntness/brevity/content of the opening sentence
   - "hundreds of others" is emphasised by use of parenthesis
   - the use of the colon isolates or enforces the pause before "Soweto"
   - the positioning of "Soweto" gives a climactic effect.

2. *Any three of the following for 1 mark each:*
   - because of the law/rule enforcing/requiring use of Afrikaans in schools
   - because they saw this as offensive/demeaning
   - because this came on top of other examples of poor treatment
   - because loss of language means loss of free thought
   - because they were generally being downtrodden, denied freedom.

3. *Any four of the following for 1 mark each:*
   - he stood up to authority
   - although he was weak, he showed he was not afraid
   - his story illustrated that there is suffering/hardship everywhere
   - he gave inspiration to young black South Africans
   - they were amazed that the book/story had not been prohibited
   - his creator seemed to understand human suffering.

4. 1 mark for selection of word and 1 for comment. *Any two of the following:*
   - "frail" – suggests undernourished, etc
   - "courageous" – suggests he was willing to stand up for himself, etc
   - "oppression" – suggests he suffered severely at the hands of his masters
   - "slave labour" – suggests he was treated cruelly, unfairly, inhumanely, etc
   - "thin rations" – suggests the extreme meagreness of his food
   - "cruel" – suggests vindictive, spiteful nature of his enemies
   - "taunts" – suggests the malicious, aggressive behaviour of his enemies.

5. It introduces an explanation of the way in which they "took Oliver to heart".

6. *Any four of the following for 1 mark each (may be in bullet point form or in prose):*
   - his books were shared among many people
   - there was a waiting list for his books
   - he inspired the formation of a committee dedicated to improving conditions among young black people
   - his characters were known well, referred to by name
   - he connected people to the great books of the world
   - he was chosen as favourite by Hugh Masakela on *Desert Island Discs*.

7. *Any two of the following for 1 mark each:*
   - they were not interested in black people improving themselves
   - they were actively opposed to black people improving themselves
   - they were tyrannical, vicious, over-severe in punishment
   - they were ruthless
   - they were dishonest/corrupt (the charge of "violence" for a non-violent act.

8. (a) • (first) the idea of grandparents carrying out initial education then strongly encouraging as much learning as possible
   - (second) the idea of encouraging isolated/primitive peoples to understand/have control over their own world/environment
   - (third) the idea of using your own language to learn about your own world.

   (b) 1 mark for selection of word or feature and 1 mark for comment.
   Any two of the following:
   - "love" – shows books were treated with respect, passion, devotion, etc
   - "inspire" – suggests leading towards something uplifting, etc
   - "mentor" – idea of helpful, inspirational teacher
   - "spent a lifetime" – idea of dedication, devotion to a worthy cause
   - "future" – suggests hope, improvement, etc
   - short sentence "And they got it." – triumphant tone
   - "sacrifices" – suggests a worthwhile, if costly, course of action, done for the benefit of others
   - "applaud" – idea of approval, support, etc.

NATIONAL 5 ENGLISH 2014

READING FOR UNDERSTANDING, ANALYSIS AND EVALUATION

1. Candidates should paraphrase "wretchedly indulgent".

   - eg appallingly/dreadfully/extremely/shamefully – ie appreciation of the intensifying function of "wretchedly"
   - eg (over-) tolerant/libertarian/lenient/non-disciplinarian (accept colloquial "soft")
   - 1 mark for reference to "revisiting one's own childhood" (eg comparing one's own childhood).

2. Candidates should identify the structural link, but may do so in either direction

   Selection and identified reference from examples below – no "mix and match"

   or

   Selection identified as looking back

   Selection identified as looking forward

   - "When I was little" looks back to (idea of) "one's own childhood"
   - "given no choices" looks forward to (list of words suggesting) idea of compulsion/(comparative) deprivation
   - "I could only choose what to read" looks forward to "we had all the books we could read".

3. Candidates should draw inferences from the writer's use of language to show appreciation of this important idea

   Word choice

   - "only once" suggests rarity of eating out
   - "motorway café" implies moderately-priced venue
   - "wincing" suggests pained reaction to perceived expense
   - "wincing" or "stomach-churning" suggests repellent nature of comestibles
   - "spag bol" suggests cheap option
   - "From the children's menu" suggests limitation of choice
   - "mainly spent "wooding" for winter fuel" suggests lack of facilities/choice/spartan nature of activity
   - "on rainswept hillsides" suggests spartan nature of activity
   - "(father would invariably book) cheap (overnight ferry crossings)" suggests thrift/parsimony
   - "He would never shell out for a cabin" suggests thrift/parsimony
   - "there was nothing to do for weeks on end except rake leaves" suggests lack of facilities/choice/spartan nature of activity.

   Sentence structure

   - (idea of) minor sentence or brevity of "From the children's menu" complements idea of lack of choice/adds emphasis

   - (idea of parenthetical) insertion of "mainly spent "wooding" for winter fuel on rainswept hillsides" illustrates/develops/exemplifies idea of lack of facilities/choice.

4. Candidates should offer a gloss of both words and a correct analytic comment

   - "benign" (eg kind/caring/compassionate/well-meant)
   - "neglect (eg ignoring/leaving alone/not paying attention to, but synonym should not have critical connotation);
   - (idea of) paradox/oxymoron/contrast.

5. Candidates will make selections and offer correct explanations of their effect – these require the drawing of inferences from connotations and/or nuances

   - "manic (mum)" suggests/indicates excess/(near-) insanity
   - "(calls herself a) Tiger Mother" suggests excessive competitiveness/ambition
   - "produce" suggests parenthood being analogous to a manufacturing process
   - Any part of "straight-A …superkids" suggests excessive ambition
   - "pushy" suggests assertiveness/forcefulness
   - "anxious" suggests over-concern/worry/angst
   - "helicopter parents" or "hover" suggests excessive proximity/involvement
   - "mothers pulled out their sons because the weather forecast was 'rainy'" suggests over-protectiveness/feather-bedding
   - "traumatic" suggests deleterious effect of parental involvement
   - "over-involvement" states excess/inappropriateness of parental attachment
   - "mummies and daddies" allows the inference that (eg) parental view of relationship is inappropriate.

6. Comment may express approval or disapproval.

   Candidates may comment on expression of

   - diversity
   - high achievement
   - preternatural quality
   - hyphenation
   - the effect of a list.

7. Candidates have to select and comment upon aspects of the writer's use of language, to show (inferred) understanding of the father's attitude.

   Apparent attitude:

   - Uses the word "great" **or** an exclamation mark **or** "cried" to suggest enthusiasm.

   Actual attitude:

   - did not miss a beat" suggests calmness
   - "astutely" suggests wisdom
   - "if he approved the plan, I would never carry it out" shows (inferable) disapproval.

8. Candidates have to identify two similarities, either by specific reference or expression of more generalised comparisons.

   Possible examples include:

   - undergoing training/going on courses/taking classes in it
   - childcare vouchers
   - aims imposed by government/rules
   - professional advice/support eg online
   - sources of advice
   - idea of multiplicity of activities
   - idea of diversity of activities
   - idea of constantly being on duty
   - idea of bureaucratic vigilance.

9. Candidates have to recognise and restate key points.

   Any five points from:

   Then

   Glosses of

   - "we were given no choices" eg children were not given options/consulted
   - "There was not so much stuff" eg children had fewer possessions
   - "we made our own fun" eg children entertained themselves
   - "Our parents provided us with the essentials" eg care was basic , parents were not so generous
   - "then got on with their own lives" eg parents were more remote/hands-off
   - "there was not the expectation of having every wish granted" eg children did not anticipate being given everything they wanted
   - "My parents were so hard-up" eg reference to spartan holiday travel and activities
   - "Keeping children busy and happy was not a parental priority" eg parents' first concern was not their children's pleasure
   - Lack of school "involvement" eg skimpy attention paid to reports, non-attendance at meetings
   - "It was the complete opposite in my day" eg lack of involvement pre-tertiary education
   - "Becoming a mother or father is no longer something you just are" eg people discovered what to do as they went along.

   Now

   Glosses of

   - "wretchedly indulgent state of modern parenting" eg parents are excessively lenient/lax/soft
   - "many of my son's 15-year-old friends have iPods, iPads, MacBooks ... Pay Pal, eBay and iTunes accounts" eg children have many/a variety of modern devices
   - "unlimited access to their parents' credit cards" eg children are given a great deal of/excessive financial extravagance
   - "I can't repeat this sensible regime ..." eg parents are unable to be as removed as hers were

   - "examples of 'wet parenting' abound" eg there are many instances of excessive/over-indulgent/over-protective behaviour
   - "(traumatic level of) parental over-involvement just at the exact moment that mummies and daddies are supposed to be letting go" eg parents are too concerned/interfering/hands-on when their children are older
   - "Parenting is something you do ... has become subsidised and professionalised" eg parents now are more rule-bound/have more people telling them what to do.

NATIONAL 5 ENGLISH
2014

CRITICAL READING

SECTION 1 — Scottish Text

SCOTTISH TEXT — DRAMA

Text 1 — Drama — *Bold Girls* by Rona Munro

1. Candidates should show how the word choice and/or sentence structure create the impression that Marie's daily life is demanding.

   (The volume/range of work she has to do and the general lack of resources is likely to be commented upon.)

   1 mark for selection of relevant quotation about **word choice**.

   1 mark for appropriate comment. 1 mark for selection of relevant reference to **sentence structure**.

   1 mark for appropriate comment.

   #### Examples of word choice include:

   - use of plural on "irons" and "boards" suggests volume of work
   - "piles" suggests the scale of the work to be undertaken
   - "waiting to be smoothed" (personification) suggests demanding nature of house work
   - Description of toys in different states of repair suggests the never ending cycle of pace of life
   - "swallowed up the year's savings" suggests money is tight
   - "pots and pans and steam..." suggests the multiplicity of the tasks to be done
   - "always hot" suggests the relentlessness of the chores
   - "furniture bald with age" suggests lack of money
   - "gleaming clean" suggests how hard Marie works/ house proud
   - "never deserted" suggests little peace
   - "too stuffed" suggests it is cramped
   - "clutter of housework" suggests she never gets to the end of her work
   - "picture of the virgin" suggests she is religious
   - "blown-up photo" suggests sentimentality.

   #### Examples of sentence structure include:

   - repeated use of "It's" suggests immediacy of domestic life
   - use of complex sentences suggests the scale of the work she does
   - use of semi-colons for expansion of detail intensifies demanding nature of Marie's remit.

2. Deirdre's words and actions create a bleak mood/ atmosphere. Candidates should demonstrate understanding of this through reference to and comment upon one aspect of the **stage directions** and one aspect of her dialogue.

   1 mark for selection of relevant quotation about stage directions.

   1 mark for appropriate comment.

   1 mark for selection of relevant quotation about **dialogue**.

   1 mark for appropriate comment.

   #### Examples of stage directions include:

   - "not in this room" suggests she is an outsider (not part of community)
   - "crouching on all fours" suggests she is afraid/or in a hostile environment
   - "darkness" suggests bleakness
   - "only her face is visible" suggests mystery/ concealment
   - "wary" suggests suspicion/danger
   - "black-out" at the end of her speech suggests she is an outsider/builds tension.

   #### Examples of dialogue include:

   - "sun going down" suggests literally lack of light/ metaphorically lack of hope
   - "sky is grey" suggests bleakness/dullness/lack of interest
   - "hills...green" suggests a contrasting brighter setting
   - "I can't hardly see them..." suggests she is cut off from (more) appealing setting
   - "stones" suggests coldness/harshness
   - repetition of "grey" suggests drabness/hopelessness
   - "Somewhere a bird is singing" suggests her environment lacks natural beauty/suggests she knows there is something better elsewhere.
   - "ice cream van" suggests a nostalgia for the past
   - "helicopter overhead" suggests military action/ urban policing/crime
   - "I hear the ice cream van... and the helicopter overhead" suggests the contrast between daily life and extreme circumstances...

3. (a) Candidates must identify Marie's attitude, eg. she treats him kindly **or** is willing to discipline him.

   Candidates might provide an example of her kindness and an example of discipline.

   #### Examples of kindness include:

   - asks him about the flavour of the crisps he wanted
   - tells him he can swap them
   - deals with him immediately ("hurls the bag")
   - she explains her decisions to him.

   #### Examples of discipline include:

   - she restricts the intake of his food
   - she tells him to pick up the crisps
   - she tells him not to be "so bold".

   (b) 1 mark for identification of/comment on Marie's attitude – eg. she accepts that she has a lot of work to do/tries to do all her chores speedily/successfully.

   Candidates should quote and comment on any one aspect of Marie's efficiency.

   1 mark for identification/comment and one mark for relevant quotation.

   or

   Relevant summary of Marie's attitude (without quotation) towards her daily routine – up to 2 marks.

Examples of Marie's efficiency include:

- "starts two jobs simultaneously" suggests competence/skill
- "First…then" suggests a logical approach to her tasks/running order
- "needs ironing and what doesn't" suggests an economy of effort/doesn't do needless jobs
- "sorts a few items then starts peeling potatoes" suggests the range of tasks to be undertaken
- "all her movements have a frenetic efficiency" suggests her competence in all respects.

4. Candidates should identify areas of difficulty in the characters' lives from this extract and elsewhere in the play.

Possible areas for comment are:

- the setting of the play is bleak and there is the constant threat of violence
- the women do not have a lot of money and struggle to make ends meet
- the women do not have a male figure at home to help them with family life
- the community in which they live is intrusive and there is a lack of privacy
- the women have committed immoral acts which they hide from others
- the women have dreams and aspirations beyond what they can secure.

Candidates may choose to answer in **bullet points** in this final question, or write a number of linked statements. There is **no requirement** to write a 'mini essay'.

Up to 2 marks can be achieved for identifying elements of **commonality** as identified in the question.

A further 2 marks can be achieved for **reference to the extract given.**

4 additional marks can be awarded for similar references to **at least one other part of the text** by the writer.

In practice this means:

Identification of commonality (eg: theme, central relationship, importance of setting, use of imagery, development in characterisation, use of personal experience, use of narrative style, or any other key element…)

from the extract:

1 × relevant reference to technique

1 × appropriate comment

or

1 × relevant reference to idea

1 × appropriate comment

or

1 × relevant reference to feature

1 × appropriate comment

or

1 × relevant reference to text

1 × appropriate comment

(maximum of 2 marks only for discussion of extract)

from **at least one other part of the text:**

as above (× 2) for **up to 4 marks**

Text 2 — Drama — *Sailmaker* by Alan Spence

5. Any two key points.

Candidates are expected to use their own words.

Possible answers include:

- Davie comes home drunk
- Alec is worried
- Alec is annoyed
- Alec complains about the state of the house
- Davie tries to defend the way things are
- Alec becomes frustrated that his father will not move on with his life and challenges him
- Davie will not admit his interest in the woman he has met in the pub
- Davie slaps Alec for his rudeness/directness …
- Alec is left reflecting on the way his relationship with his father has changed/broken down
- Alec is trying to remember something but is unsure what it is.

6. (a) Candidates should identify or comment on an appropriate feeling.

This feeling should be supported by an appropriate quotation or reference.

Possible answers include:

Alec is feeling angry/frustrated/let down …

Evidence might include:

- Alec criticises the untidy/unclean house – "Look at the state ae us"/"livin like bloody Steptoe and Son"/"Place is like a midden"/"When did we last gie it a good clean?"/"Needs gutted"
- Alec is annoyed that the electricity has been cut off – "Nae light"
- Alec criticises Davie for going to the pub instead of taking responsibility – "ye go an get bevvied"
- Alec is frustrated that Davie seems to like women but won't commit to a relationship – "That was no lady, that was a really nice person"
- Alec's sarcastic tone conveys his frustration – stage direction
- Alec's question reflects his frustration – "Why don't ye just admit that ye fancy her?".

(b) Candidates should identify at least two appropriate feelings

One quotation or reference to language technique (1 mark)

Appropriate comment about feeling (1 mark)

Possible answers include:

Davie is feeling upset/resigned/defensive/fleetingly positive or cheerful/ultimately angry …

Evidence might include:

- defends his lack of cleaning – "It's hard son"/"It's no easy on yer own"
- defensive with Alec when he mentions going to the pub – "Ye'd think ah came in steamin every night"
- feels he is entitled to a night out – "Nae harm in it"
- emphasises that by repeating it in lines 7 and 15

- cheerful when he remembers the evening and the singing – "Wee sing song"/"That lassie's a rare singer"
- angry with Alec at the end (perhaps because Alec's challenge is uncomfortable for him) – stage directions – "slaps him, exits".

7. Alec's state of mind should be justified with reference to an example of word-choice

and

appropriate comment

and

Alec's state of mind should be justified with identification of a feature of sentence structure and appropriate comment

Both word-choice and sentence structure should be justified for full marks.

Possible answers include:

Alec is confused/regretful

Word-choice:

- repetition of "somethin"/"something" vagueness suggest he is confused/seeking answers
- "sometimes" again suggests lack of pattern in his life /confusion
- "lost"/"looking for" suggests he is confused /seeking answers ...
- language is mostly English – he has moved on/ changed and doesn't understand this/thinks he no longer belongs ...

Sentence Structure:

- three questions suggests he is looking for answers
- use of ellipsis struggling to find the words to finish the sentence
- short/abrupt sentence – "God knows" suggests he cannot work out what has gone wrong
- series of short sentences/questions thoughts are not flowing well/confused ideas.

8. Candidates should identify the way in which Alec has changed with reference to this extract and to elsewhere in the play.

Both sides of the change (eg. working class to middle class/using Scots to English/school to university) should be identified for 1 mark.

Supporting evidence /comment for each side can be rewarded with 1 mark each.

- Alec has become more (openly) critical of his father/ has lost respect for him.
- he becomes increasingly more responsible and mature
- Alec becomes more distant from his father and more of a contrast to him
- ultimately, the roles reverse and Alec becomes more like the father in the relationship
- however, Alec still feels something is missing in his life.

Extract: Alec is critical of his father

Elsewhere:
At start of play Alec shows a lot of respect and admiration for his father especially in his conversations with Ian in Act 1 where he boasts of his dad's sailmaking skills and shows off his dad's tools. He also has faith in his father that he will fix the yacht that he also shows to Ian.

Extract: Alec criticises his father's drinking

Elsewhere:
Earlier in Act 1 Alec says to Davie 'You've been drinkin. I can smell it.' But that is all he says – he simply makes a statement; he does not criticise or antagonise Davie further about it.

Extract: relationship is at its lowest point as Alec is very critical and Davie ends up slapping him

Elsewhere:
Earlier in Act 2 – Alec criticises his dad's cooking so there are signs of this side of Alec before now

End of play – Alec finally questions Davie about why he gambles which he always just accepted before

End of play – Alec tells Davie he plans to move out

Prior to this event in the extract, Alec tells of a time Davie teased him about a girl to the extent Alec was so angry he hit his father; the complete opposite of what has happened here highlighting the role reversal

Extract: it is Alec who criticises the state of the house

Elsewhere:
Twice in Act 1 – at start and later on – it is Davie who comments on the state of the house – not Alec and Alec never responds showing he had no interest/this wasn't his concern before

Alec also shows his maturity and sense of responsibility when he offers Davie the money for the electricity bill.

It is also Alec who suggests burning the furniture at the end of the play to keep warm, showing his ability to present solutions to problems

Extract: Alec still questions what he has lost, what is missing from his life

Elsewhere:
Earlier, Alec has similar thoughts after the argument with Davie about his cooking

Also, earlier in the play, Alec turns to religion to try to fill a gap in his life and has doubts about his reasons for his interest in the church

Candidates may choose to answer in **bullet points** in this final question, or write a number of linked statements. There is **no requirement** to write a 'mini essay'.

Up to 2 marks can be achieved for identifying elements of **commonality** as identified in the question.

A further 2 marks can be achieved for **reference to the extract given.**

4 additional marks can be awarded for similar references to **at least one other part of the text** by the writer.

In practice this means:

Identification of commonality (eg: theme, central relationship, importance of setting, use of imagery, development in characterisation, use of personal experience, use of narrative style, or any other key element…)

from the extract:

1 × relevant reference to technique

1 × appropriate comment

or

1 × relevant reference to idea

1 × appropriate comment

or

1 × relevant reference to feature

1 × appropriate comment

or

1 × relevant reference to text

1 × appropriate comment

(maximum of 2 marks only for discussion of extract)

from **at least one other part of the text:**

as above (× 2) for up to 4 marks

Text 3 — Drama — *Tally's Blood* by Ann Marie de Mambro

9. (a) Candidates should identify two stereotypes then explain how they are shown to be false.

   - Rosinella says Italian men are willing to work hard/ no one works as hard as them
   - but Hughie is shown to be working hard/Hughie is described as "working like a trojan"
   - Rosinella says that "Nobody loves their families like the Italians"
   - but Hughie is shown to love his mum by going home to sit with her **or** Bridget is willing to help her brother out with his wedding preparations because his mum can't
   - Rosinella criticises Hughie's brother (and in effect all Scottish men) for drinking
   - but then Massimo reaches for the wine **or** Hughie refuses a drink.

   (b) Identification of reaction (1 mark)

   Explanation/justification (1 mark)

   - think it is funny
   - think it is ironic
   - think Rosinella is stupid/prejudiced for saying it
   - they might be angry
   - any other appropriate audience reaction accepted with explanation.

10. (a) Identify two examples of Rosinella's kindness/caring

   - offers Hughie food
   - knows Rigatoni is Hughie's favourite
   - gives Hughie money for a present for his brother
   - is interested in/asks about Hughie's family
   - calls Hughie "son".

   (b) Identify two examples of Rosinella's unkindness/ unpleasantness.

   - suggests Hughie's brother has got his fiancée pregnant
   - assumes Bridget is going out to see a man but calls it 'winching' to cheapen it
   - Lucia is too scared to ask her something (to go to the wedding)

   - suggests that Bridget will never get married
   - suggests that Hughie's brother will be out drinking days after his wedding
   - doesn't realise that neither Massimo or Lucia are interested in her conversation
   - keeps insisting that she is 'right' in the things she is saying
   - Rosinella makes prejudiced statements.

11. Candidates are asked to identify two examples:

   'wee bit'/'up the road'/'winching'/'up to it'/'am n't'/'poke'/'wee'/'pals'/'son'/'mammy'/'give's a hand'/'Hang on a minute'/'Help them out'/'shooshes'

12. Candidates should discuss how racism is explored in this extract and elsewhere in the play.

   Possible answers may include:

   - Rosinella's comments from elsewhere about Italians (always positive) eg makes you special, makes you more attractive, etc
   - Rosinella's comments from elsewhere about Scots (usually negative) eg can't look after their children properly, allow their girls to go out unsupervised, have looser moral standards, etc
   - Rosinella's racism towards Bridget when she is dating Franco
   - Rosinella's racism towards Hughie when he is in love with Lucia
   - the treatment of Massimo by the public at the outbreak of war/when his shop is attacked
   - the treatment of the Italian people who were taken during the war
   - Rosinella's refusal to let go of what happened to them during the war
   - Lucia's mimicry of the school teacher showing the racism she has suffered
   - there may be valid comments about the war itself as an example of Nationalism becoming racism.

   Candidates may choose to answer in **bullet points** in this final question, or write a number of linked statements. There is **no requirement** to write a 'mini essay'.

   Up to 2 marks can be achieved for identifying elements of commonality as identified in the question.

   A further 2 marks can be achieved for **reference to the extract given.**

   4 additional marks can be awarded for similar references to **at least one other part of the text** by the writer.

   <u>In practice this means:</u>

   Identification of commonality (eg: theme, central relationship, importance of setting, use of imagery, development in characterisation, use of personal experience, use of narrative style, or any other key element…)

   from the extract:

   1 × relevant reference to technique

   1 × appropriate comment

   or

   1 × relevant reference to idea

   1 × appropriate comment

or

1 × relevant reference to feature

1 × appropriate comment

or

1 × relevant reference to text

1 × appropriate comment

(maximum of 2 marks only for discussion of extract)

from at least one other part of the text:

as above (× 2) for up to 4 marks

SCOTTISH TEXT — PROSE

Text 1 — Prose — *The Cone Gatherers* by Robin Jenkins

13. Both emotions for full marks.
    - at first delight/happiness
    - then fear for the animals

14. Can have either aspect for full marks or implied recognition of contrast.

    "marvellous grace and agility" plus comment

    or

    "flew for the doom ahead" plus comment

    or

    Accept grace/doom. Accept a gloss on: they were very beautiful, but they were going to be killed anyway.

15. *Any two from:*
    - "Moaning"
    - "gasping"
    - "Impulse"
    - "Not … so swift and sure of foot"
    - "He fell and rose again"
    - "avoided one tree (only to collide with another close to it)".

16. Two quotations with references and associated comments:
    - "Wails of lament" distress being loudly expressed
    - "Dashed on at demented speed" dashed suggests speed of his movement; demented as though he is mad
    - "A deer screaming" suggests the terror of the animal
    - "Scrabbling around on its hindquarters" the struggle of the wounded animal to escape
    - "Calum saw no one else" unheeding of anything but the animal
    - "Screaming in sympathy" loud distress shared by Calum
    - "Terrified more than ever" implies losing control through fear
    - "It dragged him about with it" creature in its agony instinctively trying to escape, even with Calum holding it.
    - "In mortal agony" unaware of anything but its death throes.
    - "heedless of the danger of being shot" emphasising that he is in such a panic that his personal safety is not important to him.

17. We would expect him to be angry but instead he seems to be enjoying what he is seeing.

    or

    The others are horrified but he is laughing.

    or

    He has planned this so is pleased.

18. Candidates should discuss the portrayal of Duror in this extract and elsewhere in the novel.

    This passage is a culmination of Duror's plot to get rid of the cone gathering brothers, Callum and Neil. The passage holds a great deal of information but we will focus on the parts specifically pertaining to Duror.

    Throughout the novel there is an irrational animosity towards Callum and Neil, but mainly Callum displayed by the gamekeeper, Duror and this passage is the watershed which signals his descent into madness.

    His intention had been to use the deer hunt as a means to cause Callum harm or distress resulting in a more overt obsession.

    He has an obsessive hatred for Callum because he has detested anything misshapen since his younger days and this has manifested itself in his disgust of his bedridden wife whom he cannot even touch.

    He is embittered because of the situation he finds himself in including his relationships with his mother in law, his repeated rejection by the army as this is set during the war and his sense of frustration towards his employer Lady Runcie-Campbell whom he desires but it is a one sided desire.

    L5 **Duror caught sight of them and rushed in pursuit** this is a literal pursuit in the extract but is also the pursuit of his goal to get rid of the brothers throughout the novel, an irrational pursuit.

    L17 **The dogs barked fiercely** and **Duror fired his gun** the word choice of barked fiercely and fired contrasts with words to describe Callum in this extract such as **silent** and **desperate**.

    L22 **Duror bawled to his dogs** a line filled with hard sounding consonants and plosives

    By his would be attack on the brother, it is as if he is simultaneously acting unnaturally and attacking nature itself. This is evident through the word choice of **screaming** to describe the noise made by both Callum and the deer.

    Not only is Callum associated with animal symbolism, Duror himself latterly in the novel can be seen as embodying evil and darkness and in this rural setting can be seen to represent the serpent from the Garden of Eden. It is paradoxical in that his role within the novel is as a gamekeeper on a large estate who should maintain control of the animals.

    At the end of this extract, Duror **came leaping out of the wood** and **seemed to be laughing in some kind of berserk joy**. This overt display of madness contrasts with the reactions of the other witnesses to this event, Captain Forgan, Young Roderick and Lady Runcie-Campbell who are standing **petrified**.

    His abnormal reaction foreshadows his descent into madness and irrational behaviour which leads ultimately to the tragic ending, the murder of Callum and his own suicide.

Candidates may choose to answer in **bullet points** in this final question, or write a number of linked statements. There is **no requirement** to write a 'mini essay'.

Up to 2 marks can be achieved for identifying elements of **commonality** as identified in the question.

A further 2 marks can be achieved for **reference to the extract given**.

4 additional marks can be awarded for similar references to **at least one other part of the text** by the writer.

In practice this means:

Identification of commonality (eg: theme, central relationship, importance of setting, use of imagery, development in characterisation, use of personal experience, use of narrative style, or any other key element…)

from the extract:

1 × relevant reference to technique

1 × appropriate comment

or

1 × relevant reference to idea

1 × appropriate comment

or

1 × relevant reference to feature

1 × appropriate comment

or

1 × relevant reference to text

1 × appropriate comment

(maximum of 2 marks only for discussion of extract)

from **at least one other part of the text:**

as above (× 2) for up to 4 marks

Text 2 — Prose — *The Testament of Gideon Mack* by James Robertson

19. Full marks can be obtained in a variety of ways – by making four brief points or by making fewer, more developed points for multiple marks, adding up to 4.

Possible answers include:

- freedom ('took me out of myself'/'minister off the leash') with supplementary points about forgetting about job and wider world problems
- released energy inside him , perhaps with explanation of the candidate's understanding of what that means
- rebellion against his disapproving parishioners
- vanity, as he thinks he looks good or runs well
- loses himself in it to the point that he notices the different sounds his trainers make on different surfaces
- increased awareness and appreciation of surroundings
- sense of living life to the full.

20. 1 mark for attitude and 1 mark for appropriate evidence

Attitude identified is likely to be negative eg not committed, even interested/sees it as a burden/sees himself as a hypocrite etc.

Plus appropriate evidence.

21. (a) Example (1 mark)

NB 1 mark for each example given

or

One well developed explanation could gain all 3 marks at once.

Possible answers include:

- **extended sentence** in first paragraph **giving** all the alternative reasons for running
- using the **repetition** of 'not'/**parenthesis** adding weight to each point
- **simple sentence** to emphasise his real reason for running
- the word 'but' indicates a change in direction
- **italics** for emphasis of the word 'needed'
- **repetition** (of the sentence starter 'I ran') to emphasise how much/how freely he ran
- **use of semicolons** to separate the things he can ignore when running to emphasise the freedom from worry.

(b) Identification of image (1 mark)

Brief comment on image (1 mark)

Relation of image to running (1 mark)

Possible answers include:

- 'as if the fire blazing away in there was my fuel' suggests that the energy/heat he refers to is what is propelling him when he runs just as petrol/fuel propels a car/machinery /feels he has to run/is able to run because of this energy.
- 'emptied my head of work, the Kirk, the world' suggests that running is removing his worries from his head Mack feels free when running.
- 'difficult issues and awkward individuals were' suggests the issues and people were pushed back which removes his worries /allows him to feel free when he is running.
- 'their ghosts faded into the trees' suggests his problems disappeared from his mind when running. Mack feels free and relaxed when running.

22. Candidates should discuss one aspect of Gideon Mack's character with reference to this extract and elsewhere in the novel.

Possible answers may include:

Need to escape
Extract: *When I set off…I could feel the disapproval of some of my parishioners*
Elsewhere in novel: mountains/B and B…

Reluctance to conform
Extract: *there was something just no richt about a minister in shorts*
Elsewhere in novel: references could include wanting to be a school teacher not a minister; funeral for Catherine Craigie; didn't believe in God; Having sex on his marital bed with Elsie…

Hypocrite
Extract: *an escapee from my professional hypocrisy, a minister off the leash*
Elsewhere in novel: *Although within I had abandoned my faith, I still attended church and remained the dutiful son of the manse*; Gideon joins the Church as a minister despite his lack of belief…

Outsider
Extract: *The loneliness of the long distance runner*; references to film.
Elsewhere in novel: References could include when he met the boys in his new school in the 1970s; dual existence – pretending to be one person to satisfy his parents while being someone else to satisfy classmates.

Represses memories/feelings
Extract: *Running emptied my head of work, the Kirk, the world*
Elsewhere in novel: references to hiding feelings; Elsie says "terrible childhood which strangled love at every turn"…

Frustrated by others
Extract: *Difficult issues and awkward individuals were repelled by the force of my energy…*
Elsewhere in novel: References to relationship with father; Peter Macmurray and his dislike of Gideon.

Candidates may choose to answer in **bullet points** in this final question, or write a number of linked statements. There is **no requirement** to write a 'mini essay'.

Up to 2 marks can be achieved for identifying elements of **commonality** as identified in the question.

A further 2 marks can be achieved for **reference to the extract given**.

4 additional marks can be awarded for similar references to **at least one other part of the text** by the writer.

In practice this means:

Identification of commonality (eg: theme, central relationship, importance of setting, use of imagery, development in characterisation, use of personal experience, use of narrative style, or any other key element…)

from the extract:
1 × relevant reference to technique
1 × appropriate comment
or
1 × relevant reference to idea
1 × appropriate comment
or
1 × relevant reference to feature
1 × appropriate comment
or
1 × relevant reference to text
1 × appropriate comment
(maximum of 2 marks only for discussion of extract)
from **at least one other part of the text:**
as above (× 2) for up to 4 marks

Text 3 — Prose — *Kidnapped* by Robert Lewis Stevenson

23. Four points to be made.
1 mark for each point.
Possible answers include:

- it is foggy
- Alan's boat is struck by the *Covenant*
- Alan's boat is split in half
- Alan's boat sinks
- the whole crew die except Alan

- Alan grabs hold of the *Covenant*'s bowspirit
- Alan is saved and brought on to the *Covenant*.

24. 1 mark for each individual point about his physical appearance and his character.

Candidates must deal with both physical appearance and character for full marks but not necessarily in equal proportion.

Possible answers include:

A gloss of **physical characteristics:**
- "smallish in stature"
- "well set"
- "nimble as a goat"
- "open expression"
- "sunburnt very dark"
- "heavily freckled"
- "pitted with the small-pox"
- "eyes were unusually light"
- (eyes had) "dancing madness"

A gloss on his **character:**
- "His manners … were elegant"
- "he pledged the captain handsomely"
- "engaging"
- "alarming"
- "rather call my friend than my enemy".

25. Candidates should show an awareness of the friction between Alan and Hoseason.

Full marks for two examples with detailed comments.

Possible answers include:

Word choice:
- "still (watching him)" emphasis of the fact that Hoseason has possibly been wary of Alan
- "(still) watching (him)" watching with connotations of careful inspection emphasising possible concern
- "Oho!" exclamatory interjection of surprise and realisation indicates friction in this context
- "(laid his hand) quickly" emphasises the suddenness of Alan's response in reaching for his pistols/ emphasises Alan's concern for his situation/action could also be seen as a response to a slight by Hoseason.
- "(Don't be) hasty" emphasises Hoseason's attempt to quell Alan, or shows his concern about what Alan may do with the pistols.

Metaphor:
- "is that how the wind sets?" emphasises Alan's perception of Hoseason's now clear antagonistic attitude towards him.

Sentence structure:
- "Oho!" exclamatory nature of the interjection
- Rhetorical question – "…is that how the wind sets?" emphasis on the fact that Alan feels he knows Hoseason's antagonistic view of him.
- Repetition of "Don't be …" emphasises Hoseason's attempt to quell Alan, or shows his concern about what Alan may do with the pistols.

26. Candidates should discuss the development of David and Alan's relationship with reference to this extract and to elsewhere in the novel.

Possible references:

The idea of 'commonality' is one which may be established in several ways. It could be made explicit in the candidate response or it could be implicitly delivered through the overall answer of the candidate for this question.

Some possible aspects of the developing relationship between David and Alan which candidates may discuss are:

- the contradictory/contrasting natures of the characters as developed throughout the text;
- tensions in the relationship as it develops throughout the text;
- the theme of duality established by looking at the relationship throughout the text;
- the admiration the characters have for each other at points throughout the texts;
- the developing movement from uncertainty towards true friendship and understanding which is developed throughout the text;
- a mixture of elements from some or all of the above.

The points above could be seen as the more accepted ideas about the relationship between David and Alan in this text. Be open to accepting well-argued points which are not included within the points above.

Candidates may choose to answer in **bullet points** in this final question, or write a number of linked statements. There is **no requirement** to write a 'mini essay'.

Up to 2 marks can be achieved for identifying elements of **commonality** as identified in the question.

A further 2 marks can be achieved f**or reference to the extract given.**

4 additional marks can be awarded for similar references to **at least one other part of the text** by the writer.

In practice this means:

Identification of commonality (eg: theme, central relationship, importance of setting, use of imagery, development in characterisation, use of personal experience, use of narrative style, or any other key element...)

from the extract:

1 × relevant reference to technique
1 × appropriate comment

or

1 × relevant reference to idea
1 × appropriate comment

or

1 × relevant reference to feature
1 × appropriate comment

or

1 × relevant reference to text
1 × appropriate comment

(**maximum of 2 marks only for discussion of extract**)
from **at least one other part of the text:**
as above (× 2) for **up to 4 marks**

Text 4 — Prose — *The Telegram* by Iain Crichton Smith

27. Example/reference to language feature with comment

Suggested examples include:

Short sentences build up the pace

Sentence structure: sentence beginning 'She had dreamt...' climactic effect

Repetitive sentence structure/'She had dreamt'; 'She could see'; 'She could never..' emphasis on the rising panic of the fat woman

Word choice: we are shown fat woman's thoughts 'Oh pray God...' etc helps us to understand her rising fear/tension/panic

Repetition of 'God'/repeated references to religion like she is praying/becoming hysterical

28. (a) Example with comment

Possible examples/explanations:

- 'lips...white and bloodless' emphasises her state of shock
- 'dreaded' emphasises the worry/panic she feels that her son may be dead.

(b) Example with comment

Possible examples/explanations:

- 'lips pressed closely together' emphasises her attempt to hold back her emotion/expression
- 'wasn't crying or shaking' not showing her emotions
- 'firm voice' does not shake with emotion.

29. Candidates should give four relevant points for 4 marks.

Must be an attempt to use own words.

Suggested answers include:

- she is poor
- struggles to feed herself and her son
- she is a widow/no husband to support her/single parent
- gloss of 'bringing up a son in a village not her own' eg an outsider
- people have been unkind/unsupportive.

30. Candidates should discuss how the writer creates sympathy for a character/characters in this story and in at least one other story by Iain Crichton Smith.

Possible references:

"Mother And Son"
John, central character – Aggression of mother (may be expressed by reference to speech, "she snapped pettishly"); sustained denigration; low self-esteem (because of being butt of others' humour); joblessness; word choice such as his life being "hell", his "loneliness" ...

"The Red Door"
Murdo, central character – His unmarried status (reluctance to enter/fear of entering a relationship); his fear of breaching convention despite desire to expand horizons; lack of academic success and clumsiness at school; he has "never been [himself]"; loneliness; unhappiness at lifestyle (repetition of "he didn't like"); the difference of the red door symbolising everything that he was not

"The Painter"
William Murray, focus of account – Ill health; incongruity of this character in a conventional, inward-looking village; the fact that the painting was destroyed by the narrator; ostracisation and banishment of painter

"The Crater"
Lt Robert Mackinnon, central character – Context of war; danger of raid, hazards of No Man's Land; responsibilities of leadership; expression of fear (emphasised by repetition); the awful appearance of the victim in the crater (eg emphasis on colour green); implication of stress shown by (unusual) swearing; irony of victim dying

"In Church"
Lt Colin Macleod, central character – General context of war; specific perception that fate is indifferent to him and his comrades; discomfiting character of (lunatic) "priest"; ending where (defenceless) central character is murdered

Candidates may choose to answer in **bullet points** in this final question, or write a number of linked statements. There is **no requirement** to write a 'mini essay'.

Up to 2 marks can be achieved for identifying elements of **commonality** as identified in the question.

A further 2 marks can be achieved for **reference to the extract given**.

4 additional marks can be awarded for similar references to **at least one other short story** by the writer.

In practice this means:

Identification of commonality (eg: theme, central relationship, importance of setting, use of imagery, development in characterisation, use of personal experience, use of narrative style, or any other key element...)

from the extract:
1 × relevant reference to technique
1 × appropriate comment
or
1 × relevant reference to idea
1 × appropriate comment
or
1 × relevant reference to feature
1 × appropriate comment
or
1 × relevant reference to text
1 × appropriate comment
(maximum of 2 marks only for discussion of extract)
from **at least one other short story by the writer:**
as above (× 2) for **up to 4 marks**

Text 5 – Prose – *Away in a Manger* by Anne Donovan

31. Candidates should make two clear points
Must make an attempt to use own words.
    - the family go to see the nativity
    - in George Square
    - the mother explains the scene
    - a homeless man has climbed inside the crib to escape the cold
    - they think he is an angel.

32. Identification or exemplification of technique with comment
Possible answers could include:
    - **Personification**/'staunin' suggests bronze statues are brought to life/which makes them seem more like ordinary human beings.
    - **Metaphor**/the straw is described as a carpet as something familiar (we would see in the home).
    - **Simile**/'what looked like a hoose made of glass'. The manger/crib is surrounded by a glass screen. This is compared again to the ordinary or familiar, the 'hoose' again making it seem less unusual.

Candidate may refer to Amy from lines 11–29.

Possible answers could include:
    - questions show that she does not know who they are
    - use of dash in line 12 or 14 indicates pause for recognition
    - italics (in line 15) for emphasis
    - statements followed by question
    - exclamation marks (in line 29) for emotion/recognition.

33. Identification of language feature (1 mark)
Comment on its effect (1 mark)
    - Omission of capital letters/full stops creates the impression of changes of mind.
    - Use of commas (creates pauses), giving us the impression of an idea being challenged/altered/thought through.
    - Sentence structures suggest/sound like someone speaking (out loud).
    - Opening statement 'Sandra wisnae very religious' is then qualified with, 'no religious at all,' then a second time in, 'really'. The final part of the sentence then acts as explanation (that, despite her lack of religious conviction, 'it was nice for wee ones tae have a crib').
    - Parenthesis (line 7) – indication of thinking.

34. Two identifications of word choice with comment on effect
Possible examples of word choice include:
    - "Huddled" cold/insecure/protecting himself
    - "Hidden" doesn't want to be seen/hiding
    - "a man" no idea of age
    - "Slightly built" unhealthy/underfed
    - "Auld jeans" poverty/lack of money
    - "Thin jaicket" not suited to winter, therefore he is poor/unemployed
    - "Worn trainin shoe" poor/doesn't have a lot of money
    - "Cheapest kind" poverty
    - "Quite young" engages our sympathy/surprise
    - "Pointed face" thin/undernourished
    - "Longish dark hair" uncut as he can't afford it/reminds us of Jesus
    - "Stubbly growth covered his chin" reminds us of Jesus.
    - "Sound asleep" exhausted/tired/engages our sympathy.

35. Candidates should discuss any one theme explored in this story and in at least one other story by Donovan.

Possible references to theme:

"Away in a Manger"
Family relationships, childhood, naiveté, parent/child relationships, misunderstanding, love, generational differences, growing up, Christmas

"All that Glisters"
Family relationships, childhood, naiveté, parent/child relationships, misunderstanding, love, generational differences, growing up

"Dear Santa"
Family relationships, childhood, parent/child relationships, misunderstanding, love, growing up, Christmas

"Virtual Pals"
Childhood, naiveté, misunderstanding, growing up, love, relationships

"A Chitterin Bite"
Childhood, growing up, relationships, love

"Zimmerobics"
Relationships, generational differences

Candidates may choose to answer in **bullet points** in this final question, or write a number of linked statements. There is **no requirement** to write a 'mini essay'.

Up to 2 marks can be achieved for identifying elements of **commonality** as identified in the question.

A further 2 marks can be achieved for **reference to the extract given.**

4 additional marks can be awarded for similar references to **at least one other short story** by the writer.

<u>In practice this means:</u>

Identification of commonality (eg: theme, central relationship, importance of setting, use of imagery, development in characterisation, use of personal experience, use of narrative style, or any other key element...)

from the extract:

1 × relevant reference to technique

1 × appropriate comment

or

1 × relevant reference to idea

1 × appropriate comment

or

1 × relevant reference to feature

1 × appropriate comment

or

1 × relevant reference to text

1 × appropriate comment

(maximum of 2 marks only for discussion of extract)

from **at least one other short story by the writer:**

as above (× 2) for up to **4 marks**

SCOTTISH TEXT — POETRY

Text 1 — Poetry — *War Photographs* by Carol Ann Duffy

36. 2 marks can be awarded for two main ideas or concerns shown in stanza one.

The war photographer:

- has from become isolated from other people/needs to be alone
- has been exposed to the pain and suffering of others
- is very methodical
- feels he has a duty to inform the public about the pain he has witnessed
- has travelled to many war zones (needs more than just he is well travelled)
- has developed a pessimistic world view.

37. 4 marks can be awarded for two examples of language helping to bring out his attitude.

Example (1 mark) plus comment (1 mark) – any two will gain 4 marks.

Other examples from stanza are acceptable.

- the position of the short emphatic sentence "He has a job to do"
- suggests the photographer's professionalism/matter of fact view of his work.

or

- the need to adopt this attitude as a coping strategy given the horror of his work.
- the word choice of "... did not tremble then" suggests his need to control/suppress his feelings/ focused on his job while in the war zone
- the contrast in "though seem to now" suggests the long term emotional effect of what he witnessed abroad/having an impact on him now
- the word choice of "explode"/"nightmare heat" suggests the threat/danger
- the contrast of "Rural England" and "explode"/"nightmare heat" highlights the danger he became accustomed to in the war zone.

or

- the difficulty of re-adjusting to home
- "ordinary pain" suggests his awareness of how trivial the problems faced by people in Britain are (compared to those in the war zones)
- the word choice of "dispel" suggests how shallow/ easily addressed he feels the problems faced by people in Britain are.

38. 2 marks can be awarded for one example of dramatic language.

Example (1 mark) plus comment (1 mark)

- the positioning of the abrupt sentence "Something is happening" suggests sudden activity
- the word choice of "twist" suggests violent activity/ distorted in pain
- the ambiguity of "twist before his eyes" suggests the image being revealed but also the distressing nature of the image

- the word choice of "half formed ghost" suggests being haunted by memories/idea of memories being slowly revealed
- the word choice of "cries" suggests the anguish of the man's wife
- the use of sense words such as "blood stained"/"cries" suggests the vivacity of the memory.

39. Candidates should show an understanding of how the content of the last stanza continues ideas and/or language from the first three stanzas.

- "A hundred agonies" refers to scenes of pain and suffering mentioned earlier
- the word choice of "black and white" continues the references to the development of photographs/ suggests a truthful representation of the suffering
- the contrast in numbers – "hundred" with "five or six" continues the process of trivialising suffering/ callousness to suffering in the war zones
- the word choice of "prick with tears" is another example of the limited emotional response to the suffering in the war zone
- the juxtaposition/alliteration of "between the bath and the pre-lunch beers" suggests the brief period of concern for the suffering/suggests a contrast between the safety and comfort of life in Britain and the dangers of life in the war zone
- the word choice of "impassively" suggests the beginning of his coping strategy as he flies out to his next assignment
- the word choice of "earns his living" suggests a return of the matter of fact way of viewing his job/ beginning of his coping strategy as he returns to the war zone
- "they do not care" emphasises the indifference of people in Britain to the suffering in the war zones.

40. Candidates should show awareness of the presentation of a main character through ideas and/or language in this poem and at least one other poem by Duffy.

Candidates may refer to how the war photographer has endured an upsetting/difficult experience that has profoundly affected his view of society. This is a theme which emerges in **"Havisham"** and **"Mrs. Midas"** in which the main character has also endured such an experience.

In **"Valentine"**, the speaker is the main character. The speaker gives an account of the experience of sharing valentine's gifts.

In **"Anne Hathaway"**, the speaker is the main character. Here, she reflects on her life with her husband following his death.

In **"Originally"**, the speaker is the main character. Here she reflects on the difficulties she endured when moving from one place to another.

Candidates may choose to answer in **bullet points** in this final question, or write a number of linked statements. There is **no requirement** to write a 'mini essay'.

Up to 2 marks can be achieved for identifying elements of **commonality** as identified in the question.

A further 2 marks can be achieved for **reference to the extract given**.

4 additional marks can be awarded for similar references to **at least one other poem** by the writer.

In practice this means:

Identification of commonality (eg: theme, central relationship, importance of setting, use of imagery, development in characterisation, use of personal experience, use of narrative style, or any other key element...)

from the extract:

1 × relevant reference to technique

1 × appropriate comment

or

1 × relevant reference to idea

1 × appropriate comment

or

1 × relevant reference to feature

1 × appropriate comment

or

1 × relevant reference to text

1 × appropriate comment

(maximum of 2 marks only for discussion of extract)

from **at least one poem by the writer:**

as above (x 2) for **up to 4 marks**

Text 2 — Poetry — *In the Snack-bar* by Edwin Morgan

41. (a) Candidates should identify two of the poem's main ideas or central concerns that are introduced in this extract.

    Possible answers:

    - how the less fortunate are treated in society
    - appearance and reality
    - isolation/loneliness
    - society's selfishness/lack of interest in helping others
    - for some disabled people tasks that might seem to us to be straightforward to us can involve many potential hazards
    - public places can be full of difficulties for some disabled people
    - society fears what looks strange
    - some disabled people have no choice but to rely on strangers to help them.

    (b) Examples of use of language with comment on how it clarifies a central concern

    Possible answers:

    - use of alliteration/"cup capsizes along the formica".

    and/or

    - use of onomatopoeia/"with a dull clatter"
    - to highlight the loudness of the sound made by the old man/the fact that other customers in the snack bar would have definitely heard his attempts to stand (but do nothing to help)
    - use of contrast/"a few heads turn in the crowded evening snack bar" to highlight that though the café was full very few people were prepared to show even the slightest interest in the old man's plight.

- use of simile/"like a monstrous animal caught in a tent"
- to highlight that the old man is seen by others as a terrifying creature
- use of direct speech/"I want – to go to the – toilet" to emphasise that the old man must ask strangers to help with the necessities of life
- use of dashes/"I want – to go to the – toilet" to highlight his uncertainty/anxiety.

42. Candidates should identify the change in the poet's role between stanzas 1 and 2.

In stanza 1 the poet is a mere observer – (his only reference to himself is when he writes "I notice now his stick")

In stanza 2 the poet is a participant – (he is involved in what is going on and experiences first hand the old man's plight)

43. Candidates should comment on two ways in which the poet uses language to emphasise the difficulty of the start of the journey to the toilet.

Possible answers:

- he uses direct speech/"Give me – your arm – it's better" to emphasise the awkwardness of movement
- he says they move "Inch by inch"/reference to repetition which emphasises how slowly they move "a few yards of floor are like a landscape to be negotiated" shows how far it feels they have to travel/difficult crossing the floor is for them
- "drift"/"slow setting out"/"slow dangerous inches" suggests unfocused movement/limited progress/ threat .
- he creates a long list of all the obstacles the old man has to cope with which highlights the many everyday objects that are challenging and/or dangerous to the old man
- "concentrate my life to his" emphasises understanding of the challenges faced by the old man.

44. Candidates should show their ability to analyse the poet's characterisation by referring closely and relevantly to the text of this poem and at least one other Morgan poem.

Possible references:

In Morgan's **"In the Snack-bar"** the poet creates an interesting character – a vulnerable blind man who relies on the poet's assistance.

Other interesting characters are presented in **"Trio"** where three individuals, who embody the spirit of Christmas, are walking up Buchanan Street.

In the opening line of **"Hyena"**, Morgan creates an interesting character. 'I am waiting for you' establishes the intimidating nature of the persona. Through Morgan giving the hyena a voice, he brings the character to life by directly addressing the reader.

'Wait till he sees this but!' – Morgan's use of direct speech in **"Trio"** allows the reader to hear the excitement in the boy's voice as he anticipates the joy he will bring through his gift.

In **"Good Friday"** the drunk man is an interesting character because he openly acknowledges to a complete stranger his own lack of knowledge about Easter. This allows Morgan to explore the idea of the value of religion in modern society.

In 'Trio' all three characters are interesting because through them Morgan explores the central idea of love. He details the objects they carry and celebrates the happiness they radiate.

Candidates may choose to answer in **bullet points** in this final question, or write a number of linked statements. There is **no requirement** to write a 'mini essay'.

Up to 2 marks can be achieved for identifying elements of **commonality** as identified in the question.

A further 2 marks can be achieved for **reference to the extract given**.

4 additional marks can be awarded for similar references to **at least one other poem** by the writer.

In practice this means:

Identification of commonality (eg: theme, central relationship, importance of setting, use of imagery, development in characterisation, use of personal experience, use of narrative style, or any other key element...)

from the extract:

1 × relevant reference to technique

1 × appropriate comment

or

1 × relevant reference to idea

1 × appropriate comment

or

1 × relevant reference to feature

1 × appropriate comment

or

1 × relevant reference to text

1 × appropriate comment

(maximum of 2 marks only for discussion of extract)

from **at least one other poem by the writer:**

as above (× 2) for **up to 4 marks**

Text 3 — Poetry — *Basking Shark* by Norman MacCaig

45. Incident (1 mark)

Relevant reference to text (1 mark)

Reaction (1 mark)

At sea/rowing/sticks oar in water/disturbs/hits a shark/ shark rises up

and

disorientated "a rock where none should be"

or

threatened "rise with a slounge"

46. Two references (1 mark) with comment (1 mark)

"not too often though enough" rare occurrence but still prompted reflection

and/or

"I count as gain" valuable/thought-provoking experience

and/or

"roomsized monster with a/matchbox brain" humorous/ not that frightening/insulting

47. Upset/changed/questioned MacCaig's certainty/ perspective/view of evolution

    and

    "he shoggled me centuries back" use of humour/made MacCaig think about origins/evolution/life

    or

    "this decadent townee" thinks of his own position culturally

    or

    "Shook on a branch of his family tree" evolution/that they are different/same origin

48. *Possible answers:*

    "Swish up the dirt" disturbance of the water and disturbance of MacCaig's thoughts/views

    or

    "a spring is all the clearer" once water settles, it is clearer as are MacCaig's thoughts/views

    or

    "I saw me in one fling, emerging from the slime of everything" makes him reflect on his own origins/"slime" – primordial, viscous

49. Candidates should discuss how MacCaig uses personal experience in this poem and in at least one other poem to explore wider themes.

    Themes explored through experience:

    - the temporariness/insignificance of man
    - the relationship between man and other species, man and nature
    - the randomness of the process of evolution
    - the scale of human evolution vs species which have remained unchanged/unevolved.

    Possible references:

    "Assisi" The hypocrisy of the church/desensitization to poverty and suffering.

    "Aunt Julia" – How lack of common language prevents can be frustrating/prevent communication BUT despite this a real bond between speaker and Aunt is clear. On a wider level, this experience is a comment on the loss of some traditional aspects of Scottish heritage that is in danger of being lost.

    "Memorial" – Grief/Permanence, lack of relief from sense of loss/Impact on death and grief on the artistic process.

    "Sounds of the Day" – Impact of love and loss on the psyche/Whether experience of relationship worth the pain.

    "Visiting Hour" – Death and loss and our own attitudes towards mortality.

    Candidates may choose to answer in **bullet points** in this final question, or write a number of linked statements. There is **no requirement** to write a 'mini essay'.

    Up to 2 marks can be achieved for identifying elements of **commonality** as identified in the question.

    A further 2 marks can be achieved for **reference to the extract given**.

    4 additional marks can be awarded for similar references to **at least one other poem** by the writer.

<u>In practice this means:</u>

Identification of commonality (eg: theme, central relationship, importance of setting, use of imagery, development in characterisation, use of personal experience, use of narrative style, or any other key element…)

from the extract:

1 × relevant reference to technique

1 × appropriate comment

or

1 × relevant reference to idea

1 × appropriate comment

or

1 × relevant reference to feature

1 × appropriate comment

or

1 × relevant reference to text

1 × appropriate comment

(maximum of 2 marks only for discussion of extract)

from at least one other poem by the writer:

as above (× 2) for up to **4 marks**

Text 4 — Poetry — *Lucozade* by Jackie Kay

50. Two points for 2 marks:
    - Flowers wilt/die. This reminds her of illness/death/ being in hospital.
    - Ref to "sad chrysanthemums". Flowers don't make her happy/she thinks they are pointless.
    - Lucozade reminds her of past. This brings thoughts of possibility of death.

51. Two references with comment:
    - ref to "doctors with their white lies" she doesn't trust doctors/like being in hospital
    - ref to "Don't bring magazines, too much about size" she doesn't like media images of women/approve of diets etc
    - ref. to "groggy and low" she is down/depressed
    - ref to any of "Big brandy … meringue" doesn't approve of diets/she is unconventional/not a stereotypical mother/likes to live for moment/has her own opinions etc
    - ref to "luxury" she likes indulgence
    - ref to "grapes" she's not keen on conventions/ healthy eating
    - ref to "stop the neighbours coming" she is bored/ irritated by neighbours/small talk etc.

52. To be awarded full marks, candidates should identify through references and comments some change – eg sadness to celebration, negative to positive.

    Any three references plus acceptable comments for 6 marks.

    To gain 6 marks, both sides of change must be dealt with.

    - "sad (chrysanthemums)" she is upset
    - "weighted (down)" she is burdened/full of negative thoughts

    CHANGES TO

    - "high hospital bed" girl sees that mother is raised up/not low (connotations of being elevated)

- "light"/"radiant" positive connotations/optimistic
- "billow and whirl" full of life/energy
- "beautiful" admiration, pleasure
- "divine" elevated etc
- "(singing) an old song" good memories of the past

53. Candidates should identify a theme or themes from the poetry of Kay, and be able to show how it is explored in this poem and in at least one other poem by Kay.

Candidates are probably likely to identify one of the following themes:

Illness/death, Family Relationships, Parent/Child relationships

Possible references:

"Bed" – themes of **illness/infirmity/impending death AND/OR mother – daughter relationships**

"Gap Year" – Closeness of parent/child bond.

Candidates may also make reference to the CONTRAST between the obvious bond between the mother and daughter in **"Lucozade"** with the very different exploration of the parent/child relationships considered in **"Divorce"**, **"Keeping Orchids"** and to a lesser extent also in **"Bed"**

Candidates may choose to answer in **bullet points** in this final question, or write a number of linked statements. There is **no requirement** to write a 'mini essay'.

Up to 2 marks can be achieved for identifying elements of **commonality** as identified in the question.

A further 2 marks can be achieved for **reference to the extract given**.

4 additional marks can be awarded for similar references to **at least one other poem** by the writer.

In practice this means:

Identification of commonality (eg: theme, central relationship, importance of setting, use of imagery, development in characterisation, use of personal experience, use of narrative style, or any other key element...)

from the extract:

1 × relevant reference to technique

1 × appropriate comment

or

1 × relevant reference to idea

1 × appropriate comment

or

1 × relevant reference to feature

1 × appropriate comment

or

1 × relevant reference to text

1 × appropriate comment

(maximum of 2 marks only for discussion of extract)

from **at least one other poem by the writer:**

as above (× 2) for **up to 4 marks**

SECTION 2 – Critical Essay

Please see the assessment criteria for the Critical Essay on page 169.

Acknowledgements

Permission has been sought from all relevant copyright holders and Hodder Gibson is grateful for the use of the following:

An extract fom the article 'Reassuring message of Rowling's wizard world' taken from The Scotsman, June 2003 © The Scotsman Publications Ltd (SQP Reading for Understanding, Analysis and Evaluation pages 2 to 3);

An extract from 'Tally's Blood' by Ann Marie di Mambro, published by Education Scotland. Reprinted by permission of Ann Marie di Mambro/MacFarlane Chard Associates (SQP Critical Reading pages 2 to 3);

An extract from Bold Girls copyright © 1991 Rona Munro. Excerpted with permission of Nick Hern Books Ltd: www.nickhernbooks.co.uk (SQP Critical Reading pages 4 to 5);

An extract from ' Sailmaker' by Alan Spence. Reproduced by permission of Hodder Education (SQP Critical Reading page 6);

An extract from 'Telegram' by Iain Crichton Smith, taken from 'The Red Door: The Complete English Stories 1949-76', published by Birlinn. Reproduced by permission of Birlinn Ltd. www.birlinn.co.uk (SQP Critical Reading page 8);

An extract from 'A Chitterin' Bite' by Anne Donovan from 'Hieroglyphics and Other Stories' published by Canongate Books Ltd. (SQP Critical Reading page 10);

An extract from 'The Cone Gatherers' by Robin Jenkins published by Canongate Books Ltd. (SQP Critical Reading page 12);

An extract from 'The Testament Of Gideon Mack' (Hamish Hamilton 2006, Penguin Books 2007). Copyright © James Robertson, 2006. Reproduced by permission of Penguin Books Ltd. (SQP Critical Reading page 14 to 15);

An extract from 'Kidnapped' by Robert Louis Stevenson, published by Cassell and Company Ltd 1886. Public domain (SQP Critical Reading page 16);

The poem 'Havisham' by Carol Ann Duffy from New Selected Poems 1984-2004 (Picador, 2004). Reproduced by permission of the author c/o Rogers, Coleridge & White Ltd., 20 Powis Mews, London W11 1JN (SQP Critical Reading page 18);

The poem, 'Bed' Jackie Kay, from 'Darling: New & Selected Poems' (Bloodaxe Books, 2007) Reprinted with permission of Bloodaxe Books, on behalf of the author. www.bloodaxebooks.com (SQP Critical Reading pages 20 to 21);

The poem, 'Aunt Julia' by Norman MacCaig, is taken from 'The Poems of Norman MacCaig' edited by Ewan MacCaig, published by Polygon. Reproduced by permission of Birlinn Ltd. www.birlinn.co.uk (SQP Critical Reading pages 22 to 23);

The poem 'Trio' by Edwin Morgan, from 'New Selected Poems' published by Carcanet Press Limited 2000 (SQP Critical Reading page 24);

The article 'Superstition' by Matthew Syed © The Times/News Syndication, 1st July 2009 (Model Paper 1 Reading for Understanding, Analysis and Evaluation pages 2 to 3);

An extract from 'Bold Girls' copyright © 1991 Rona Munro. Excerpted with permission of Nick Hern Books Ltd: www.nickhernbooks.co.uk (Model Paper 1 Critical Reading pages 2 to 3);

An extract from 'Sailmaker' by Alan Spence. Reproduced by permission of Hodder Education (Model Paper 1 Critic Reading pages 4 to 5);

An extract from 'Tally's Blood' by Ann Marie di Mambro, published by Education Scotland. Reprinted by permission of Ann Marie di Mambro/MacFarlane Chard Associates (Model Paper 1 Critical Reading pages 6 to 7);

An extract from 'The Cone Gatherers' by Robin Jenkins published by Canongate Books Ltd. (Model Paper 1 Critical Reading page 8);

An extract from 'The Testament Of Gideon Mack' (Hamish Hamilton 2006, Penguin Books 2007). Copyright © James Robertson, 2006. Reproduced by permission of Penguin Books Ltd. (Model Paper 1 Critical Reading page 10);

An extract from 'Kidnapped' by Robert Louis Stevenson, published by Cassell and Company Ltd 1886. Public domain. (Model Paper 1 Critical Reading page 12);

An extract from 'Mother and Son' by Iain Crichton Smith, taken from 'The Red Door: The Complete English Stories 1949-76', published by Birlinn. Reproduced by permission of Birlinn Ltd. www.birlinn.co.uk (Model Paper 1 Critical Reading page 14);

An extract from 'Zimmerobics' by Anne Donovan, taken from 'Hieroglyphics and Other Stories' published by Canongate Books Ltd. (Model Paper 1 Critical Reading page 16);

The poem 'Originally' by Carol Ann Duffy from 'The Other Country' (Anvil, 1990). Reproduced by permission of the author c/o Rogers, Coleridge & White Ltd., 20 Powis Mews, London W11 1JN (Model Paper 1 Critical Reading page 18);

The poem 'Hyena' by Edwin Morgan, from 'From Glasgow to Saturn' published by Carcanet Press Limited 1973 (Model Paper 1 Critical Reading page 20);

The poem 'Assisi' by Norman MacCaig from 'The Many Days: Selected Poems of Norman MacCaig' published by Polygon. Reproduced by permission of Birlinn Ltd. www.birlinn.co.uk (Model Paper 1 Critical Reading page 22);

The poem 'My Grandmother's Houses' by Jackie Kay, from 'Darling: New & Selected Poems' (Bloodaxe Books, 2007). Reprinted with permission of Bloodaxe Books, on behalf of the author. www.bloodaxebooks.com (Model Paper 1 Critical Reading page 24);